Love &

RULES

This book is dedicated to all the girls like me —
longing to live our lives well, on foot and in the saddle.

PRAISE FOR *Love & * RULES

"Down-to-earth with a heartfelt sense of humour, Lee's rich writing blends her common sense with clarity as she shares her life and soul alongside horses."

— Tom Bews, Five-time Canadian Champion All-Around Cowboy

"Brave, honest and intentional. Will tug at your heart from every direction and resonate with you whether you are a horse person or not. The life lessons throughout are bountiful. I felt as though I was sitting down with an old friend, nodding my head in agreement the whole way through. I will go back to *Love & Rules* again and again as it has earned a permanent place in my heart and on my bookshelf!"

— Gail Greenough, Former World Show Jumping Champion

"Lee McLean is a wonderful storyteller with an art for seeing the bigger picture. With horses, finding a balance between affection and respect can be difficult, but Lee uncovers some beautiful truth in her latest book *Love & Rules*. The rawness and honesty in Lee's storytelling leaves the reader feeling inspired and ready to tackle the next storm."

— Amber Marshall, Award-winning Actor & Star of Heartland

"Lee is indeed the 'Boss Hoss' and this book is a treasure. Her struggles, victories, setbacks and lessons are a feast for the soul, and a powerful glimpse into the world of real ranchers and horse people."

— *Ingo Neuhaus, Award-winning Hollywood Actor & Producer*

"As you read Lee McLean's short stories in *Love & Rules,* you feel like you're sitting with your best friend, having coffee, and listening to fun and beautiful tales about ideas you're glad you heard for the first time, or thank goodness, you were reminded of them once again. Lee's willingness to be vulnerable will open your heart and inspire you to keep going for your dreams — in life and with horses."

— *Barbra Schulte, Author, High-Performance Coach & Cutting Horse Trainer*

"An inspiring and courageous account of life and love. There are so many lessons, horse lover or not, that every reader will relate to. It is a bold, authentic telling of hardships, celebrations and overcoming all the twists in the road life poses for each of us, as well as the consequences of the decisions we make — good and bad. Most importantly, I was left with the reminder that with a good heart, sense of purpose, determination and perseverance, we *can* make dreams come true!"

— *Nancy Southern, Business Leader & EVP of Spruce Meadows*

RED BARN BOOKS INC.
CARSTAIRS, ALBERTA, CANADA
REDBARNBOOKS.CA

DESIGN: LIA GOLEMBA | PINK SPOT STUDIOS
COVER IMAGES: MARY DURANT PHOTOGRAPHY

#LOVE&RULES
To book a talk, bookstore visit, or book club Q&A, email info@redbarnbooks.ca. Follow Lee McLean's blog at Keystone Equine on Facebook.

DELUXE EDITION
ISBN 978-1-989915-08-0
PRINTED IN CANADA

red barn
- BOOKS -

Love &
RULES

Life Lessons
Learned with Horses

LEE M^cLEAN

Best-selling Author of Horse Woman
& the Keystone Equine blog

SAFETY
DISCLAIMER

Please note that by taking part in horsemanship or any of the suggestions
herein, you are agreeing to not hold liable Lee McLean, her family,
Keystone Equine, Red Barn Books Inc., or employees thereof, should any
misfortune occur as a result of your training or actions.

We recommend that you seek the help of a professional
and use an approved helmet and correct riding footwear
when working with any pony or horse.

Archival photos used in this book may predate modern safety standards.
The content herein is anecdotal. Your own common
sense and safety must be uppermost. Horses can be
dangerous, handle them at your own risk.

HOW TO READ
THIS BOOK

At first, I tried organizing *Love & Rule*s into sections, using chapters, themes, concepts, and all the right stuff. Like real life, however, it said, 'I don't think so.' Instead, it wants to come as a surprise. The book asks the reader to wait — to cope, accept, fight or simply learn from — all the lessons that life with horses offers. How we react to the up-and-down journey is ultimately up to us.

If you'd like to look something up, to be able to reference one of the stories or lessons later, there is an index that refers to each by number. There is no chronological order, and while some of the words have appeared on Keystone Equine, much of the book is seen here for the first time.

As our horses would teach us, some of the lessons learned are about joy, wonder and hope. Some are about heartbreak.

Most of the photographs I have chosen are humble ones, gathered from my personal collection to illustrate each horse's own story.

I hope you will love getting to know these wonderful animals, as has been my great privilege.

LEE MᶜLEAN
AUTHOR. HORSE WOMAN. STUDENT.

CONTENTS

Lee McLean (Mary Durant Photography)

INTRODUCTION
LEAD LINES

One day, I took my old habit of journaling about my horsemanship and I put it online. I called my blog Keystone Equine, after my horse business and in honour of our family's century-old brand. Each day that I came in from riding — either with a breakthrough; or black, blue and feeling beaten — I'd put the kettle on and I'd write it down. In the beginning, there were not many people hearing what I had to say. Eventually, they told two friends, and they told two friends, and so on. Today, my online diary has many followers worldwide. The Keystone horses and ponies are the main players in my stories. Their adventures are always received with love and encouragement, which means so much to me. You cheer when they finally get something with which they've struggled. You cry with me when they are hurt.

These horses, with all my memories of them, have sown the seeds for *Love & Rules*.

There was a period of adjustment, changing my writing from a personal diary — meant to be read by no one — to words that would be read by thousands of strangers. What I did was to simply imagine myself hosting a dinner party of diverse characters. I would sit people of widely-ranging interests side-by-side. I would pour the wine, serve the food, sit back, and hope for the best. Our conversation would most likely drift towards all the life lessons we have learned with horses.

You are at this party because you want to be. I am here because I believe that, more than ever, we need people who will tell their stories, real-life experiences about honest horsemanship. We need more willingness to openly educate, to build up, and to make the people who read these words feel empowered and understood. Today, more than ever, we need to share what we have learned.

I am mother to three grown children, all of whom rode well. I have made some very good horses and sadly, terribly, I have ruined a few. (Yes, that happens). I am a stroke survivor. I know what it's like to be so frightened to put a leg over a horse, that you can no longer breathe. I have had to put my saddle on the high rack and leave my riding, so that I could raise children and help make a living, doing my best at a job that sure as heck wasn't my dream. I've stayed awake nights, worrying about

1

money. I have needed to sell my best horse, so that the furnace would be fixed and the car have safe tires. Like so many of you, I have come back, dusted myself off and got back in the game.

I, myself, am not discipline-specific. There are many horsemen and women who are better-suited to tell you how things should be done. The diverse camps I have spent time in have shown me one thing with clarity. The older I get and the more I see, I have this unshakeable feeling that we're all riding down the same trail. We may climb into our dusty chaps, or halt and salute at 'X', read from our favourite chairs, follow the mountain trails, live for our Tuesday night lessons, lead the children on their ponies, drive a chore team, help with therapeutic riding, work the big pastures doctoring calves, teach in Pony Club or 4-H, count strides to the oxer, toil at the vet clinic, go down the fence, settle into the carriage, sit tall on our sidesaddles, or any of the myriad adventures these horses offer us. While the details are seemingly everything, in the end, none of them really matters.

I have learned that to study the ways of the horse is to be a keen student of life. The one is forever running parallel to the other. You and I are here for the horsemanship. Reading about it, dreaming about it, learning from it — this is where we belong.

.I.

LOVE AND RULES

The door to the arena slid closed behind me. In that moment, Eddie and I knew that we were on our own. One of us would hold fast, while the other would have to soften. Eddie was quite clear about which of these would be him. In the heartbeat in which I was processing this, the chestnut smoothly swung 'round in an arc, pinned his ears and came straight for me. At the last moment, I was forced to give ground. The young stallion let loose with a pair of flying heels as he shot past. Luckily, I was out of reach, for his feet fanned the air uncomfortably close to my head.

Three strides beyond and Eddie had wheeled again. Neither of us was playing around now. We were engaged in lunges, turns and flourishes, me an awkward matador, a dance that would eventually have one of us backing down. I could taste blood where I'd bitten my lip and, in that one instant, I resolved that the domineering Welsh Cob would be my second-in-command, or I would die trying. Eventually — eventually — Eddie got the memo. Our family would spend the coming years sending him occasional reminders.

It's easy to take this sort of behaviour in a horse personally. He is trying to hurt me, we think, but no. He is actually just being a horse. In the herd, any horse of dominant character spends his hours jockeying for position in the hierarchy. He is just waiting for the fellow above him to either leave, die, or slip up. Understanding this can help us when dealing with any forceful personality. That said, keeping our spot in the pecking order can be easier said than done. This is also why leadership, in a horse's eyes, cannot be bought with bribes, love, or treats. You either earn your place, or you lose it. This is the way of the horse.

So many horses — and some people — will fight all authority until they learn to trust in a larger plan. This learning to trust requires an equilibrium. In addition to convincing someone of the necessity of playing by the rules, it is all too easy to come on too strong, to frighten a sensitive nature, to overpower a free spirit, and to replace this innate fire with resentment or fear. Whether we're faced with extreme dominants or submissives — humans or horses — we need to uphold inborn confidence. It's a delicate balance and therein lies the challenge.

Whether training my ponies or raising my children, 'love and rules' has become my mantra. It holds fast with co-workers who are behaving badly, clients who overstep boundaries, friendships that have somehow gone awry. It even holds meaning for the way I talk to myself. Love and rules, love and rules, love and rules.

. 2 .

HERE COMES THE JUDGE

It's so easy to sit in judgment of other riders and their horses.

We mightn't even know them, and yet we'll watch. We're looking for that chink in the armour, that weak spot that comforts us. It could be the low-budget turnout with the out-of-date saddle or ill-fitting chaps. It could be the high-end horse and rider who "should be good because they can just buy their way to the top."

We'll see the young horse who's losing his marbles, just a bit, and find fault with the trainer's program. "He's putting too much pressure on," we'll think. We may even voice that opinion out loud. We'll see the green horse in the hands of the nervous beginner and scoff, "Green-plus-green equals black-and-blue. Why don't they get a coach and some guidance?"

We'll see someone who works hard to compete and think, "He'll do anything to win." We'll see someone who stays home and works for the sheer joy of it and disclaim, "If she was any kind of serious, she wouldn't be afraid to compete."

We Western riders will watch the English horses and think, "Why do they put up with such bad ground manners?" We English riders will watch the Western crowd and say, "Why do they use such harsh bits?" What would happen if we could watch these horses and riders, in all manner of disciplines, and say instead, "Wow, what beautiful work."

I am very aware of this tendency within myself, and perhaps you might recognize it in yourself as well. The message here? Other people are outside our control. I myself am able to change, if I am willing. No matter my age, experience or gender, good medicine is getting myself 'out there' on all manner of horses. They alone are brilliant at finding ego — and in knowing how to administer the right antidote.

Like a cold-water hosing, horses can get our attention pretty fast.

I have learned that showing up with the colt who is kicking the trailer; the pony

who is too small, too slow and too fat; sitting the forty-year-old saddle; or the horse who bucks when changing leads are good for me. They remind me that each of us must embark on our own journeys. We're all riding the same trail, even though we are camped at different spots.

· 3 ·

GROUND TIED

More money. More skill. More courage. Fewer responsibilities. Fewer self-doubts.

"When the children leave home."
"If my partner supported me."

Better horses. Better chances of winning. Better health. More time. More experience. More resolve.

"Maybe next year ... my horse and I are not going to be ready."

Fear of failure. Fear of trying. Fear of being judged. Ageing. Learning. Changing. Growing.

"I've got too much on my plate."
"I am still too fat."

Trust me when I say that I understand. These are things I am tempted to tell myself almost daily. But life is short and, for many of us, the next stop will not involve horses. Or fresh air. Or taking chances. Or really, really challenging ourselves to be bold and have fun.

Gently, respectfully, lovingly, dear reader ... I'll ask again. What are we waiting for?

· 4 ·

ALONE, BUT NOT LONELY

I think it's important to teach our horses to be alone. Yes, horses are herd animals. They socialize and find safety in a group. In the wild, to be separated from the others is a huge threat that might well mean death. Problem is, our horses are no longer in the wild. If they're going to make it in this world, they're going to have to get along with just us.

Herdboundness is an issue that can really make us question the relationship we have with our horse. It can even make us question the reliability of the horse itself. I blame two things for this. One, that we think it's mean and unnatural to make our horses be without their friends. And, two, that it's now considered unsafe and irresponsible to ride alone.

We don't feel good around horses who shriek and carry on when they can't see their buddies. It's dangerous and annoying. Horse or human, the spectrum between being able to socialize well and being able to enjoy one's own company is a learned skill. So many of us feel lonely and vulnerable whenever we find ourselves alone.

Pamela is one such horse. While young and impressionable, she should have been fed in the barn by herself, then turned back out with her herd. She should have been tied for short periods on opposite sides of the corral, then the barn, from her friends. As she grew, she should have been hauled alone to get groceries and to pick up the mail. She should have learned the valuable lesson that no matter where she went in the world, she would, in turn, come home. She would, once again, see all her friends. Like so many horses, unfortunately, Pamela did not.

'Objection!' she has learned to shout. Now, finding herself a problem that needs fixing, she must be saddled up and ridden out on her own, the small herd of just me and herself. This is not easy. We stick close to home and gradually, ever so gradually, range farther afield. If Pamela gets upset — no, when she gets upset — she is ridden homeward smartly and really put to work, right near her friends. Huffing, puffing, sweating, lacking any sort of payoff, we will try to ride out, alone, again. This will need to be repeated many times. Eventually, I know that Pamela will figure this out. No matter where we go, we will come home again.

My goal is to try and set each horse or pony up to have their own confidence. By mindfully facing this elemental fear of being alone, horses like Pamela can learn how to cope. It's a socializing skill that is as important as learning how to get along with others.

Thanks to my horses, I have learned that being alone does not mean we have to be lonely.

· 5 ·

HANGING UP OUR SPURS

It's taken me a while to admit that my body is an amazing machine. I've been mad at it for a long time now. Since the morning I awoke at age fourteen and knew, instinctively, that my life would never be the same, it has been one long sickness after another. Never mind that this body didn't look like the cute girls in the Sears catalogue, either. Somehow, when they were handing out physiques at birth, I'd got into the manly lineup instead of the one meant for girls.

Those of us who've followed athletic endeavours can often add injury to this list of physical challenges. Strangely, after fifty years of being horseback, my worst break was one made while jumping down from the flatbed chore truck one winter. Cr-rack went my ankle as I made my landing on a frozen boulder, hidden under the snow. My doctor smiled knowingly when I complained of pain and stiffness a year later.

"My dear, your bones will heal just fine. It's the soft tissue you need to worry about." He was right. The ankle healed in a fused and frozen state and didn't 'free up' until one day, seven years later, as I long-trotted a horse across a windswept field. Another cr-rack but I regained almost full use of the joint. What I'm getting around to saying is this — while our bodies are amazing machines, if we don't use 'em, we'll lose 'em.

I teach a number of students who have limited mobility, either through osteoarthritis or prior injury. Hips and knees, especially, are good at getting our attention when they're feeling cranky. They start complaining and next thing we know, we're letting them get out of work. I urge you to strengthen the muscles around these joints, to take whatever pain meds you can tolerate, then to use your body as best you can. Riding is particularly good for maintaining our flexibility, and yes, some horses and some saddles are easier on us than others. Plain old walking, if and when we can manage it, is also good.

Don't be too proud to use a mounting block. Yes, even for stepping off. Your horse and your body will thank you. A safe horse, narrowly-built and smooth-moving if you've the luxury of choosing, will allow your riding to continue. When I'm having my worst days, shorter rides done more often can keep me in the saddle. My lower back pain, especially, seems more manageable when I 'treat' it with the movement of a horse.

For some time now, I've been eating cleanly. By avoiding certain inflammatory foods and all pre-packaged ones, I've lost over thirty pounds, along with gaining a renewed range of motion. Was it easy? Not really. But was it worth it? Oh, yes.

Lastly, I've learned to listen to myself. There's a line I do not force myself across without dire consequences. Some days, it's a matter of a pep-talk and a pain pill before pulling on my boots and getting out there. Other days, I remind myself that 'my body is an amazing machine and it will feel better again', while I head to bed with a hot water bottle. I know that just as soon as I'm able, I'll be back out the door, itching to ride.

If you're having joint trouble and are wondering whether it's time to hang up your spurs, I urge you to talk to your doctor. Then, if you can, go saddle up. Horses can heal us — mentally and physically — and it's not just woo-woo stuff.

. 6 .

EXTENSIONS

One of the biggest brouhahas I ever caused with my writing was to suggest that 'our horses are reflections of ourselves'. Oh, the uproar. The accusations of anthropomorphism, which has surely become the catchword of the decade.

We may not be able to pronounce it but, by golly, we sure can sling it around. Therefore, risking the onslaught of certain readers' fury, I still believe the truth behind the concept of 'show me your horse and I will tell you who you are'. This quote, by the way, has unknown attribution but is believed to be an old English saying. This means that we have suspected as much, for many years.

"Don't be putting your human emotions and tags upon your horses," I am told. But wait. Whether we tend to be guarded with strangers, impatient, afraid of being hurt, fiery and achieving, fearless, soft and searching, distrustful, strong-willed, cautious, harried and rushing, in search of better leadership, highly reactive, angry or joyful — I believe that our horses can and eventually will become our mirrors.

That's a lot of responsibility, this notion of turning others into versions of ourselves.

· 7 ·

LONG RIDERS

There's a famous quote by John Wooden: "It's what you learn after you know it all that counts." As with serious gardening and music, the more we learn about horsemanship, it seems the less we feel good about what we do know for sure.

Horses have long been both a passion and a torment of mine. I'm either lying awake at night because of their possibilities, or I'm lying awake because I have failed them. I'm sure some of you will understand. Lately, I've been learning more about riding from my sister, Kerry. Let me explain.

The history shared with family is common ground, but our decisions and life paths shape us differently. Here, my big sister Kerry and I are ready to ride in our brand-new boots, the thrill of which has never grown old. (Author's Collection)

Ours was a normal family of the 1970s, with two hardworking parents and kids who took them for granted. Kerry, my older sister, was the smart one. I was the kid who was happiest outdoors. In our own ways, each of us decided this meant that one couldn't do anything with feeling, while the other couldn't do anything needing a brain. My sister would go on to university and the corporate life. I, the drop-out, would do well to stay home and balance her cheque book.

9

While we were growing up, Kerry got only difficult horses. Given their personalities and her age, she was doing well just to pilot them around the show ring. I was blessed with superstars, either horses that had put Kerry into hospital long before I ever climbed aboard, or horses who were already household names. I learned a lot from these animals, enough that I was accepted into a very picky riding program as a teen. I mean, *the* Richard Waetjen was my teacher's teacher. So, one kid worked hard and got shown the out-gate, while the other kid worked no harder and found riding a breeze.

My sister married a city boy and raised her family. I married my rancher and did the same. Kerry learned how to navigate city traffic, all the while I was spending more than those fabled 'ten-thousand hours' in the saddle. Just two more people whose few pivotal decisions would dictate the course of their lives. Last year, Kerry decided to get back to her riding. It's a brave move for someone who last wore boots with patent hunt tops and two-way-stretch breeches when they were newly trending.

My only advice for her was to tell her to find an excellent teacher. So, she did. All went well until this good riding school closed its doors. Kerry phoned every barn in the area, asking if they would take on an ageing adult beginner — just a once-keen student who has probably forgotten more than she's remembered. There were no takers. I had no idea that such teachers were so hard to find, teachers who will take an adult rider all the way through the chapters of the old blue *Manual of Horsemanship*.

Finally, in desperation, Kerry came to me. It was a little weird, I'll have you know. We have this shared history of galloping ponies down the trails of the Cariboo country; of riding with the Alderwood Horse Club in borrowed clothes; of riding before judges the likes of Jim Wyatt, Chick Miller and Art Anderson; of trying, in the August heat, to get boots on without zippers; of sewing our groovy fortrel equitation suits; of saving up babysitting money for chaps; of reading and then trying every bit of horse lore we could get our hands on. But that was then, and this is now. Kerry eases into my old dressage saddle at the mounting block. She gives me a wry, "Oh, what the hell?" sort of smile and we begin our lesson.

"Okay," I say, walking level with Brown Betty's shoulder, feeling the grinding and stiffness in my worn-out knees. Our shared history feels a very long time ago. "I want you to breathe deeply and bend your elbows. I want you to think about riding with a soft feel ..."

. 8 .

HORSING AROUND

A few days ago, I'd groomed Pilot, then left him to graze loose in the yard. We were getting set to head down the highway to our regular lesson. I'd also left the trailer's tack room door open for just a few minutes, don't you know?

I changed my shirt, brushed my teeth, grabbed my hat and pulled on my boots. In that time, Pi had certainly been busy. Tack had been pulled from the racks and was strewn everywhere. Ditto, my saddle and blankets. The grooming toolbox was empty. I came upon several of my brushes, dropped in the raised garden, where he'd strolled over to pick some beets.

Returning to the trailer, Pi dug out an old lariat, my hobbles and a hot pink short line string. These were duly added to the pile. Finally, not one to shirk work, he grabbed a brimful bag of horse cookies, ones I'd just bought to serve old Cody his meds. By carefully shaking out the bag, Pilot managed to eat all but one of them — no mean feat, as I'd snipped off only one tiny corner from the bag.

When I went out, about ten minutes later, he was so proud of himself! The gelding followed me carefully as I picked up and replaced each thing into the trailer. Strangely, not one stray cookie was to be found. The whole incident brought to mind some of my memories of my children when they were toddlers. They were healthy, confident and intelligent, and in the time that it took to turn my back, they sometimes made questionable choices.

"You! Are! An incredibly! Exasperating! Horse!" I gasped at each bending down and picking up. Pilot's expressive face told me that the whole thing had been lots of fun. Later on, at the lesson, he gave me the best ride we've ever had. Our turnarounds, both ways, were fast, smooth and correct. He willingly backed beautiful circles. He rolled the cricket in his bit smugly, confidently, as he answered each and every one of my questions. We bridled up, one-handed, to work at the lope. First on one track, then on two. Pi yielded his quarters and gave me two perfect flying lead changes when asked. Then, he showed me that he's starting to understand this whole 'working the flag' thing. He watched the flag, he stopped and backed up, he made the turn, and he did it again and again. Don't you just love a joyful horse?

I realized my error. As a serious horsewoman, I was missing so many of the opportunities these horses gave me, just to smile and have fun. They were telling me to get over myself.

· 9 ·

TENDER LOVING CARE

When it comes to good, older horses, a lot of folks want something for nothing. Here's why it doesn't work that way.

The horse who is safe in all situations, with all types of riders, is most usually a high-mileage horse. There are some young horses who can roll with the punches, but it's safe to say that when we're nervous and looking for a solid ride, we're looking for a well-ridden teenager.

Here's the problem. For a horse to have enough mileage to be proven, he'll often be showing some wear 'n' tear on his body. The perfect joints and lungs often belong to the greener horse. The catch lies in the fact that if we want experience, we usually must sign up for maintenance. This rule holds true for the point-and-shoot amateur-friendly jumper, to the beginner-safe ranch horse, to the children's first pony.

'Maintenance' — that dirty word. Folks will back away from a great, older horse who needs cold-weather blanketing, or supplemental feeding, or shoes with pads, or low-dose painkillers, or meds for his airways, or more-than-average dental care and bodywork; rather than ride safe. When we put it that way, in black and white, we see that so many people would rather put themselves or their children in danger, than do the upkeep on a trail-worn but wonderful horse.

Is there a difference between doing what is necessary to keep a working horse comfortable in his twilight years and riding a chronically-sore horse? Yes. Your equine healthcare team will help set you straight, if you've any doubts. Are there older, perfectly-sound horses available? Are there beautifully-honest, young horses around? Sure. But I think many of us are too quick to look askance at horses who would take pride in serving us well, if only they had some support.

I urge you, if you've the time and love to put into an older horse, just do it. Senior horses, if they were good horses once upon a time, come with a wisdom and energy that is worth every bit of effort and every penny. They have so much to give us in return for our safekeeping. I cringe when I see ads in search of excellent, experienced performance horses requiring no maintenance. We can't get something for nothing. Loving care is an especially valuable teaching opportunity for our children. It's our chance to really show them what horsemanship is all about.

Old horses rank high among my blessings. Some might say they need maintenance; I prefer to call it tender loving care.

. 10 .

WELL IN HAND

Write. Write! Just write it all down. If you have been dealing with recurring themes in your life, write them down. If you're struggling in your lessons or wondering if any headway is being made with the new horse, write it down. If you have been thinking of phrases or lyrics, write of them before you forget them. You don't have to call yourself a poet or a songsmith to have something worthwhile to say.

Whenever I'm teaching, I always speak of the practical uses of recording our lessons on paper. Writing is such a lasting way to learn. Often, I will mention the benefits of putting our deepest vulnerabilities into words. This sharing is usually met with snorts of laughter, or sadness, or real regret.

"I'm not a writer, but I'd love to be able to put my thoughts down," people will say. You know, I'm a big believer in just starting on that first clean page. Not in setting out to write the next great novel. Not in writing anything that someone else might read and judge. No, I believe in starting with something you feel the need to speak out loud. Without writing as though our thoughts are going to be published, just begin.

Sometimes I tear pages out, or scribble over them when I've either settled down, solved the problem, or have just maybe told myself to grow up. Writing, when done authentically, is an effective map to self-knowledge. We all have some sort of a truth that dwells within us and many times, the rest of the world is not interested — or not ready — to hear what we have to say. One day last year, I burned some old journals that were so full of raw hurt and disappointment that I decided it was time for me to hold a ceremony of goodbyes. Wow. It was a powerful act of self-care.

Ernest Hemingway famously said, "All you have to do is write one true sentence. Write the truest sentence that you know." He may well have been talking about crafting a great novel. But for me, the truest sentence I know is the pure essence of journaling. It is telling my own personal gospel. It is asking the hard questions. It is being openly afraid. It is celebration, it is learning.

Writing unplugs us and turns off all the machinery that so noisily wants to be heard. Writing is like putting down a heavy suitcase, even if we write only about our riding. When we go back and read, we see that, yes, everything is going to be all right.

Now, writing takes practice. It is a meditation. Cheap therapy, reading what we've written is like holding up a mirror. It shows us where we're stuck and where we're gaining ground. Rich with memories, our journals will be what remains of our horsemanship when this riding gig is done.

. II .

ROLL BACKS

It's a curious thing, running into people who have known you a long time. "I've known you since when ..." they like to say, and usually this involves a memory that doesn't put you in your best light. Without saying so, exactly, many of these old chums like to put you in your place. I still run across people who have known me since I was a child. To them, it matters not one iota that I have spent six decades in the saddle, perfecting my skills, trying to stay abreast of all the new thoughts and techniques that have come about in my lifetime. Nope. They see me as a freckle-faced, pig-tailed child on a chubby pony. They remember when they were better than I, or in something of a position of power. They wonder, quite openly and with an ill-hidden show of humour, what I could possibly have to write about, and why all these strangers from around the world would bother to read it?

I have neighbours and family members who still ask me, every single time I see them, if I'm still buying and selling antiques, or driving the school bus? It doesn't matter to them that I have not done so in almost twenty years, the time that I've gone full-time into training and selling horses. They like to bring up our years in 4-H together, or their achievements from back in 1978, or how good their own horses are showing right now. They never once think to ask me about my business, or my health, or what I'm doing day-to-day, or what I'm currently writing and thinking about. You know, what I'm currently doing to evolve.

The older I get, the better I was.

It's a thing that happens to us whenever we've been a long time away from horses. Or any other endeavour requiring skill, fitness and dexterity, come to think of it. I got a good lesson about this a few years ago.

As a teen, I belonged to an extraordinary high school basketball team. We were provincial champions two years out of three, and the one year we were not, we lost the championship game in overtime. It was a huge achievement for a small-town school, back in an era before tiered ranking, a fair system where like-sized schools played one other, based on student enrolment. It was the norm to find ourselves pitted against inner-city high schools with almost as many students as our town had citizens. But we loved the game, we were extremely well-coached and we played to win. I was a point guard on this team, starting line-up my final two years. I haven't talked basketball or thought much about it in almost forty years. It comes as a shock to realize that I thought nothing of a five-mile run, then hitting the showers before school even started. I worked hard at my ball handling and passing, setting up plays and making it all happen. I had a decent three-point shot for when the opposing team's defence was too tight to crack.

When a local charity game was organized to pit past team members against the current ones, I — along with a few otherwise sane people who should've known better — jumped at the chance. This would be awesome, for we'd show those kids a thing or two. Some of us weren't that long out of high school or college, while a few of us hadn't been playing basketball since gas was thirty cents a gallon, since pay phones needed ten cents to make a call, since chocolate bars were ten for a dollar. You get my drift.

I stood in the new high school gym, proudly raising my eyes to our two provincial banners that hung from the rafters. My, they looked faded and old. Within thirty seconds of the opening tip-off, I learned that I hadn't played basketball in a very long time. There was only one other person on the court older than me and it wasn't by much. She and I ran hard for the first two trips up and down the court. I tried to pass the ball but it was constantly intercepted. The offence and defence didn't look like anything I remembered. I dribbled on my own toe more than once. I didn't make one single shot that night. My lungs felt as though they were being pulled through my nostrils as the young current team handed us our tired arses on a platter. With a shock, I knew I was finished before the game even really started. All night long, I only saw other peoples' tail lights.

Yep, the older I get, the better I was. This is a truism in so much of what we did in our youth, including our horsemanship. If you're not currently out there in the arena — or the pastures — still striving, still fighting the weather, still teaching youth, still learning from every single horse you come across, I think you'd be surprised if you were again given the chance. Horsemanship is constantly evolving. It might not be one hundred per cent better than it once was, but I'm here to tell you that it has changed. I, too, have known a number of people who have put in their 'more than ten thousand hours' to become industry bright lights. It is not a kindness for me to bring up their humble beginnings on the way to becoming household names. No, I need to applaud their long and rocky roads to success.

Those who were around a long time ago might want to remember this — as should we all — with newcomers, people and horses. Bettering themselves and honing their sports, constantly rising, aiming for the stars. Nothing stays the same and there will always be someone who wants what we had, but even more so. The older I get, the better I was. It's a thing, all right.

. 12 .

SEEING SPOTS

Coming home with Rockabilly, Johnny Cash and Spot Me A Dollar,
I always say, "There's an App for that." (Author's Collection)

. 13 .

FEELING OUR OATS

Today, every day, I dare you. For just ten or fifteen minutes, do what makes you feel like a kid. That is, if you remember.

. 14 .

TRUST IS EARNED

Trust. What is it? How do we lose it and, if so, how do we gain it back?

When it comes to horsemanship, we're the ultimate salesmen. We're promising our horses happiness and safety, all the while trying to convince them that, more than anything, they need to 'buy in' to what we're trying so hard to sell. Like all salesmen, some of us are more-or-less honest — and some of us are just trying to cut a quick deal.

We horse people have gone from 'my way or the highway' all the way to 'horse whispering', if you want to call it that. From our horses' points of view, when they finally decide to trust us, they're really just hoping that we're not going to let them down. Many of them have been hurt, cheated, lied to and disappointed by so many people, it always amazes me that they — for the most part — continue to trust.

Trust, by definition, is the firm belief in the reliability, truth, ability or strength of someone or something. When we lose trust, we have the strong feeling that someone or something cannot be relied upon. To regain lost trust, we must decide to forgive and let go of the past. None of this is easy. Horse or human, we have to be open to self-growth and improvement — and then we have to want the relationship to work. Whether it's better horsemanship or homegrown hay we're selling, we have to know ourselves well enough that we'll not make the mistake of promising what we cannot give. By speaking the truth and always delivering, this is how we earn trust.

Life, of course, has other plans. We fall through the ice when we finally convince our horse to cross the stream. Our girth straps break during the heroic jump. We expect our horse to walk with us, and then, we inadvertently jerk his mouth when we drop the rein. Innocent mistakes, all are very hard on regaining and holding the horse's trust. All we can do when working with them is to try our best, say we're sorry and mean it, and then vow to do better the next time.

Like people, some horses are more forgiving and more trusting than others. Some allow us to make mistakes, while others will never allow us to make those same mistakes again. All we can do is to be our most honest, genuine selves and never, ever promise more than we can give.

Now, because you've read this far, I'm going to repay your trust with a kindness. Here it is, from the depths of my grandmother's 1930s apple green Bakelite recipe box. Lardy, jammy, oatmealy goodness — and hey, if you trust me enough to go ahead and make them, you're welcome.

. 15 .
NANNY'S BIRDS' NESTS

In a large bowl, stir together with a wooden spoon:
2 cups flour
1 cup brown sugar
2 tsp. baking powder

With two knives, or your fingers, mix in until 'shotty':
½ cup butter
½ cup lard (or any mixture of the two)

Work in:
½ cup sour milk

Roll in 1" balls, make imprint with finger, bake at 325F/160C until just slightly browned. Resist the urge to overbake. Re-press fingerprints and while cooling, fill with leftover jellies and jams.

Don't worry too much about how to store these humble little cookies. They'll easily keep long enough for you to snuggle down, enjoy with a cup of tea, and finish reading your book.

. 16 .

OF MEN AND HORSES

It's been a long, hard one. I am bone tired and looking forward to a soak in the tub. In short, I have had enough.

Men 'n' horses. Gotta love 'em. Most days.

. 17 .

TURNAROUNDS

Hard-luck ponies. We've all seen them, those sad cases in the local buy-sell pages, neglected and mishandled from day one. They call out to me and no matter how hard I try, I cannot scroll by them. I will make arrangements to go see such a pony. Invariably, it is in such dire straits that even if I don't see a spark of something good inside, it is next-to-impossible to go home with an empty trailer. And so it begins.

One particular chestnut pony was one of the saddest cases imaginable. I think of forsaken horses and hers is the face I see. There was no sign of the beauty hidden within when I first met this pony, several hours' drive from home. When the door of her pen swung open, out walked one of the worst-neglected animals I've seen. She stood all of 13:1 hands, but she was immense. Just stepping across the yard had the mare gasping for air. Her toes were long and starting to curl. Somehow, a rusty shoe swung from her front foot, holding on by one nail. Scrape, clunk, ching! went her every step. The pony's one blue eye was glued shut with an infection and, worse, a revolting malodorous discharge coated her tail and hind legs.

I stood there, holding on to her with a baler twine neck rope, wondering what on earth I should do. She struck out at me, hard, across the knee. How could I leave her? When the pony refused to load onto my trailer, it seemed as though a higher power was telling me to change my mind. I did not, of course, and once the little mare agreed to come home with me, her life was set to change. It wasn't easy. There were daily regrets. Many hours and dollars were spent, working on basic physical care, installing manners, paying for ongoing vetting, dentistry, farrier and chiro, teaching her how to walk, trot and canter on the lunge line before we could begin any time under saddle. When we did start riding out, the pony alternated between balking and bolting for home. There were some scary and frustrating rides for both of us, along the rocky road to wellness.

In the end, she became Nelly, a beautiful warrior princess, fierce competitor and loyal friend. My one last job was to find her a new home, a soft spot where she would be valued for who she was, a place where her talents would shine. When she met her people, two keen and talented sisters, there was no stopping her. The one-time hard-luck pony became a household name in junior rodeo. Nelly's consistency in barrels, pole bending, breakaway and team roping grew legendary. I think of Nelly and all the others like her, whenever I bring another hard-luck pony home. Not all can make the changes needed to turn their lives around. Some have such dire health, or troubled characters, they cannot take these last chances offered them. Others need only to have someone believe in them, to have faith in a happy ending.

While I will always want to ride and sell good horses who have everything going for them, in my corral, there will always be one more hard-luck pony, doing its level best to turn his, or her, life around.

. 18 .

HORSE POWER

Are you feeling despairing? Or are you feeling invincible? Wait, just for one moment. Such is the power of horses.

Once upon a time, I had a nice horse coming on. A very nice horse. We were riding in a full-time program and this horse was telling us that he might be the best horse I would ever ride. There is a certain amount of pressure in suspecting such a thing. We began to produce this horse carefully, putting off the moment when he would step out and compete. Though unspoken, I think both the trainer and I were a little afraid of outside opinions. Finally, it could wait no longer. There was no reason to hide, and he was entered in a large regional show.

Our first class, for maiden hacks, was chosen because it would be a relaxing jaunt without undue pressure. Alas, there were sixty-five other horses entered in this class. My heart sank. I had zero expectations. My horse, of course, rose to the occasion and shone above all others. He won and qualified for the overall ridden championship, to be held the next night.

With heart soaring, that next evening, I rode in on a winner. My horse, of course, came apart at the seams as a line of wheelchairs was rolled down a long ramp at the end of the arena. Within seconds, the ring was a seething mass of dappled and

braided bucking horses. The judge was so overwhelmed that the ring was cleared. We were generously rescheduled, the entire championship class, one hour later. Now feeling unsure, I rode in the second time, quietly and without any real hope of winning. You guessed it. My horse was star-powered and, despite his first showing, won the championship that night. The memory still brings a smile to my face many years later. I knew then, beyond any doubt, that I had the best ever horse.

Later that night, I was reduced to tears of frustration on the deserted show ground. Waiting for the hurly burly of the show ground to clear, I was the last competitor to load out. My champion, still green as grass, had finally broken under the unaccustomed pressure of our public outing. He flatly refused to get on the trailer for the long haul home. A rest and some supper were needed, he said, before he could do this one last thing for me. The gelding was young, large and overwhelmed by his anxiety. I was tired and alone.

Though my default setting was of impatience, to show him who's boss, I had no choice but to stop and listen to him. It was a lesson of greater importance, than being a winner, earlier that day.

I say, are you feeling despairing? Or are you feeling invincible? Wait for just one moment. Such is the power of horses.

. 19 .

LETTING THE FIRE GO OUT

How many of us struggle mightily with making the time to ride?

As we find ourselves more and more mired down in this muddy business that is life, time becomes truly precious. As we age, our responsibilities pile up, just like unopened mail. Somewhere along the line, it becomes our habit to say 'no' to ourselves — and never to anyone else.

I can remember, in my final year as a competing junior, dreading the day that I would have to ride against the adult amateurs. Silly me. I was afraid that with their age 'advantage', I would be in over my head. What I didn't realize was this — as a kid, I had only to worry about school and my few chores. The rest of the time, including two months over summer vacation, I literally lived on my horses. Fast forward a few years and that's when I got a real education.

Love & RULES

As a young rural wife and mother, I was juggling bills and running a household on pennies. There was endless cooking, cleaning and laundry. Three babies in cloth diapers really amped up the pressure. To ease our situation, I got a job. For eighteen years, I drove other peoples' children to school, in order to help pave the way for my own. My riding suffered while I laboured, working for other people and at my own home business, to pay the bills. My riding suffered a little more.

The kids grew and my daughter ended up with a phenomenal horse. Her involvement in 4-H seemed to help her transition through the difficult teen years. For several years, we would be heading down the road, both showing and rodeoing. I would joke to friends that I was the only mother who knew where her teenaged daughter was every Saturday night. My oldest son was into sports and my younger son was an aspiring drummer. I was so proud of these kids and loved driving them back and forth to their commitments. These were the whirlwind years and during them my riding suffered, still.

Just when there was an end in sight, just when Mike and I were kissing the kids goodbye and packing their things for college, I had a stroke. Wham. Everything in my life screeched to a halt. I saw, with some surprise, that the world intended to go on, without me. Learning to swallow and concentrate, coping with new depression and a backward body, riding wasn't even on the radar.

Before I knew it, I was too far gone to saddle up. Riding, the one thing that I'd lived for since childhood, had been put on the back burner for so many years, I'd almost let the fire go out.

Almost. A wise counsellor realized where I'd gone wrong and urged me to reconfigure my life. The day that I did so was one of my greatest victories. There was no trophy, no picture in the local paper, no fanfare of any kind. I started out small, by committing myself to signing up for one weekly group riding lesson. I promised myself that I would do this one thing for myself for one winter. If I was missed too much in the real world, I would reconsider. That was many years ago.

Today, my weekly lesson is still something I do just for me. Selfish? Perhaps. But I learned that if I didn't make the time to ride, my life would go by, regardless. As it is, it's speeding by at an alarming pace. If your horse is standing there, waiting for you to find some time in your day, please know that you never will find it. Extra time does not exist. Instead, you will have to somehow make it, starting from scratch.

Making the time to ride is a lot like making homemade bread. You start with an empty bowl. It seems an insurmountable task, until that moment when you pull that golden loaf from the oven. After measuring and mixing, kneading and waiting, it will rise and fall, rise and fall.

You will watch anxiously, pulling it out at just the right moment. You will take that first bite and just like me, you will savour the quiet, uplifting result.

. 20 .

DOWN AT THE OL' WATERING HOLE

There aren't all that many horses, anymore, who know how to navigate a water hole. It takes a fair bit of equine know-how, gleaned from the wisest members of the herd — so often, the oldest mares — to leave the feed grounds or winter pasture and lead the horses, slip-sliding down the hills, all the way to the creek. If there has been a spell of warmer weather, the snow cover will have melted and then it's a treacherous trip out over the ice for a drink. If the barometric pressure changes, the water level will drop in the creek far enough that the horses and cattle must fall to their knees, in order to slake their thirst.

Nowadays, so few of our modern horses have been raised to understand such things as surviving amid wild animals and nature. Like those of us lining up to buy our expensive coffees to go, they far prefer to gather around the heated trough. I, too, like the convenience of automatic waterers, but am compelled to admit that I miss the character-building of heading out, alone, in the frosty mornings, wielding my axe. That old-fashioned chore is among my fondest memories.

For a long time, it was Mike's or my job to ride a saddle horse, or the snowmobile, down with an axe and keep the water holes open. I always felt that I was being watched by cougars, making my hair stand on end, and adding to the similarly vivid imaginings of my horses. Once, I followed some enormous, clawed tracks in the snow a fair way up the creek, only to find that they belonged to Ella, our Basset Hound. Looking back, this was probably a stroke of luck.

. 21 .

TALL IN THE SADDLE

"It ain't whatcha ride, it's how you ride it." That, ladies 'n' gentlemen,
is a metaphor for life. (Public domain image)

. 22 .

COWGIRL UP

Learning, learning, always learning. The Art of the Cowgirl festival is over. My suitcase is unpacked, my boots and hats are wiped clean and back on their shelves. The old sidesaddle, new in the 1880s, has been reconditioned, her bruises kissed, and then safely put away.

"'Til next time," I have said. For there will be a next time and a different place. I have learned, just last weekend, that I can survive away from home, that I can step away from my home corrals and share this horsemanship thing that I love. I have learned that I'm smarter than I've thought. That I can get in the right lineup at the airport. That I can ask the right people. That I can back the strange rental car out of the underground parkade and merge onto a dark and terrifying six-lane interstate at eighty miles per hour. I have learned that I can handle unknown horses and people. That I can, despite all my best intentions, still forget key interviews and make poor decisions, like foregoing enough water and the essential twenty-minute nap. I have learned that I can shake off my personal shortfalls and keep chugging.

I have learned that no matter my prior planning, my heartfelt pep-talks, I will still walk into a crowded cocktail party feeling fat and gauche. I am learning that this old high school feeling will present itself, over and over, until I decide to take a deep breath, smile and boldly say hello. This real-life vulnerability is something I still struggle with, but I am learning to carry it with grace and perhaps even a pinch of self-love. I have learned that it's a great big sea out there and that we women are well represented in all the cowboy arts. In art, literally, and in making the good bridle horse, just as well as any man. We can ride hard, 'read' cattle, and rope — and in doing so, protect our shared and oft-forgotten history, both in music and the spoken word.

I have learned that I crave watching and learning from the women who have gone forth and blazed trails before me.

I have learned that at my age, it is a good thing to go ahead and do something that scares me to death. That when I'm so intimidated that I long to say, "I'm sorry, but I can't," to just go do it, anyway. I hope this knowledge sticks with me, for I miss so many opportunities when I automatically say no. I have learned, despite years of mindful nutrition and moving my dear bod, that I still want to hide under my eating in the times I am struggling with stress. I am learning, right now, that this is a part of who I am, and that I will simply forgive myself, blend up a green smoothie, and move on.

I have learned that those of us who constantly struggle to fit in are actually meant to forge our own paths. This is as it should be. Young or old, this is something that we who are somehow 'different' must learn to embrace. While we do so, however, it strikes me that the living — wholly, mindfully, joyfully — comes as we learn to live in grace as much as in fearlessness. That my being somewhat ballsy doesn't mean that I can't be a lady. That it is fitting to care about our deportment, to use an old-fashioned word. Girls, this includes learning the gentle art of conversation, of knowing how to support others without feeling that we're falling behind or that we're not enough.

For we are enough. Part fearless warrior, part nurturing soul and inquisitive explorer, I have learned that being a cowgirl — a modern western woman — is indeed a fine balance. I have learned that while I still have a lot to master, I am more than ready. It is never too late to learn.

· 23 ·
GOING FORWARD

It's my birthday. If I was given the chance to go back to being younger, would it be all that I remember? Would it be as good? Would having shiny brown hair and straighter, whiter teeth be any compensation for self-doubt and inexperience? Would years of mixed-up living really be preferable to my wonky knee and bigger jeans? When put that way, I doubt that they would.

Instead of setting our hearts on looking and feeling younger, why don't we vow to be a little wiser, a little kinder, a little more aware of what's going on around us, with each and every year? Let us look after ourselves so that we may age with grace. Let us strive to be whole enough, well enough, involved enough, to somehow serve. That's a good wish, and now may God grant me the strength to blow out this raging bonfire of candles without growing faint.

· 24 ·
RIDING HIGH

Most days, I'm stomping around with a scowl on my face. It's not that I try to be cranky, but I'm usually deep in thought, talking to myself trying to figure things out. When I'm concentrating, it ain't pretty. But when I ride, it's different somehow.

Handling a horse is the one place I don't feel like an awkward misfit.

My heart soars and, so help me God, I always end up with a huge smile on my face. It has always been thus. At a long-ago show I rode in as a child, I remember the judge coming along the lineup, to talk to those of us who might benefit from his advice.

"As for you," he said, "you'd look better if you'd wipe that cheesy grin off your face." I remember my eyes welling up in surprise, for I was unaware of anything

beyond feeling joyful. There are several reasons why I think that old curmudgeon was wrong, not the least of which, impressing upon a pure young soul that she should dim her sparkle. Happily, I didn't take his advice.

I have noticed over the ensuing years, that when I smile, my eyes go up and my heart fills. I breathe deeply. My horses, if they've been feeling uninspired, hard done by, or the ill effects of my critical gaze, always go more lightly. They have a spring in their step when they feel the invitation to live life fully. Dogs will wag their tails and welcome my touch. Aloof strangers will soften and make friendly eye contact in the street. As the old song said, "When you're smilin', the whole world smiles with you." I still say, if we're fortunate enough to be doing what we love, we shouldn't ever be ashamed or afraid to show it.

. 25 .

RIDING BOLDLY

Let's dare to love and respect someone whose views differ from our own — and no, it isn't easy.

. 26 .

RIDING FOR A FALL

Recently, I went on a road trip with my grown daughter and two horses, promoting the art of riding sidesaddle, at a large indoor agricultural show. Every effort was made to ensure that our tack was right and the horses ready. Our clothing was carefully chosen to add to the overall picture of elegance. Other than being made to travel during a bout of freezing rain, it was all shaping up quite nicely.

I love when I'm on top of things and organized, don't you?

Three strides into our performance, all hell broke loose. With a little 'pfft!' I suddenly felt my bra give way. Surely not, my mind reasoned. Why, I was wearing the trusty 'Goddess', a veritable straitjacket of hooks, eyes and tie down straps. Never once had this contraption failed me! A quick glance southward confirmed my worst fears. If ever I needed incentive to sit quietly, with my elbows pinned to my sides, this was it.

While packing, I'd vetoed my first choice of a modest black vest and shirt with matching apron, in favour of a metallic, reflective copper dress that would boldly catch the light as sorrel Cinnabar strode around the arena.

My mother's daughter, I learned long ago to paste a smile on my face, no matter what fresh hell was brewing beneath the surface. The show must go on! Meanwhile under my blouse, video footage of our choreographed ride appears to show two badgers engaged in mortal combat.

Henry and Cinnabar accompanied me and my daughter Cait to demonstrate the womanly art of riding sidesaddle at Canada's main agricultural exhibition. It was definitely not the place I'd have chosen for my wardrobe malfunction. (Author's Collection)

On a happy note, my daughter looked glam, and I think both of our horses went pretty well. Still, there's a moral to this story. You think you want to be bold and catch somebody's eye? I say, be careful what you wish for.

· 27 ·

PUNCHING NEW HOLES

I knew, when I met Sarcee, that I would learn a lot from this horse. He, who has gone ten or twelve years an untouched stallion, has not had his thoughts coloured with imprinting, or the sharing of treats. He has not grown up at the heels of a mother whose life was one of servitude. No. Sarcee thinks in terms of black and white. If given the gift of vocalization, his words to me would be in short, complete sentences.

"You were sneaky." "I am afraid." "I do not understand." "Why?" "Why not?" "Why now?"

So much of what I have long taken for granted with other horses has had no bearing on Sarcee. Petting or praising, in any form, was seen more as a pressure, than a reassurance. Being turned out with the other horses, for the longest time, was of no consequence to the little horse who was happiest standing alone, with his nostrils to the wind.

I have been asked why I would choose to ride a horse who appears to have stepped straight from a Charlie Russell painting. The large head with its convex profile, held aloft a short and tensely upright neck, the narrow shoulders and small wiry stature, supported by short, dense legs and frypan feet. Why him — when the equestrian world is clamouring for gifted stock horses and warmbloods?

Honestly, I do not know. I see now that my apprenticeship in the school of horsemanship has gone off on an interesting tangent, a place that I have never imagined myself, even after a lifetime of teaching diverse equine characters. Sarcee will never show — for where would he? — and more and more, it is feeling as though I shall not, ever again, myself. Still, we try, and we fall short, then we try once more.

Ordinary yet extraordinary days, one woman and one horse. Together, alone.

My hours are filled with wanting to teach him to carry himself in a softness so needed, yet unnatural to a horse who has had to survive on his wits and quick reactions. To teach a relaxed and sustained lope in an animal who has only used the gallop as a short-lived bolting to escape danger. To teach bend and guidance in a horse who has learned to follow well-known trails and his instincts — and little else.

Sarcee came to me in the form of a sage. The fact that he would threaten to part my hair with his lightning-fast front feet, should I sneeze, laugh or move suddenly, has receded in importance to us.

Yes, the student has somehow become the teacher.

When first we met, I wondered how many months he would be in my hands before he was ready. Now? I'm wondering how many years I will be in his presence before I begin to understand.

ON A TIGHT REIN

Working around the house, I had the radio tuned to a talk show. It was keeping me company, but only just. I wasn't paying much attention until, suddenly, I was.

"In order to improve, we must allow ourselves to be judged." Whoa, stop the bus. "Is it easy? No. Is it painful? It can be." The guest speaker happened to be a classical pianist. He could as easily have been a writer, or a painter, or an equestrian. His words would have still hit home.

There are a lot of us in the horse business who do not compete. We say, often with some smugness, that we ride for the purity of whatever it is we hold dear. That we aren't interested in the physical demands, or political manipulations of the show pen, let alone the opinion of some judge. Okay, fine. I get it. If we never put ourselves in a place of vulnerability and transparency, though, is there just the tiniest chance that our thoughts and methods will go unchallenged? Does any of this — let's call it seclusion — come at a risk to the horse?

I think it might. I know that I will dust off my show clothes a few times each year and get out there, if only to see how my methods stand up. Because if I stay home, I stay safe. I tend not to stretch my boundaries. I tend not to ask myself the hard questions. Showing horses isn't the only way to find if we're on the right track. We can sign up for more advanced lessons with a tougher coach. We can get ourselves to the big, scary clinic. We can ride a few dressage tests, if our scene isn't western pleasure.

Social media might be the most terrifying arena of all. Posting videos of our own riding ranks right up there when it comes to vulnerability, same as writing of one's training methods and personal thoughts. People, bless their hearts, have no problem with telling the world that you stink. Every now and then, someone will say something that cuts to the quick. The shame! The outrage! Though usually, there's a grain of truth in what they're braying. It's up to me, then, to decide if I want to nurse my hurt feelings — or do I quietly try again, figuring out a way to do better? Bingo. Being held accountable is the first side effect of being judged.

For many years, horse showing for me was a dog-and-pony show, an endeavour where, no matter how deep my exhaustion, I knew that one day, I'd be grateful for these memories. Yes. Though I was also grateful when the children moved on to other pursuits (with the exception of our youngest child, and more on her elsewhere). But first, picture three little kids and their ponies in various stages of training and, of course, my husband and I, still trying to ride our own horses and keep our marriage intact. Like most mothers, I remember late nights sewing a lot of chaps and costumes.

We bribed our babies into holding their reins with the promise of ice cream cones. We saved frustrated children from bad ends by scaling their intractable steeds in the hitching ring, re-installing last-minute stops and leads. Once, we narrowly avoided all-out warfare by negotiating the exchange of one child's red ribbon for his brother's highly-regarded 'John Deere' green, using the skills of international diplomats. Always, we are shown smiling for the camera.

The toddler years morphed into the teens. One-by-one, our boys elected to forego show-ring honours for the likes of school sports and other things — anything — that might be considered cooler than a weekend spent showing with Mother. Excepting our youngest. She, alone, was the reason Mike and I kept the local tire shop and bulk-fuel dealer solvent. Good years, focused years, saving money for lessons, better saddles, custom clothes, steeper entry fees, nights spent in hilariously dodgy hotel rooms. The girl and her horse were beautiful. Who can blame me for choosing only to remember their moments of glory, rather than all the times I drove our rig home with both of us arguing and in tears?

And then it was over.

The kids went off to school and their own lives, the beloved horses passed to other hands, the show clothes sold before they became too 'last year'. It was down to Mike and I and he, bless him, was flying the white flag of surrender. He craved staying home with the dog. Could I, after all this time, fly solo? Riding, training, feeding, washing, clipping, loading out on dark mornings, hauling to God-knows-where, backing my rig in, then getting to the ring on time? Marshalling my thoughts, learning the patterns, then mounting the fresh, green horse in skin-tight show chaps. Only to find, with dismay, that I'd not got my number on.

There's a gentle kind of buzz in not beating all comers, but in sharing a marshmallow square with one's horse on the shady side of the trailer at noon. Alas, this meeting of our minds comes far easier over the hay bag, than it does when we're actually performing. I wrestle with the knowledge that while we should be doing better — I've been in lessons a good four decades now — I don't seem to know how, or to care enough, to ever change.

My current travelling partner is a disinterested broodmare, one who reluctantly allowed herself to be dragged into this riding gig at age twelve. We understand one another. Many days, the apex of our performance is jumping into the trailer for the welcome haul home. Still, we are out there, waiting for the soft feel for one, two, three strides — and when it happens, it lifts me higher than anything else I know.

. 29 .

HANGING ON FOR DEAR LIFE

About this thing we do, of hanging on to horses that we fear, but are somehow guilted into riding and loving, anyway ... Many of us, I think, were simply raised to be good.

"Be a good girl!" we were told, which often gave the perpetrator license to do whatever he, or she, wanted to do with us. Our minds were so malleable that we learned to make excuses on their behalf.

It was my fault; I was in the wrong place at the wrong time; I should have known better; you don't know him, or how kind and sweet he can be. Now, exchange this for how many of us approach our riding. I didn't read the signs; it's not easy to predict her moods; I never know how far I can push him; she is so good to handle on the ground; when he's in the right mood, he's the best horse, ever! We have no doubt heard — and maybe even said — them all.

I will never understand why everything has to be somebody's fault. It doesn't change a blessed thing and blaming just gets in the way of our healing. One thing I do know is this. It is not my job, or your job, to love and enable something, or someone, who isn't bothered if we get hurt. It doesn't matter whether they knowingly put us in danger or whether they're just untrustworthy flakes. It doesn't matter if they've had a negative upbringing and never knew love. It doesn't change anything, even if they've been abused or spoiled. It just doesn't matter. Your well-being and my well-being were never meant to come at such high cost. That said, there are riders who are the walking wounded. They are seemingly hurt as often as they are well. They might be made of sterner stuff than the average person, or perhaps they have less imagination than many of us? They don't seem to worry, ever, or have foreboding thoughts. Maybe they're just meant to ride tougher horses. If so, this discussion probably isn't meant for them.

It might be time for some practical talk on where we go after we've been hurt. Very few of us, when we've had kindness thrown back in our faces, can exchange this feeling of 'disloyalty' for continued happiness. Our memories are not that short. We are not that dumb. After serious injury, we will be replaying all the details in a brand-new blockbuster thriller, _Boots, Saddles & PTSD._ This is nothing to be ashamed of. It is natural that our fears try to keep us safe.

When we are made to be afraid, we are not unworthy. We are not meant to hang up our spurs and live our lives in fear. Now, whether or not the horse that hurt us can be our own trusted saddle horse again is questionable. He may need to go on to other hands, as might you. I repeat, our memories are not short. We are not dumb. Experience has shown me that unless it was a fluke accident — such as an equipment malfunction or falling while having fun — it is next-to-impossible to forgive and forget. Which, if you've been paying attention, is what is needed between trusted friends.

Perhaps you can put your horse into serious training while you are healing and getting counselling. By the way, get the counselling. Your very well-being has been compromised and you deserve help with that. Perhaps your tough horse will learn to go from daily hard riding to more occasional trail rides, if you are not into serious mileage (though it is doubtful that he can). Perhaps you will be able to sign up for weekly lessons from the trainer, once you are ready. Perhaps this person can eliminate the dark place between you and your horse, the spot where the two of you went wrong. Perhaps the horse, now working at his finest, can be offered for sale by your trainer, to find a more suitable home. There are worse things.

I strongly recommend that if you've been shaken to the core, you heal as best you can, then when you are ready to ride, arrange for lessons. Find an emotionally stable teacher and plan to use that person's most trustworthy horse. Place yourself in the care of someone who understands but will help you overcome your fear. Also, do not buy another horse while you are in recovery. Just like a rebound relationship between people, buying a horse while you are on the mend isn't always wise. Riding a good horse while you are mending means that you can start memorizing what it feels like to expect obedience and good behaviour. This is just another way of saying that we need to learn what it feels like to feel safe.

If these things can't happen, it is not on you to patch them. There are many honest, undamaged horses who would be honoured to serve you. When we feel guilt-ridden and honour-bound to hang on to the misfits, we never open the door to the ones without baggage. Yes, I just said that out loud. Finally, we are not always going to want or need the same type of horses throughout our lifetimes. Our physical bodies, requirements and courage all wax and wane, just like the moon. This is normal. Please, don't get upset with me. Don't let's talk about the horses you need to rescue and the cruelty of selling or putting any animal down. This isn't about letting anyone guilt you into giving your poor horse one more try. For once, I want you to stop and breathe and cry and shake and pound your fist against the wall. For once, I want you to get real about how it feels to be frightened badly.

Yes, it hurts — and both you and your horse deserve better.

. 30 .

GOING THE DISTANCE

I am not feeling well, and this looks to be a day spent in bed. Hacking away at this heaviness in my chest, my voice sounds as though I've been living on whisky. To be honest, I've been indulging in the odd hot toddy, if not two, at night. Mike's toddies are the best. Dreadfully strong — a shot of whiskey, a spoonful of honey, another of lemon juice, then the mug is filled with boiling water. Drinking this will bring tears to your eyes, along with an hour or two of blessed sleep.

Finally, morning. Mike brings a hot water bottle and a cup of coffee to be had in bed. Propped up on my pillows, I'm lying here while the sun makes its age-old climb over the big hill. Low, golden sunrays angle through the attic window and begin warming my toes. The only sounds are of my dog Glen, dancing on the kitchen floor to hurry up a ride in the chore truck, and the measured tick-tock of an old black mantle clock. This has sat on my bedroom dresser since I was a kid.

I chart the sun's progress, noting how far to the south is its path in winter. In the far distance, there is one dark speck, a lone animal, slowly grazing along the fenceline. This does not alarm me, for I know it is Bobby. The young Welsh Cob has been gelded and is now turned out with the main herd. He joins the others on his trips in for water and salt. Otherwise, he enjoys his solitude, bravely searching for better forage than is found nearer the home corrals. I smile at this, for in my experience, these horses who can take or leave the security of the herd are good ones. Fearless and thoughtful, they are their own guiding lights.

Mike climbs the stairs, bringing me a steaming second cup. A good man this, and I would do well to remember during my next marital vexations. I've just finished pulling an all-nighter, working my way, incredulously, through my first published

book, *Horse Woman*. Like the recalling of all great adventures, there are perhaps a few things I wish had been done differently, but there are not too many. Perhaps like the old quilters from years past, we should claim that our errors are planted a-purpose, out of deference to the only possible perfection being the handwork of God.

It relieves me to find that the book is an honest read. There is no pretention, just simply these written words that unite my heart with those of my readers. Some stories are humorous, some are for learning, while others still have the power to hurt. Almost all are based on the things I have learned through my lifelong journey in horsemanship. I note, with some satisfaction, that when I come to the last page, I am sorry that I am done. I think that's a good sign, don't you? Shutting the book and closing my eyes, to better savour this moment of coming to the end — of finally, finally, finishing something that I had started, long ago. I am not a quitter, after all.

Then, once more, I open the book and begin to read.

· 3 1 ·
A PRAYER FOR GOING RIDING

Me: feeling a little jagged, a little niggle of foreboding, a little too much fault-finding and discontent. I stop. With my hands on my midriff, I close my eyes and breathe deeply. I say:

"Thank you, Self, for all the times you keep me safe, make good decisions, forgive my mistakes. Yes, even the boots and chaps that no longer fit, the times I go off course, the horses I wrong or give up on, all the people I hurt and disappoint.

"Thank you, Self, for forgiving all the shady backroom deals I make with you, telling you that I'm not enough, or that I'm a sham, an impostor, or that I don't belong, but that if I change who I really am, I will be worthy.

"Thank you, Self, for looking out for me even when I question myself. Thank you for saying, "Enough!" whenever I replay the mean things, those 'truths' I tell myself so often, I forget that they're actually old lies.

"Thank you, Self, for reminding me that I deserve my own loyalty. That I may listen to the gut feelings of what isn't sitting right, to follow my personal compass, to recognize safe haven among friends, to quietly shed people and situations who don't wish me beauty and light.

"Thank you, Self, for nodding to fear and panic. Thank you for reminding me to breathe and ask: am I getting close to breaking through to a greater truth? Or am I ignoring all the signs of being unsafe?

"Thank you, Self, for making sure that despite everything I have said and done, deep down, I am exactly who I was meant to be. Today, I promise that I have your back; I trust and know that you have mine."

Then stilled, comforted, listened to ... I open my eyes, exhale and ride. This is a help whenever I am too upset, worried, distracted, ashamed, scared or otherwise too much of anything to just breathe, be fair to myself and settle down.

· 32 ·

UNBRIDLED

Trail courses, back in the dark ages, were very different from what they are now.

Rather than counted strides with lengthenings and shortenings, lope-overs and trot poles, trail was judged on a horse's ability to bravely and safely negotiate obstacles. I happened to really like this class, mostly because I thought it was useful and had some day-to-day benefit to real-life working horses. So, from horse showing all the way to my fashion wardrobe, it would seem that I'm hopelessly out of date.

This is an old-time trail horse story, from way back when. My horse, a beautiful black mare, is schooled to be bridled up, Californio style, in rawhide romals and a gorgeous silver bit. We're at a significant show and Shadow has made the trail horse finals. To us, it's a pretty big deal. After scoring highest in the preliminaries run earlier in the afternoon, we will be last to go in the finals at night. All the while we are getting ready, I can hear the crowd building in the arena, the organist playing 4/4 time and waltzes as the pleasure horses go 'round and 'round.

I groom Shadow to a blue-black shine, chalk her white socks, polish her feet and pick through her wavy tail. I grease up her nose, then begin to saddle her with care. First, the thin felt pad, the red and black Navajo blanket, then my stock saddle, riata and matching rawhide hobbles. My little black slicker is rolled as tight and neat as a foot-long pool noodle. There's a bit of an art to this and I stand back, observing my efforts with satisfaction.

I told you this was a story from long ago.

Then, up with my hair in a low, neat bun and I fasten it with a silver clip. Earrings to match. Mascara, three coats, some colour on my cheeks and lips. That'll do. Next, I slide into my red fortrel equitation suit. Yes. It has low belt loops for the black-and-red buck-stitched Tony Lama belt that matches my boots, all from Bradley's Western Wear. A tiny neckerchief with a silver concha pin finishes off the look. I buckle my spurs and the bell-bottomed, hipster show chaps (with a fringed back-belt that cleverly conceals my bottom). Finally, I pull on my black high-crown hat.

It's but a moment to slip on the mare's bridle and I am ready. A few rolls of her cricket and Shadow is ready, too.

We wait in the hitching ring after jogging and loping around to warm up. Scattered applause follows each of the seven horses to go in ahead of us. My mare is very brave, and she loves her job. I can't help but start smiling. The ringmaster waves us in as the announcer introduces us and so we begin our round.

First, the gate. Smoothly, rhythmically, make it look like she needs no help, Lee. Check. Jog over to the big log to side-pass, first to the right. Stop and set down the reins, pick up the yellow slicker on the edge of the arena and put it on. It's twelve sizes too big! Looking like a little kid now, I ask the mare to side-pass left again, all the way off the big log. Check.

Lope to the brush pile. Let her put her head down to pick her way through. Check. Jog over to the wooden bridge, which is kind of scary because it has side railings that are a squeeze, just to fit through. Check. Next, a water obstacle made of a large piece of plywood floating in a kiddie pool. Be careful, here, because the plywood is drilled with holes that gush water, as the horse steps in. Nothing more than a flinch from Shadow as she figures it out. Ask her to put her head down and pause in the middle. Good girl!

After this, we pick up a wire basket of eggs and carefully make our way through an L-shaped back-through. Shadow is always very careful of her feet and if I just keep my eyes on the left side, close to the rails, she'll look after the right. She keeps her part of the bargain and we set down the eggs. Check. Oops, my big slicker has slid down in a sexy off-the-shoulder look, so I reef it back up again. We lope for the next obstacle, a small brushy jump with a bear hide rug sprawled over it, something that has stopped a few horses. Shadow doesn't even glance at it as she makes the leap. Check.

I know that the second last test is going to be difficult. A large tractor tire must be dragged a set distance with a lariat. So far, only two horses have leaned into the rope with enough heft to move the thing through the deep sand. We dally up, grateful for the addition of some last-minute rubber horn wrap. My little mare, veteran of long branding days and calvings, digs deep and gets it done. Check. The crowd claps appreciatively and misty-eyed, I rein Shadow around for the final obstacle.

This is the one thing that none of the horses yet have done faultlessly. I can see what is causing all the trouble. It's a nice bale of hay, sitting about six feet away from a chalk-lined square box.

We lope over to the box and stop. A slow, smooth turnaround one way and then the other. Check. Then, I'm to dismount and either ground-tie or hobble my horse, depending on whether we're using split reins or romals. With shaking, nervous hands and my long rubber sleeves trailing, I pull up the cuffs on my chaps and take the rawhide hobbles off my saddle, crouch down and put them on my mare. Right leg first, pull 'em together, then button the left. Whoa, Shad.

Now, I'm to leave my horse and exit the arena. Going around the outside to where I'd first picked up the slicker, I'm to take it off and leave it hanging in the same spot. Only then can I go back in to Shadow, remount and leave the ring. It sounds easy enough and oh, my word, we've had a glorious run.

I am first alerted to a hitch in my plans as the crowd begins to laugh. No scattered tittering, this, but great guffaws. The organist is playing the theme from *The Lone Ranger*. More laughter. This can't be good. By the time I'm past the end boards of the arena, where I'm to leave my slicker, I can see the cause of their mirth.

There is Shadow, out on the rail, head up and tail streaming — loping, loping, loping. Not fooling, not missing a beat, not looking left or right. Her knees are almost hitting her chin in that high bounding peculiar to hobbled, running horses. Wisely, she has had the foresight to grab the huge chunk of hay that now trails from her mouth. Smart mare, to pack a snack for the road. My jaw drops in disbelief, but I do remember to shuck the raincoat.

I race into the ring, on foot, my long chaps dragging, without any real hope of getting her stopped. Here is a mare who can — and will — go for miles. In the end, with the help of the judge, his ringmaster and a number of handy fellows, the mare finally stops in one corner. We're all short of breath, just gasping away, while she calmly finishes her snack.

Afterward, the show resumes with the results of the Trail Horse final. Shadow and I ride out, amid more laughter, to accept the ribbon and cheque for second place. Meanwhile back at the ranch ...

Fine art is wherever we find it. Even the humblest things, if they bring a smile or a happy memory, deserve to be framed and enjoyed. (Author's Collection)

My pre-school son, Duncan, draws a picture to cheer me. A perfectionist, even at age four, Duncan makes sure to get the amused crowd and my basket of eggs just right. Frustrated at not finding the black crayon, he chooses indigo blue, and very reasonably informs me, "I made Shadow the next darkest thing."

Time flies. My little boy is now the fire chief of a nearby town.

· 33 ·

GIVING A LEG UP

I rode with my friend yesterday. As always, we shared some hard truths, some good laughs, and then we shared horses.

I love riding my friends' horses. They almost always remind me of my friends. Emily, a much-loved sorrel mare, is serious, honest and hard-working. Salt of the earth, she has a generous heart underneath a downright crusty exterior. More to the point, Emily is not about to take any guff from the likes of me.

Even more telling, however, is when the friend throws a leg over one of my horses. It is a real-life snapshot into what is really going on. I watch my friend gather Charlie's reins and then move him off at the trot and lope through a few simple manoeuvres. What a gorgeous guy. I feel myself flush with pride.

Next, of course, comes the embarrassment of noticing that Charlie doesn't neck rein very well without me on board. Now, why would that be? My friend wisely points out that he isn't really neck reining, but rather he is relying upon my legs. Nor can he stop without reefing down, just a little bit, upon the reins. My friend is not causing these things, they are well and truly established. I've just got good at hiding them. Sliding by.

So, I pay attention. I see that there is much about my current project pony that fills my heart with happiness. I see that there are two or three things that need work. That is all. It's like getting a free professional consultation. Now, this only works if your friends happen to be riders you trust and respect. Because Charlie is not a beginner's horse — not yet — I am careful to not offer him up to just anyone to ride. But I like the exposure that other hands can give him. By watching how he processes different methods of mounting and handling, I know that it is keeping him from that dreaded condition of becoming too precious. Making such a horse is bordering on a disservice as, most of all, I want to make a resilient horse or pony who is comfortable and capable of going on without me. It's a lot like parenting, actually.

When I follow this credo, I am trying to give my horse the skills he will need to live a safe and cared-for life. When it comes to my horses, I welcome the village that will help me raise up my 'child'.

· 34 ·

JUMP FOR JOY

If I resolve to do anything, might I be more mindful of my gratitude? In that case, here goes. I give thanks for Mike. Beautiful grandbaby Ruby! Our three kids and their special others. My unstoppable mum. Glen and Pan, the Border Collies. That first coffee. Digging in the dirt. Fringed gauntlets. Riding. Better yet, riding well.

Old houses, new toothbrushes. Mike's bread, with real butter. Laughter. Sidesaddles. Singing, made richer with the harmony of friends. My country. Good horses and clients. Just the right bit of a westerly wind. My banjo. Reading, dancing. Parade Day. Artists. Canning all manner of things. Chinooks. Long skirts. Clean sheets. Wearing hats. These hills. Cody and Harry. Questionable jokes. Ponies! Loud music (like there's any other kind).

Firing up the cookstove. Gingerbread. Beautiful gear. Finding joy. The long view. Tartan, tartan, everywhere. Delphiniums. Old photos. The stars. Turned stirrups and broken-in chaps. Basset Hounds. Heated conversation. Pilot. Unusual people. Really great boots! Tough roses. Sarah Brightman, The Black Keys, Mark Knopfler, The Tragically Hip, Tom Petty, The Stones.

Writing. Really setting the table. Fireworks! Scotch caps. Artists. My teachers. Brown Betty. Taking Cypress down to soak in the creek. Cottonwoods, better yet, with hammocks. Antiques. One very good beer. Sleighing with bells on. Sanchez. Tight harmony. Going to the fair. Believe it or not, Facebook. The smell of mowing the lawn. Saying yes and really meaning it. The colour orange. Art of the Cowgirl. Pamela. Well-ironed shirts. Old '78s. Rain. Nanny's dishes. This creaky house. Did I say ponies? Dark fruitcake, not light. Jazz chords. Trucks. Cows — bulls, not so much. My Cattle Cait purse. Chickadee. Robbie Burns night. Old jewellery, new pyjamas. Silver bits. Good hay. Heartfelt hugs.

My lovely publisher. Cathedral choirs. 'Lip grease' to ward off evil. Old clocks. Honest-to-goodness linen napkins. A few good friends. Hoar frost. Fresh snow. The open road. An accountant to do all my heavy lifting. My bathtub. Real Christmas trees. Tee, Bobby and Atticus. A delicious, new book. Planning a garden and eating the first peas. Knowing there are people in the world who are genuinely cheering me on.

My only want in the face of these blessings? Let there be love and light, for us all.

· 35 ·

STANDING HOBBLED

"What are we waiting for?"

Do you remember? We talked about this question in my first book, *Horse Woman*. Beyond the usual weather and bad roads, beyond new fears of money and social distancing, I'll ask again: What are we waiting for?

Get the paper and pencil. Make the list. Name three things you really want to try this year, before you get any older. Note the word 'try' here — I've not said anything about mastering, nor winning champion of the world. Just to try. Now, stick this note on the mirror where you brush your teeth.

Me? Seek better fitness (again). 'Camp' on this particular horse (still). Enter the dressage show, no matter how I look in my white breeches (see the first point) or how well I think young Atticus will behave (read the second). I can do these things, even if I don't win.

What about you? What would you try this year, if we weren't all so scared of being judged?

· 36 ·

SOAKING

There are days we're plumb hard on ourselves. Our biggest hurts are not always about wrecks from riding. For me, the biggest pains come from fencing, choring and gardening, just. Whenever I've any minor cuts, scrapes or bits of infection brewing, I treat myself as I do my horses. It's time to brew up some 'Tea for Ten'. The kettle goes on and I'll throw a few Red Rose black tea bags into a mug or small bowl. When the liquid is viciously strong and just comfortably hot, I will soak my fingers. There's always time for a healing soak in black tea — ten minutes, to be exact — and though simple, this is bliss. My horses, when cut, or on a course of antibiotics, would agree, though their tea is steeped in a bucket.

· 37 ·

LONG MAY SHE RUN

When it comes to my being a horsewoman, and starting a family, I went many years without riding enough.

I remember mainly angst and tears during that time as the study of riding — or more rightly, being a rider — had always been who I was. Because I was so very young at the time, I didn't fully grasp the fleeting nature of those years.

Boom. Boom. Boom. We had three babies, almost overlapping, they were so close together. Looking back, chronic tonsillitis that went untreated, along with undiagnosed post-partum depression. "Go clean your house, you'll feel better" did not help. The best years of my life, or so I was told, were feeling bleak. Rather than celebrate life with my beautiful children, I stood sobbing at the diaper pail by the window, watching, while others in the family headed out every morning to work cattle, to ride the hills. They were so free! Those years were agony, if I'm honest. My time in the saddle became odd stolen moments after hours, when my husband came in from his ranch job, exhausted. I would barter his time to watch our dear children while I saddled my snuffy, unridden horse and rode until darkness set. On many nights, I just went out to groom her and shed my tears.

This quiet time became both my salvation and my torment.

Eventually, of course, I was able to ride more often, once the children were old enough to accompany us, either in front of me on the saddle, or on ponies of their own. This was better, but it still was thin gruel for someone who had apprenticed almost five years with a dressage master. I somehow nourished myself by teaching other riders and competing with the children's ponies in combined driving. Early mornings were spent schooling dressage on quiet roads, the afternoons for designing my show turnout around my latest guiltily-purchased hat.

The children grew. I veered dangerously into the uncharted waters of becoming 'that' parent. You know who I mean — the mother who rides through her kids. It wasn't pretty and while I treasure the memories and old photographs of well-schooled young riders in their made-to-measure chaps, I realize that they put up with an awful lot from me. That we still speak says a lot for my grown kids' forgiving natures.

Six-year-old Iain and me, with the beloved family horses, Kinistino and Playgirl,
in Adult-and-Child Pairs. "Sit tall and hold your reins like an ice cream cone!"
Iain still mimics his mother, three decades later. (Author's Collection)

By the time my daughter was competing as a junior, I'd made the move to embrace better fitness — I mean, starve myself — and get back into my custom boots and regular lessons. At long last! Six months later, at the age of forty-two, I had a stroke. So began months spent in bed, in darkened rooms, learning how to swallow and focus my eyes in bright sunlight. Again, my horses waited.

Riding, for me, has meant decades of forging ahead and then falling behind. I wish I'd known then what I'm just now starting to learn — that horsemanship, however it comes to us, is a lifelong thing. There is learning and reconsidering, embracing challenge and fear, along with all our demons, the things we've long tried to hide. There is joy and, if we're lucky, one or two excellent horses who will allow us to go beyond any places we might have imagined. In the end, while I feel some regret about the years that my saddles sat, untouched, on the hard-to-reach racks in the tack room, I know now that it was all meant to be.

I was not made to ride expensive horses and compete in faraway lands. Rather, I was a rural farm wife and a mother, going to town for parts, growing a garden, taking cookies to the class party, becoming a small business owner, raising kind children into responsible adults. I would have my time in the sun, riding and teaching new riders, new horses and then — somehow, magically — writing to you all, here, right now.

Our own brand of horsemanship. It comes to us in untold ways, and despite what we may hope and dream, is never one-size-fits-all. Years later, I can only look back and thank heaven.

. 38 .

OLD RAWHIDE

There is this thing with social media. We put ourselves 'out there' in a way that isn't quite real or true. I'm no exception, giving impressions that I don't try very hard to disprove — that I never lose my temper with a horse; that I feel good about being the size I am; that my husband and I are so in love, we're like newlyweds; that I don't live in a falling-down house with a teeny-tiny mousey trap-line; that when it comes to horses, I pretty much know it all. Yeah, right.

I went to town for groceries a few days ago. It was bloody hot, and I wasn't feeling well. I manage my rheumatoid arthritis, to a point, but every so often, it sits up and manages me. This week, this familiar, chronic illness has kicked the feet out from under me. Just when I was staggering out of the grocery store, my cart brimful, a voice called out from behind.

"Lee McLean? Is that really you?!" I turned and made polite conversation with this stranger, a lady who faithfully follows Keystone and has kindly shelled out to buy my first book, both for herself and several friends. Why did I? Because it is what polite and grateful people do. I got a little uncomfortable when she stopped a second stranger to take our picture. We laughed because with Covid and social distancing, it was actually a picture of a dusty station wagon, bookended by two random women. This sweet person was so excited to have her picture taken 'with someone famous', in the grocery store parking lot, no less. But no, my dear, that's not quite right. That's not who I am.

When people come up to me, excited to meet the person behind the words, it embarrasses me. I'm not Elvis. To be honest, I feel like a fraud. I'll tell you about my latest horsey misadventure, so that you'll get a better idea of the real me. Yesterday, I'd signed up to take part in a clinic on competing in Ranch Horse Versatility. I was excited a few weeks ago, but this week, with my illness and the added complication of selling every single one of my well-broke horses, everything had changed. I'd decided this was something I was just going to have to muscle through, even if it killed me. I showed up, saddled poor old Sanchez, then swallowed a hefty dose of painkiller. Even the horse was on Previcox, because he's not actually serviceably sound.

Maybe it was the heat, the travel, the stress of learning something new, but Sanchez had to pack it up partway through the riding portion of the clinic. I was so ashamed that I had put my horse in a position to fail that it overshadowed my own shame at being fragile and drugged, myself. What a pair we were! A kind and observant friend who was there auditing the clinic came out to help me unsaddle and wash Sanchez down, to try and make him more comfortable. As she led him away to put him in his stall, I returned to the clinic on foot. It was actually good for me and, you know, I learned a few things.

In addition to gaining some new knowledge on an up 'n' coming horse sport, I learned that I am not in control of how things will work out. I am not above putting my horse in a bad situation. I am as subject to disappointment and failure, as is anyone. I am not above needing and asking for help. I am still in the position of driving home into the setting sun with humility, let-down, self-pity and even a few tears.

Every now and then, we will have one of those days. Nope, it's not all photo ops and autographs.

· 39 ·

IN AND OUT OBSTACLES

Golly, we know it's true and yet why do we still wonder about ourselves? The five-hundred-billion-dollar beauty industry knows this about us and banks upon our losing these battles with our inner demons. A lot of money, made by others and lost by us, flowing simply because we can never quite believe that we are good enough, as is.

The mindset is learned young. I figured out very quickly the power behind a pretty face, when I was driving a school bus in my early twenties. No matter the age of the students, from kindergarten kids to high schoolers, girls and boys, if my make-up was solid and my hair on trend, I was taken seriously. I counted. I mattered. I was obeyed. Never once did I have to stop the bus or raise my voice. Whenever I'd rush out the door with unwashed hair and in my old sweats, it was altogether a different story. It didn't take me long to see a pattern. On any given day, to these kids, I was only as good as I looked.

Grudgingly, somewhat annoyed with myself, I have since done my best to meet others' approval. Somehow, it's just easier on everyone if we go along. This knowledge that our worth is displayed for all to see by our outside appearance is certainly no news to anyone who has spent time in the corporate world. Power dressing, being stylish, knowing our daytime wear versus softer nighttime looks, blonde or brunette, up-dos and letting our hair down, flats or heels, another round of dieting. It is what it is.

Or is it? As I've aged, I've tried hard to be truer to myself. All along, that little girl within has known what is best for me. More and more, I am wanting to find sustainable health in my quest for growth and learning. It has taken me a lifetime to get beyond the first lessons learned from Barbie. Namely, that I will be happy and valued just so long as I can manage to pull off a great body with impossibly long legs. Without voice or opinion, but with a pretty face. Of course, if we were to have a real heart-to-heart with all our sisters who actually possess great long legs and pretty faces, we'd be surprised and disheartened to find that neither does anything to guarantee any sort of happiness. Who knew that the hard work of living with self-worth would fall to us?

You might be surprised to find that this thinking we do seeps into other areas of our lives, including our horsemanship. Would it shock you to be told that a beautifully well-schooled and correct horse is worth considerably more money if he has a symmetrical face marking and four white feet? Hence all the white-wrapped legs on the sales pages. That the seeming perfection of these bandages means more to our eye, than the ability to see puffy joints or crooked legs? That too often, we will pick the poor-quality or troubled horse, if he is of an eye-catching colour? That any horse sale will attest to the fact that the blue roans, true blacks and palominos top out the averages, all day long. That the hardest horse to sell is the chestnut mare, unless she has a considerable list of performance earnings to offset her appearance? That too many people will judge a horse by its colour if not its sex and, surprisingly, the harshest critics when it comes to a horse's looks can be us women.

Because I buy unstarted horses for resale, I am always looking at prospects who catch the eye. I have learned, the hard way, that a horse's colour will make it easier to sell him again, once he is trained. His colour might well matter more than the fact that he shows a balanced topline, a beautifully-schooled canter or even, a functionally-sound set of legs.

Case in point, dear Henry, who in anyone's eyes should have been the perfect horse. Ridden English, Western or Sidesaddle, in the show pen or out on the range, Henry was safe for any level of rider. Imagine that. Sound as a bell, he was without need of shoes or meds of any kind. Fifteen hands of handsome and only twelve years of age. But the money-earning reiner was an ordinary, orangey-sort of sorrel with a decidedly skimpy tail and mane. Reasonably priced and well-presented, it took me what seemed forever to find Henry a worthy home.

Babe was different. She was not even remotely schooled and there was very little about her conformation that might be considered a plus. With a cresty neck that appeared a good six inches too short for a body that bordered on obesity, Babe had little to commend her. When the mare repeatedly struck at me with a front foot during our first introduction, I should have walked away and left her right where she was. Still, there was something about this horse that made me stop for a second look. Surprised at myself, I tried to dig down to the root cause. Was I was finding myself drawn to her luxuriant mane and tail, blood bay dapples, and four stockings? It came as a shock to realize that, of course, I was.

No matter how obstreperous her behaviour, I wanted to take this little cutie home.

The next morning, I observed my new horse from outside the corral. She would need a laundry list of work and procedures done to gain back her health and decorum, but first things first. She needed a new name. I looked at the rudely-mannered mare and imagined what ideal we would be working toward. I saw a reliable, sparkling character who would be a joy to be around. She would be safe and comfortable to ride in the arenas and along the trails. Her rotundity would morph into a fit, large pony with a body that could easily absorb an adult rider's leg. She would bring nothing but happiness to her new family. I smiled when, for some reason, I thought of the old, brown teapot that has served in my kitchen for many years. In that moment, Babe became Brown Betty.

I would like to say that in that one instant, everything about my new mare changed. This would be untrue, of course, for in the coming months, we waged many a battle royal over trailer loading, standing tied, walking, trotting and cantering, steering, getting stopped, standing still and, yes, even just guiding obediently down the lane. Through it all, one defining thought stayed foremost in my mind. I vowed that Betty would be so honest and genuine in her character, the last thing people would notice would be her cuteness.

With my faith in her largely unwavering, Betty eventually rose to the heights of my belief. With time and mileage, she began to act as I'd imagined her. I would ride her out in public, so proud of all we'd accomplished, only to be surprised by the laughter of those mounted on more talented horses. To be fair, it took most of a winter for dear, unathletic Betty to manage a canter through the bend of the arena's short wall. It was a good lesson for me, a person who has always wanted recognition and justification for my work. Together, Betty and I somehow brought about slow change from the inside out. Because she strived to be a force of integrity in the world, because she grew to be loved for who she was and not because of how she looked, Betty's changes were profound. They were lasting.

Don't know about you, but I wanna be like Betty. As she neared middle age, she had finally come to understand her own value and visibly showed unshakeable confidence in who she was. Brown Betty was more than her short neck, her rotund body or her stocky legs. She was truly beautiful because she was kind and brave, using her God-given powers for good.

· 40 ·
PASSING THE VETTING

I have just gone in to the Big Smoke, to see a doctor who specializes in sports medicine. He led me to believe that by the time a physically-adventurous person is nearing sixty years on this earth, they will — ahem — be wearing out. That their parts are no longer covered by any sort of warranty. He also led me to believe that an otherwise sane person who messes around with horses is more likely to wear out, even faster. I was beginning to get the feeling that I was one in a l-o-n-g line of people who came to him with similar complaints. It was while I was explaining what had happened to my knee that he stopped short in his taking of notes. Now, I had his attention.

"Whoa, whoa, whoa!" The doctor looked up from his screen and held up a hand. "I'd have bet that I've treated every possible sports injury known to mankind, but you might be one for the diary. I have never been presented with someone who was hurt while racing sidesaddle. Is that even a thing?!"

We shared a good laugh, before getting back to the serious business of 'living well and riding better'. I'm still smiling and, you know, it feels good to see to my own health for a change. Our horses have their teeth and chiro done regularly and yet it's all too easy for an owner to go years without taking the needed time and money.

I was left with a scolding that I'm going to pass along to any of you who might be doing what I have been doing for the past several years now. I know exactly where and when I hurt myself and yet I did nothing about it. If we are presented with a searing pain that does not lessen, does not go away, it is not going to go away on its own. We are not going to 'walk it off' or magically resolve with 'turnout'. We are not going to 'Bute it better'.

Today's hard diagnosis would have been very, very different had I seen to this knee back when I hurt it. My friends, you wouldn't do it to your horses, don't do it to yourselves. Don't make yourself ride sore. Go to the doctors and physical therapists until you've got some real answers. Then, do the homework and follow the rules.

Why do we do this to ourselves? Why do we take our horses to the vet, the dentist, the massage therapist, the chiropractor, and then we put our own complaints on the back burner, all the while knowing that this active life we lead is only possible while our health holds? This is but another lesson I am learning, thanks to my horses. How much I matter is up to me.

Riding on the circuit with the Sidesaddle Racers taught me that while we may be serious competitors, it is healthy and powerful when women can support one another, no matter what. (Lorraine Hjalte Photo)

. 41 .

CIRCLE THE WAGONS

I turn off the news, particularly in time of war or pandemic. Good sleep is aided by avoiding the landslide of frightening headlines. While we need to stay informed, this is best done during the day and not just before bed. Mike and I are listening to favourite music and watching old movies that have long delighted us. There is never too much comedy at a time like now. We're having a bit of fun, inventing recipes with whatever we're digging from dark corners of the pantry and the deepfreeze. I'm doing a lot of quiet walking. I take the dogs and we just go make tracks.

One of my favourite things in the whole world is a clean bed. I've been treating myself to fresh sheets more often than is usual. This one thing brings me a surprising amount of joy. I'm being tight with my money because it is one thing that I can do, here, now, to lower the stress of job loss. I'm slowly, slowly facing my clothes closets and kitchen cupboards, putting up new shelf liners — well, I've actually owned the roll of paper for about eight years, but who's counting? — washing and boxing items that I will never, ever again wear or use. Someday, these will go to the charity shop, or be the basis of a garage sale. Some day.

I've been plugging along at my tack, cleaning and conditioning the stuff that needs it, fixing the stitching that with hard use, has let go. I've brought in a favourite bridle to hang on the hook by the door. I've just needed something horsey here to comfort me in the house. Yesterday, I dumped all my old grooming tools in the washing machine. They came out looking like new. My poor washer was a whole other story but, hey, with job loss, we've suddenly got the time to deal with that.

Day before yesterday, I was sad. I ate as well as I could, found my blankie and let myself, for an hour or two, just feel how I was really feeling. I breathed in and out and let myself rest. I'm falling in love with twenty-minute naps again. Your homework, if you feel the need, is to distill everything you're feeling and taste it. Give your emotions a name. If you're feeling productive, finding healing in being busy, then go for it. If you're feeling as though you need to curl up and hide, then nurture yourself. Let it happen. Prioritize the things that are sitting heavily and just try to sit with one thing at a time. While some days may be lonely, I'm learning that they are also a gift. For so many years, I dreamed of being able to stay home and rest.

Today, I will lift up my eyes unto the hills, trusting in good times ahead.

. 42 .

BARN SOURED

I once told a confidante that I still didn't know what I wanted to be 'when I grew up'.

"The trick is, not to," she laughed. But I think she knew what I was hinting at. Were we always going to be in a soulless existence of showing up for work and trying to pay bills? Where was the joy in all that? Was this, whatever it was, the reason we were put on this earth? Surely not. So, I called myself 'just a student', 'just a ranch wife', then, 'just a mother'. I did short-term jobs like taking the federal census and, let me tell you, there are still people I can't look in the eye because of how they treated me. I went partners with my mother-in-law in a hardcore guest-ranching venture, when Mother Nature and twenty-three per cent interest rates turned turtle on agriculture in the 1980s.

But I didn't quit.

I went out on a limb and became a school bus driver because I'd get three weeks off over Christmas and an entire summer to languish, I mean, ride herd on paying guests. That first year somehow grew into eighteen seasons in the driver's seat. Imagine, if you will, piloting a portable greenhouse that smelled of diesel, vomit and liverwurst sandwiches. Weirdly, I loved it. Most of the parents treated me as a human being, not 'just the bus driver'. Most of the kids were awesome. I marvelled at their clever minds and the way they helped me with the profoundly handicapped student who also rode our bus. I was the benevolent dictator of a small country called Bus Number Seven. These years will remain among the best of my life. Still, a little voice inside me said, "Surely, you weren't made just for this?" I got very sick around the same time I began to wonder.

But I didn't quit.

On a whim borne of desperation, I decided to open an antiques shop in our ranch home. I loved old things! That afternoon had me ordering a three-hundred-dollar grand opening ad in our local paper — remember, it was long before the internet — and then later that week, I presented my case to municipal council. They turned me down, citing my urge to run a small home-based business an affront to traditional values. That I would do better to go home and raise my kids. The second time I went before them, council deemed that I could run a business in the country only if they redesignated all the prime agricultural land in our township as commercial. The notice went out in the local paper and, as you can imagine, this motion went over in our community like a lead balloon. It took me years to swallow the anger of being outfoxed by this old boys' club.

But I didn't quit.

Finally, later that year, with the council on summer recess, a kind clerk notified me to try again with my request for a business licence. It was rubber-stamped by the woman put in temporary charge, and with the newly-printed licence in my hand, I did not look back.

Cottonwood House Antiques went on for twelve wonderful years to buy and sell antiques, make appraisals, hold teas and summer garden parties, culminating in an annual pine-scented extravaganza each Christmas. My antiques business helped pay a mortgage, the horse show entries, bought a sweet little slant-haul trailer and some nice horses. It sent kids on school ski trips and Mike and I on a few well-deserved vacations. During this time, I taught 4-H, wrote a weekly newspaper column, and published two books on collecting antiques.

But I didn't quit.

Every morning, I vacuumed my shop/house. I cleaned the washrooms and railed at three kids who didn't care to fold or hang up a towel. I gardened like a madwoman. I dusted and made Welsh Cakes for tea parties on the verandah. I baked and put all my spoils in tins marked "COLOSTRUM" in the deep-freeze. This, to outfox three hungry teens and a sweet-toothed husband. I will say that the whole family worked very hard, kids and grandparents included. We gave up our privacy and our holidays, but we were well-rewarded. Then, surprise. I got very sick around the same time I began to grow restless.

Yes, there was a pattern. Around the times I'd grow despairing of doing these things I no longer loved, I would grow exhausted, and then failing to listen to my body, I would get sick. You see, there were only two things that I had loved with a passion since childhood. Since I would probably never realize my longstanding dream of being a jazz singer in a red satin dress and a smoke-filled nightclub, I decided to ride and sell horses. But this time, I didn't make the same mistake I had made so many times before.

I was very careful to not turn this thing I loved into a means to a paycheque. My burgeoning horse business would have nothing to do with being responsible for other people, or for getting rich.

I was mindful to not label myself a riding teacher or a horse trainer. Even the new author label, I was reluctant to make stick. I learned that whenever we turn our passions into jobs, we run the risk of ruining that one precious thing we have long loved.

In the years since, I've seen a lot of young people hang out their shingles as horse professionals. This can work if they've put in the time. Time for an education beyond ag college, more than a few years to apprentice at the hands of a master — learning the grunt work, the bookkeeping, the technical riding, the horsemanship and the people skills — soaking in all the sheer fortitude it takes to show up in this business, day after relentless day.

You will ride sore and you will turn your back, many times, on your families' needs, because your clients need you more. This isn't a choice in the business, it is a fact. If you are in a domestic relationship, where both of you are horse professionals, you will need the grace of your guardian angels.

Soon, if we are not careful, we can grow hard and resentful of this thing we once loved.

I still don't know what I want to be when I grow up. I have, however, endeavoured to keep a light-hearted mix in my business — riding only the horses I truly like, buying and selling, boarding and doctoring, training, repairing broken equipment, teaching, and building sidesaddles, balancing my clients' needs with my family's and my own, keeping up with my own continual learning, coming home to build a social media presence, nurturing longstanding friendships and mentorship, saving enough wonder in my own heart to try new things — like writing books on lessons learned and of women's horsemanship.

And so we evolve. While I will never regret doing what I do with horses, I would urge those of you who are thinking of becoming 'more of' what you so admire, to go carefully. Proceed with caution, knowing that you must want this thing, more than any other earthly happiness. Recently, somebody called me 'an overnight success'. Sweetie, when you've been pulling paycheques as long as my generation has, you're not an overnight anything. All you can do is go at that job, whatever it is, as though you're trying to change the world. What I am saying is this. There is nothing wrong with riding simply because you love it. There is nothing wrong with working for someone else. There is nothing wrong with pursuing a separate career that will allow you to enjoy having horses. There is nothing wrong with wanting to be a trainer. But listen.

Though you may never tire of riding, you will grow very tired. Fair warning. When we 'job out' our greatest passions, we run the risk of watching another good love go bad.

· 43 ·
HOLD YOUR HORSES

Opening my email account is a lesson in patience. Tap, tap, tap, go my fingernails and I drain what's left of my cold coffee. 'Round and 'round goes the aptly-named cursor. My tension begins to rise. It's like watching one's partner chew with his, or her, mouth open.

Out of interest, I've been timing my laptop between pressing 'enter' and its acknowledgement of my commands. Thirty-three seconds. A mere half-a-minute and yet I'm ready to explode.

All of a sudden, I'm realizing what is wrong with so much of today's horsemanship. This may pertain especially to children, who have not been brought up to wait for results. I, who am old enough to know better — a person who once sent cereal box tops away, for weeks on end, for a plastic decoder ring — should not need instant results. But I do.

We know in our hearts that when we're riding, we have to ask and then wait until the horse understands. It's quite a bit like teaching someone how to speak a language that we, ourselves, have never really mastered.

We have to slow our hands down. We have to wait until the horse gives the right response and then to generously reward him. We have to do this over and over until the horse learns his new default setting. We know in our hearts that we'll be working on a horse for years to get to that place where we both feel confident and satisfied. Our hearts are one thing. Our heads mightn't be so quick to accept this old-fashioned notion of time without measure.

Empathy and patience are a tall order in a society that tends to go off the deep end waiting thirty seconds for a command to be fulfilled. We want what we want now, with the click of a button. We're no longer hard-wired to stay in the moment and calmly wait, until. You might want to read that last sentence again.

We grow tense and unhappy without our instant fixes. This is an addiction at odds with good riding, good parenting and plain ol' good living. It's just another thing to think about, all the while we're tapping our fingers and revving our jets.

· 4 4 ·

A LEAP OF FAITH

Those of us who grew up as horse-crazy kids often spent a lot of time creating. We drew horses, however well, listening to the Beatles on our transistor radios. We made up horse show games with daring jump-offs. We wrote stories about ponies and kept company with our red vinyl diaries into the wee hours.

Me? I wrote poetry and drew pictures. Reams of illustrated poems of horses and nothing else.

Miss Young was my teacher in the grade three/four class. She, a horse lover herself, understood this thing that fuelled me. I was allowed a free rein. One weekend, we were given the task of writing about something we had seen that changed us. Just a month or so before, I had ridden in my very first pony show. Until then, I had never seen such beautiful animals in my life.

My poem, *I'm Proud I'm a Hunter*, had the distinction of being pinned, until Christmas, on the bulletin board just outside the school staff room. I was gazing in wonder at this singular honour, when two teachers paused behind me.

"Her mother must have written this. You should've made an example of her, not given the girl a reward!" said the one. Then, flowing quietly over my shame, came the fair and resolute voice of Miss Young.

"If this was about any other subject, I might wonder," said my teacher. "But when it comes to horses, this child has something inside her that begs to be let out. These words belong to Lee."

I never forgot this moment. Talk about something that has the power to change us! Just one teacher, in the face of something ugly, who chose to believe. Miss Young, it is high time I thanked you.

As for my poem, I don't believe it was ever returned to me, but I still remember the last bit. Here goes:

> I must screw up my courage, without a fault,
> I'll discourage my rider, if I come to a halt.
>
> *(Mumble, mumble,*
> *I forget what comes next.)*
>
> Hey, what is this? I'm best out of all!
> For that is my number the announcer did call.
>
> On goes my ribbon, of red, white and blue ...
> And a cup for my rider, she deserves something, too.

Peter and I at our first show. Fifty years later, my riding jacket, made by Grammie Duncan, still hangs in my closet. (Author's Collection)

· 45 ·

PULLING OUR WEIGHT

People often say that their horses keep them sane.

It's nice to show gratitude to our four-footed friends, but I'm not so sure I agree with this idea wholly. I am mindful to not saddle my horses with such a heavy job. My moods and depressions are my responsibility, not theirs. I can be grateful to them for listening, ever-so-happy that they're in my life — but it is not their job to keep me level or emotionally-balanced. That, my friends, is squarely up to me.

Horses have garnered the role of becoming our healers. This is beautiful, believable and entirely within the equine realm. These animals are so dialed in to us that many of them already seemingly know what we'll be thinking about next week. The problem lies in the fact that many of us are unwell — mentally, emotionally — and because of this, we're drawn to horses. We get involved without doing our own work.

So many times, the wrong sort of horses end up in the hands of the wrong sort of people. The horses go down a bad road and their people often get hurt. The wheels inevitably fall off because neither party is quite able to lead the other to safety.

There is no shame in this. Just know that not all horses are able to do the work of helping us. We can groom them and say that the smells and sounds of the barn are balm to our souls. They are to mine, too, if you must know the truth. But having horses in our lives does not let us off from attending to our own therapy — getting honest, seeking qualified help, admitting our own needs to be victims and/or perpetrators, being open and willing to be the change. Horses will help us, but the real lasting healing is ours alone.

· 46 ·

BACK IN THE SADDLE AGAIN

After some time away, there's nothing like being back in the saddle. However we may ride, no matter our boots and saddles, let it be with joyful intent.

· 47 ·

FREE REIN

Both Mike and I are unusual in that we didn't ride bikes as kids. We had ponies. Best of all, both of us lived within striking distance of old-time country stores. He and his brothers rode to South Fork Trading Post, while my sister and I frequented Little Horse Store. By the way, Little Horse was a lake, it wasn't a store that sold little horses, but I digress.

White cream sodas were our absolute favourites. Soda pop and chocolate bars were a dime each. Oh, to decide between the Chunks Bars, Eat Mores and Cuban Lunches! Cherry Blossoms in little cardboard boxes were always a lure, but they invariably made me sick after eating them on the ride home. Mojos were for filling one's pockets, two for a penny. I remember the old log store's screen door with the deer antler handle. Times have certainly changed because the reason we kids were going to the store in the first place was to fetch my father his cigarettes. The elderly couple who ran the store were lovely people. Often, we'd tie our ponies to the hitching rail and stay for tea. It never once occurred to my sister and me to question equine patience. We never doubted their willingness to wait, even while hitched by their bridle reins. This is what happens when our horses become our modes of transportation. We appreciate them, yes, but we do tend to take them for granted. This patient stoicism is something I miss in many of today's horses. Like so many of us, they have lost the ability to breathe and wait.

Mike remembers pocketing the antique, curlicued key to the post office desk when he was tiny. This move drew the business of the surrounding ranching community to a halt — until the key was later recovered by his mother in a load of laundry.

Few kids ride as a means of transportation anymore. Unmanaged and unsupervised, it was a delightful way to grow up.

· 48 ·

TURNED OUT

That's the best thing about horses. They might have a disagreement, make their point, and then get over it. Back to the serious business of grazing, they leave the bearing of grudges to us.

· 49 ·

ONCE MORE, WITH FEELING

It came to me, as these things do, on the way home from my lesson. I don't know whether I'm just feeling sorry for myself or having an existential crisis! I've been having a few days, or a week, or maybe even three weeks, of uncharacteristic struggle in the saddle. It's been a long time since I've been so down about my riding. I can barely get myself and my horses out to my lessons and back home again. Today was another one of those days.

My thoughts are riding on my four someday sale-horses. Right now, two of these are lame. The one hurt herself in a heart-stopping instance while I was schooling her on the flag. Oh, my guilt and remorse! While much improved, she has been slow to heal. The other has recently fallen, or slipped with his shoes still on, during a freak snowstorm. These are both active, fit horses whom I've been enjoying in this year's lessons with my mentor. They have challenged me to be a better horsewoman. They have given meaning to my own learning. They have been long-term, technical projects who are just starting to see the light. That is, until now.

This planning, and then being disappointed, is a constant in a life spent with horses.

With this pair on the sidelines, I've been splitting my riding between new-to-me nineteen-year-old Harry, and Rockabilly, a large spotted pony who is still very green. A well-broke horse nearing retirement, Harry's modus operandi is seemingly to have his rider work at the level of exertion to which he, himself, is being held. Billy tries his best, but unaccustomed to the discipline of schooling indoors, let alone in a group of performance horses, he is finding it a challenge. Bottom line, neither horse is ready to pick up where my other two have left off.

I've taken myself to task by saying that the mark of any rider is to get the best from every single horse she handles. Harry and Billy, unfortunately, have not read the memo. They are quite content sailing through life, without honing their advanced cowhorse skills. Still, I've been showing up with a determined smile, happy with their dogged steps towards improvement, trying my best not to feel as though I'm wading against a strong current and losing ground.

I love horses, all horses. It bothers me to learn that shallowly, I'd rather ride something 'edgy', with some jam.

I want to honour these two boys and their honest personalities. Both deserve my kindness, best horsemanship, and a real chance to improve. But I'm pushing the one fellow with every blessed step, and I know that Rockabilly is already doing his level best for me. If I ask any more of them, I will be bordering on abuse. But wait. I'm schooling with people who are competitive sorts, mounted on beautiful, high-dollar horses. I'm admiring them as they ride, wishing I belonged with them, all the while my self-esteem plummets.

If you must know, this both surprises and shames me.

How can I possibly feel sad and stalled-out doing what is a dream for most people, locked in their office jobs? Am I the worst sort of flake? It is but a short path before I settle upon the thought that I'm a fraud, wasting my time and money without ever making a difference in the real world. Who am I to think I have a place in the horse business? Who am I to have the nerve to write a book?! What am I doing on the busy highway at two o'clock in the afternoon, pulling a listless horse who just wants to stay home and eat? Why am I wasting good money on learning anymore, at my age? My next thought, invariably, is that it's time to quit.

It came to me, as my old Chevy laboured up the coulee into the howling west wind, that my riding, like a piece of lasagna, is made of several layers. One is bettering my project horses. Another is enjoying my time with the 'going' family horses who will always live here. A third layer is riding out to clear my head and put on honest miles in beautiful country. Always, I am trying to do better at all of these than I did the day before. My own lessons, while I will probably never again grace a show ring, have a fourth layer of getting me out among like-minded people. Without them, I might go weeks without ever seeing another human being beyond my husband. I wouldn't know what it was to watch, to cheer, to try and laugh, then to try again. I wouldn't know about gathering enough courage to start anew with each fresh horse, the well-baked layer that tops my comfort zone.

I'm still out there, still trying to perfect my feel and timing, still trying to do my best to get out of the way of each new horse. Some days, I'm sniffling and blinking back tears as I pull through the overhead gates at home, feeling the same as I once did, when a frustrated teen.

"You ain't learnin' if you ain't cryin'," one of my hard-nosed old mentors used to drawl. If that's true, I've been learning a pile, thank you very much. Mustering a wry smile, I park the truck and trailer, stepping out into the cold wind to unload my honest-but-ordinary horses. They've done their best for me. Already, I'm thinking about our next ride and what I can do to better help them. Self-pity, be damned. I'm ready to step up and try again.

· 50 ·

GOING STEADY

Here we are, Three Caballeros from Long Ago. If it's in your heart to come back, it doesn't matter how long you have been away. With some faith, the right people and horses, you can do it again. (Maggi McIvor Photo)

Hey, it's been a while. The last time, you were maybe sixteen? Seventeen? Remember, that summer you traded your bad fingernails and high ponytail for a letterman's jacket and a ring that hung from a cheap chain? The year you let the smell of the horses go, in favour of Revlon's Charlie? It was the summer you said goodbye to rides to the barn; to packed brown bag lunches that always included a huge carrot; to learning the old *Manual of Horsemanship* by heart before Pony Club exams; to cleaning stalls in exchange for free lessons; to babysitting at twenty-five cents an hour to save up for your first real riding boots; to learning to tie a hay net and pull a mane and do a turn on the forehand; to wishing, every Christmas, for your own horse; to spending entire days and evenings with the horse-crazy girls you've known since you were ten.

Love & RULES

You stopped being a barn rat and went on to be something else. What happened? Was it a boy? A family move to a new city? Selling your beloved horse to pay for college? What steered you away from the world of horses, way back when?

So many of you are here, 'coming back' after decades away. Years spent being the good wife and mother, the breadwinner, the corporate achiever. Years spent making memories with your growing family, all the while knowing that a small pot of unrequited horse love was still simmering quietly on the back burner. Years where you promised yourself that someday, you would ride again. So, here you are. It's been three or four decades since last you gathered your reins and reached for the stirrup. While your heart and soul remember, your body is telling you that things have sure changed.

Your body is right. For not only has your health and often, your courage, morphed into strangers, horses and equestrian endeavours have also evolved. In the last thirty years, we are seeing more specialized horses, animals trained with one particular skill set, rather than the forgiving jacks of all trades with whom we grew up. With encroaching urbanization, we are seeing fewer horses who live out comfortably year-round. Fewer horses are confident riding out in all kinds of wind and weather, down the ditches and across the fields, like the stoic horses of our past. We are seeing rising costs from those we remember. Not only is the beginner-friendly horse no longer twelve hundred dollars, the truck and trailer to haul him is worth more than we paid for our first house! From funding our horse council memberships for insurance, to the monthly board bills, new equipment and group lessons, it feels as though your newfound horsemanship is a euphemism for a black money hole.

You are noticing that all the movers and shakers, the gurus, seem awfully young.

And yet you're here. We're in this together. If you're just getting back into the world of horses after a long, long time away, welcome! You have waited a long time for this. Be excited. Feel the joy and nurture your old dreams. Please, be patient, kind and loving with yourself, too. For while you've always loved horses — they were your first great passion — both you and this horsemanship thing have changed. Don't despair. Don't buy the first horse you see because you're raring to get back in the game. Do find a trustworthy mentor and a good group of likeminded people. Do get into lessons. Do work a little bit at getting yourself into physical shape. There is a place for you in today's horse business, but like all the key things in our lives, you will be faced with some important decisions.

Your safety must rank first among all your considerations. The biggest surprise in store for any returning warrior? You are not the same resilient spirit as you were at sixteen.

· 51 ·

HEADING HOME

It is the morning after saying 'so long' to my horse. Selling my horses is what allows me to ride nice horses. While I may wish for champagne and caviar, the bank account allows for canned beans. Worse, as anyone who owns horses knows, the actual cost of the horse is only a drop in the bucket. There are the farrier, dentist, vet, feed, registration, board, transportation and training costs. Just the upkeep, alone, makes one weak at the knees. We're not even going to mention how to finance that truck and trailer!

So, the passion morphs into the business of trying to stay afloat.

As these beautiful horses come into my life, I tell them — to remind myself as much as anything — that my time with them will become the needed link to mend their broken chain. I can provide the happy ending to their story. They will grow to love it here, but this time will not last forever.

Their years with me give them the tools needed to be valued and loved by somebody else. Otherwise, without solid skills and a safe mindset, the average horse is worth maybe thirty cents a pound. Think about that for a minute. I wish more horse owners realized this hard truth of the unskilled horse. It's not the signed transfer of ownership or the carefully-applied freeze brand that promises tender loving care. Oh, no. Rather, it's the work we do, training them while we're able, that keeps an ordinary horse from the possibility of a bad end.

Their years with me give all the opportunity I could ever want, to ride and train and learn. Our growth has been a two-way street.

This morning, I will head out to the tack room and bring in Win's bridle for safekeeping. It no longer needs to hang from the hook nearest the door. Instead, I will wash his bit, cleaning that last stolen mouthful of hay from the roller. I will smile, then condition the leather and reach to hang it on a high hook in the safety of the house. It will wait here, a token of remembrance, until it is needed on a good horse, once more.

I get a little sniffly, thinking about this, if you want to know the truth. When my horses are finally good enough to sell, they're good enough to be missed.

People so often judge those of us who sell our horses. They forget that if we didn't sell these good, safe horses, it would be next-to-impossible to buy one. Sadly, the two go hand-in-hand.

Unlike most amateurs who are advised to sell horses that are proving unpredictable or scary to ride, those of us in the business are selling horses once they are predictable in their reactions to our aids. They have seen and done a lot of good, consistent work. They have become the horses on which most riders can build or maintain their confidence. The horses we keep are the ones still giving us those white-knuckle rides!

As a seller who is always trying to maintain her reputation, I am only thinking of selling my horses once they are as healthy, mannerly and reliable as I can possibly make them. If they are falling short in any one of these areas, it is not yet time to say goodbye.

Bringing a horse to the point that safety is 'job one' for him is no quick task. Though I have tried, I have yet to find a way around putting on those dodgy first rides. There is only one way to bring a horse to a state of reliability in the real world — and that is to put as much time and knowledge into him, as one can. For a long time, maybe even a few years, there will be bad days that seemingly outnumber the good. Days of broken reins, rolled-on saddles, cold hands, sleepless nights, buyer's remorse, errors in judgment, going back to square one, emergency vet visits, miles of long-trotting, wild rides at the lope, learning to steer, to stop, to go calmly forward, in and out of the arena, on and off the trailer, on the ranch and at the shows, in company and alone.

There will be days when you would literally rather ride any other horse, than this one project horse you currently own.

You keep plugging away, doing your best to keep yourself and your training-horse safe and engaged in learning to honestly work. Days, weeks and months add up to years. One day — and it starts out an ordinary sort of day — you throw your leg over and sigh. Without knowing quite how it has happened, you settle into the saddle and feel as though you are safely home.

Only then is your sale-horse is ready to go on without you. Only then.

· 52 ·
DOING CHORES

Some days, the only thing we can do is to 'keep on keepin' on'. Such is the powerful lesson, the character-building, and the meditation to be found in the daily slog of doing chores.

· 53 ·
RIDING LESSONS

Horsemanship, in particular, seems ripe to attract almost a cult following when it comes to our greatest teachers. This makes me uncomfortable, even though I've been blessed with a few extraordinary mentors of my own. I'm aware that many of our horsemanship heroes, while brilliant with horses, lean towards painful, broken or toxic human relationships. This isn't to point fingers. It's to suggest perhaps that they're really no different than we are, other than they are at their best when on a horse. It's made me realize that our work with horses must extend to all areas of ourselves and not just with riding's technicalities. This one thing is what gives me courage when I feel the need to write of my own personal failings and shortcomings. When I do so, I'm not wanting sympathy. No, I'm wanting to share that I'm like anyone else, trying to do my best and sometimes — so many times — letting myself, my family, my friends and my horses down.

I wish that more of our gurus, these household names, would own up to their weaker moments. Surely, they too deal with nerves and fear? The horses that disappoint or let us down? The issue of depression? Money woes and trying to pay for these dreams? Anger and ego? Ageing? Family, versus horses? All the times they may have dropped their health and wellness balls? The stories of training gone wrong and all the thousand other little things that can trip us up, every single day? If our gurus would just allow it, they could be even more valuable to us as teachers.

Today, I will be grateful for the mentors who have made me who I am, for better and for worse. I will embrace truth in my own horsemanship, enjoying the relief that comes from being open with others and in knowing that I am doing my personal best. Even when I leave the gate open. Even when I forget the hose that's filling the water trough. Even when my horse could be better for the farrier. Even when I back the trailer into the huge tree. Even when I show up at the wrong time for my lesson. Even when my breeches won't zip. Yes, even then. Today, I am going to be grateful for all I've been taught — and for all that I've yet to learn.

· 54 ·

SHOULDERS BACK

John Wayne famously said, "Courage is being scared to death, but saddling up anyway." I don't know for sure about that. Seems to me, there are way too many of us riding scared. I think courage is being scared to death and then admitting it. Next, in deciding that we're going to do something about it, whether it's finding a safer horse, a more nurturing coach, or choosing to live in a safer, kinder home environment. That, my friends, is courage.

· 55 ·

MENDING FENCES

I am going to tell you a story that still has the power to bring me to tears. I am going to tell you about Bingo.

I was scrolling the online marketplace when a beautiful grey pony's picture came across my screen. His quality oozed from my laptop. I clicked on the whole ad and read it through, first with breathless excitement, and then much more carefully. Here was my pony. Here was my chance to short-circuit all those dramas in the round pen, to skip all those wet saddle blankets and head straight to that place where you 'Collect $200 As You Pass Go'. I bookmarked the ad, saving it to read again in the morning, believing that a good sleep always tells us whether we're meant to proceed, or to stop and heed those sober second thoughts.

There were no sober second thoughts for me. I spent the night dreaming of light grey ponies with perfect braids and tidy knees, carrying their pigtailed little jockeys to glory.

A phone call the next morning confirmed my suspicions, that this pony had indeed competed in the U.S. pony hunter circuit, in the east. This is the holy grail of raising and training ponies, akin to sending your hockey-playing son to the NHL. When I asked the seller, quite pointedly, what such a pony was doing back here in western Canada, I remember only a general, jokey sort of reply. I should have stopped her

and pressed for some clarification. I did not because as yet I did not want to hear an honest reply. My need for truth would not come until much later.

Instead, I focused on the facts that appealed to me. I checked the seller's claims with Google show results and video footage. Yes, that was him, all right. Instead, I should have been contacting the breed registry to see how many owners this pony had sifted through in the past three years. I should have asked why such a pony would be for sale here in the hinterland and why he was priced as he was. I should have, could have, would have. But I did not.

Instead, I sent a modest deposit to the seller, along with notification that I would like to arrange a pre-purchase vetting. The next day, with a snowstorm screaming in from the north, I received an email with an attached copy of a recent exam, rather than confirmation that I could proceed with hiring a third-party vet of my choosing. Ignoring that little voice inside, I read through the form. Failing to see anything untoward, I said that I would like to purchase the pony. Hasty arrangements were made to haul the four-hour drive to our chosen meeting point.

When Bingo stepped off the seller's trailer, something like an alarm bell went off in my head. I quickly silenced it. For he was a stunner, a classically-beautiful 12:2 Welsh pony, with the look and mannerisms that only the royally-bred ones have. He had a delightful way about him, awake and observant, yet fully respectful of my space. Waiting to be asked to move, then loading into my trailer with a studied calm amid the busy-ness of the highway truck stop. Obviously, this middle-aged pony had been around. It would seem that he had, indeed, been well-taught and well-handled in the years previous. I paid the seller in full, congratulated myself on the buy of the century, and drove my little treasure home.

The next morning, I went out to feed my new pony and get to know him a bit. Rather than finding joy at seeing him, however, my heart was heavy with a feeling of dread. Again, I shook off the inconvenient hunch. Bingo just needed building up, some tender loving care to improve his coat, maybe have his teeth done and see if he wouldn't fill out, put on a tad more weight.

The dentist was booked, the farrier visit ordered. I wanted to start Bingo's schooling, to have him fit and ready for spring, but was it my imagination, or did he seem to be losing weight? I increased the amount of his feed — he was already eating as much as my 16:0 hand, twenty-year-old horse — but I wasn't ready to start worrying and wondering. Yet. After the dental appointment, while Bingo was still sedated,

I asked my veterinarian to please clean his sheath. A routine procedure, it came as a shock when the kneeling and prodding vet swore softly under his breath. It was obvious that even he was alarmed.

Bingo was full of cancer. Melanomas, insidious in too many grey Welsh ponies, Thoroughbreds and Arabians, had metastasized throughout his little body. The mass up inside his sheath was the size of a good-sized cauliflower. My treasure, my quick link to the big league, was dying a slow but sure death.

It was a quiet haul home. In the weeks that followed, Bingo's registration papers arrived. The transfers that lined the lower half of his certificate were numerous and they told a grim story. I read one licensed company name after another, in the three years that this pony was supposedly making his mark. For these people had only done what I had hoped to do, they were wanting to make some good money on a pony who was priced so reasonably that he seemed too good to be true. Instead, they bailed when his poor health was discovered, hoping to sell him quickly enough to recoup their investment. With a heavy heart, I realized what was really going on. I had been duped, outsmarted at my own game. The difference was that here the buck would stop.

I don't know whether or not I really learned my lesson. I rather suspect that greed and a horse trader's heart still lie deep within me. What I did learn, however, was of the honour and character of my mother. It was she who proclaimed to me that "an education is never free" and that if I'd learned my lesson, namely, to never buy another horse or pony without a proper pre-purchase exam, it was money well spent. Meanwhile, she asked me, what was I going to do about that poor pony? I could only shrug miserably in reply, for I feared that I was losing my shirt, so to speak. Mum only rose from her chair and went to fetch her cheque book.

"I've always wanted my own pony, but I've never been keen on doing all those chores," she quipped, while handing me payment for Bingo, in full. With tears in my eyes and an unbelieving gratitude, I went home and thought about what I needed to do, to do right by the little Welshman. He was still comfortable and full of the joys of life, so with my vet's blessing, I felt that it was not, as yet, the time to be putting him down. Instead, I called the horsey mother of two lovely young children. Before she'd married her ranching husband, she had been a show jumping groom. She knew the value of good hunter ponies and she would know what a treasure Bingo was, still.

I asked, would she be willing to give a terminally-ill but very nice show pony a loving place? More to the point, would she promise to do what had to be done when came the inevitable day? Yes. And yes. Bingo went on to thrive with his new family. His cancer went into remission and the huge tumours magically began to shrink. The old fellow had six happy years before he was finally laid to rest in the hilly, green pasture of his last — and best — home. I think of him still with gratitude, for this one small pony and all the good that he brought me.

. 56 .

CULLING THE HERD

'Tis the season of damp 'n' chill. We wake up in the dark, go about our business and head home in the dark too. Before long, we find ourselves turning inward.

I start feeling as though I'm drowning under the weight of all my stuff. This sounds a little over the top, until I remember that each thing that comes into this house brings its own energy. Its own little story of good or evil. Do you know what I mean? Entire rooms in our homes tell these same tales. We start out in life, young and wanting to feather our own little nests. Each year, it adds up. So many sofa cushions, there's nowhere to sit. So many pictures on the wall, there's nothing to see. So many occasional tables we can't steer the vacuum cleaner. We must get some sort of thrill from dusting and rearranging, if we take into account all the tchotchkes just sitting around.

Each year, sometime in winter, I start with two empty boxes in each room, along with a garbage bag. One box holds things that I still love and am not quite ready to part with. Mostly, I'm just a little tired of them. Every so often, we need a break to see them anew, to feel that gladness that they belong to us. The other box is for recycling those things that have served me and are ready to move along — either by being cleaned and donated to a worthy cause, or recycled for their materials, or if really worn out, to be thrown into the trash bag. My goal is to keep clearing until I can see that space where the floor meets the walls. Until I can feel the expanse of each room. Until I can breathe again.

I put beloved music on and just putter. Every unnecessary thing in that room, I want to hold in my hands and remember. Is my first thought one of gladness? Or am I remembering a friendship turned sour? Or an era of unhappiness? Or a reminder of someone who abused my trust? Or have I simply become a different person, since vowing to love this thing for ever and always? Long before the teachings of 'keeping only that which sparks joy', I have known that I, for one, am in danger of drowning under my belongings. Generally, my first thought is the one that is most true to me. I can choose whether I want to continue sharing my journey with the cat-scratched old chair, or have it re-covered to better suit me, or just send it packing. I've stopped keeping things that I don't really like, just because they are worth a lot of money. I either sell them now, or I give them away.

I've just spent a wonderful two hours in my tack room. This is the place in my home that is most dear to me, alive with the ghosts of horses and mentors passed. I start cleaning, really noticing how some of my keepsakes make me feel. Here, a black-and-white photo of me, all smiles, aboard a beautiful horse. I sniff a bit and take the photo gently from its frame and put it into an album. Finally, I'm ready to admit that the photograph brings feelings of guilt about how I rode that horse in order to win. I've beaten myself up enough now and have asked her forgiveness. Instead, I will remember this mare with private and heartfelt gratitude.

The bookshelf, groaning outward, needs a cull. How I love my horse books! Some, however, I have read and was disappointed. Some were written by people who aren't mentors — I just wanted to read about them, to better understand. They have served me and will go to an upcoming tack sale. Now, I've the room on my shelves for when I find another classic, or a new title that is groundbreaking. It surprises me to find that the empty space left on these bookshelves is not lacking or wanting, rather, it is rich with possibility.

Oh, the bits and gear I've purchased over the years, thinking they would make my horses better, or that I would find a renewed passion, if only I had the right stuff! Thousands of dollars in hats and brass-and-patent harness and formal carriages, only to finally admit that driving, for me, will be just as fulfilling with the battered training cart in summer, or snuggling down in the old calf sled over wintry snow-covered fields. Silver bits that may be beautiful, with valuable makers' stamps, but with surprisingly unappealing mouthpieces shunned by over forty years' worth of horses. Saddles that never seem to fit anything well. Training aids I will never again use, because I am beyond them. All are feeling ready to leave, for good.

During this clearing, this purging of negative stuff, I am reminded of the things that uplift me. I've decided that it's all right to love certain things, so long as they still work well or bring joy. I fill empty boxes and then all the nail holes in the walls. I rearrange the dearest of my things, to be enjoyed again with more space around them. I put the kettle on, make a cup of tea and sit with beautiful music, surrounded only by that which I love. William Morris, that great Victorian decorator, the man who birthed Arts and Crafts design, is remembered for saying, "Have nothing in your house that you do not know to be useful or believe to be beautiful." This ritual of self-care has become an annual event for me. As soon as the days shorten and darken, I know that it is time to dig in and let go.

· 57 ·

WEARING BLINKERS

Good horsemanship is a never-ending quest for betterment.

Why? Because it is a fine balance between the concrete and the intangible. You know, the 'heads up, heels down' part versus heeding our woo-woo inner-voice. One can never outweigh the other, yet in reality, a fundamental imbalance is all too easy. One is very teachable, the other, in my experience, not so much.

Let's take a closer look at the subject of discipline. What is the meaning of this word to you? It could mean getting off the couch and saddling up when you're at the end of a hard day. It could mean calmly but mindfully teaching a horse to stop nipping. It might be something as obvious as persuading a balky horse to go down the driveway when he's telling you he'd rather park himself at the barn. These, while big and essential, are tangible. These meaty ones are easy to pick up on, even if they're not always an easy fix. But what about the little things, those 'whispers of mutiny'? Do we recognize those? They can be harder to get a read on, especially when we are talking about our own horses.

The pony who stops to eat grass while we're leading him. The fellow who throws his head and looks back over his shoulder when we are wanting him to load. The dropped lead at the out gate, the swishy overdue canter departure, the horse who crowds us while grooming, or steps close enough to our toes that we involuntarily draw back?

What about the horse who moves his head higher or farther away while we're bridling? The rushing when leading through a doorway or gate? The horse who moves off before being told, the foot that isn't as freely given for picking out, as it once was?

All are signals that something in the horse-and-rider relationship is amiss.

This isn't nitpicking and it certainly isn't about being a discipline junkie. But these little things, these mere moments, are pointing the way to a greater disobedience. Some riders ignore these and choose to turn a blind eye. I do not. But here's where the tough part comes in — what is the difference between heeding the whispers of mutiny and flat-out babysitting the horse? Here's where we must heed our gut feelings. Is this little moment of discord a hint of discontent, a place where the horse, ever so slightly, asks you to prove yourself? Or is it an honest moment of learning, where you allow your horse to make her mistake, then calmly go back and work on the fix? Herein lies the rub, being aware enough to recognize that something isn't there, and then taking the appropriate measures to put it right.

Our awareness, this constant searching for what is an honest try and what is not, is a key part of good horsemanship. It's the difference between being a rider and merely sitting pretty. Seeing — and meeting — these little things will so often prevent the all-out wreck or monumental fight.

Some horses are forgiving of error, stress or doubt. Some require us to find the balance of love and rules. Kananaskis was one such individual, and whenever I met her standards, she was an incredible performer. If I did not, all bets were off. (Author's Collection)

Next time you reach for the stirrup and feel a clutching at your heart, ask yourself, have you been mindful of brewing little disobediences? Have you listened to the latest whispers of mutiny? An unspoken tension can be a clue that you've not.

TRANSITIONS

I am wending my way south-eastward, along with my favourite pillow, two horses and a few changes of clothes. Why? I am going to sit with my daughter, who is waiting patiently to greet her first child.

To get there, I am crossing an inhospitable, demanding country. Lonely homesteads, dreams forgotten and tilting in the relentless wind, islands in huge pastures of sage and buckbrush. I keep my eyes resolutely on the road, my truck running steady between miles of yellow lines. So much change upon this landscape, while so much has stayed the same.

At one point, I am stopped by the side of the road. A sign nearby warns of rattlesnakes, and I am careful as I peel my boiled eggs and settle down for an impromptu picnic, to scan for snakes in the parched grass. The wind makes a keening sound in the overhead telephone lines. Nearby, meadowlarks are singing their springtime arias. Since the settlers pulled out in the 1930s, this is a land that belongs to no one. This is the country that my new grandchild is going to call home. Sarcee stamps once back in the trailer, and I'm reminded that we've still hundreds of miles of empty highway before we reach our journey's end. It is time to shake out the crumbs from my blanket and get back underway.

Later on, my daughter greets me shyly and with unspoken relief. We have not seen each other since last summer, when we had a quick visit during the early days of Covid. She looks tired. Her face is flushed and her small body is unaccustomed to moving under the additional weight of late pregnancy. She is now two days overdue. On her face is a mixture of impatience and the drain of being with child, along with fear of what is yet to come. Instantly, I remember and, like untold women before me, I can only do my best to lend her strength and resolve.

My daughter has been nesting. The small prairie home she shares with my son-in-law is spotless and beautifully decorated. She takes me to the new nursery, once the guest room where I have stayed. I see glimpses of the little girl she once was, as she excitedly shows me the new wallpaper, the second-hand crib and chair. There are sweet little dresses and overalls, bought from the local thrift shop for mere dollars, brought home to be washed and pressed. Receiving blankets and onesies sit in readiness on the shelves, along with the stuffed animals and favourite books from her own childhood. I smile and recall little clips from her past, from my own early parenting. Did I do well, doing that? Did I do well enough?

I still think of myself as a young wife and mother. How can it be that I am waiting to be a grandmother for the first time? Why didn't anyone warn me that life would go by so very fast? Or, if they had, would I have listened?

One day of waiting stretches into the next. We pick garbage from beside the old two-lane highway, that has blown into the native pastures. We cut a bit of wayward brush and help repair the pulled staples and downed wires of an old fence. We groom the ranch horses who, once again, are shedding their ragged coats. It was a long, hard winter. All look as though they're needing green grass. Soon, boys. Soon. We talk about past hurts and long-gone family members. We laugh about old arguments and the fights we had when she was a teen. We look at old photographs and tell well-loved stories. Bit-by-bit, we heal as we reminisce.

Still, we wait.

I do up a few horse chores and fold some laundry. Cait has come back from her last doctor's appointment before the birth. It's a five-hour round trip, not counting the wait at the clinic. Overdue now, she will be induced into labour by this Sunday — fittingly, Mother's Day — if the baby is not born before then. Cait looks tired and after a restless supper in front of the TV, she heads to bed. My son-in-law, Lee, expecting the arrival of some twenty-five-hundred cow-calf pairs this week, is looking worried.

We pass the next day doing a photoshoot of sorts, of me and my older horse, Tee. Tee lopes once or twice around the heavy, worked-up arena and says, "Enough of that." We stop, take a posed shot with three generations of horsewomen — or so I wonder — and then head for the pasture to get a few pictures on the grass. The native vegetation is different here. Spiky, clumpy, with bare sand between, there are places where the ground meets the sky in a peculiar way only seen here on this particular sweep of prairie. The rocks, ancient and covered with green and pink lichen, are more beautiful here than any manmade work of art. The wind blows and blows. It is lonely and crazy-making and still wild and breathtaking.

A person could either fall in love here or go mad.

Getting closer. Today, a last-minute trip to Maple Creek to have a government inspection done on the newly-installed car seat. The lady, methodically ticking off

items from a sheet on her clipboard, warns that the base of the car seat will leave an indentation on the seat of their truck. This, for some funny reason, strikes me as symbolic of the whole new parent-and-child relationship — oh, so many indents to come. We finish our trip with a masked shopping spree at a wonderful toy store on the main street. A bunny for baby and a sorrel pony, more for Caiti and me. I ask if the store has a hardcover copy of *The Velveteen Rabbit.*

"Oh, that's the saddest book ever," says the young man behind the counter. Yes, maybe. But it is a wonderful story for teaching young children to have a heart. He presents a beautiful anniversary edition with lovely, original illustrations and we add it to the pile of plush animals. Happy as children, we rein the Ford around and head back southward, over the high park road and through heavy, driving rain. Tomorrow is the day of the planned induction.

We awake to an arctic front blowing in from the northeast. Wet snow and ice cling to the sides of buildings and vehicles, while the horses and cattle hunker down in misery. Fears are voiced about the state of the roads to Swift Current. It is decided that my son-in-law Lee and Cait will quickly pack up and head out just after lunch. They will get to the city, two and a half hours' drive from the pasture, and take a hotel room, where Cait can perhaps rest and have a real bath, without fear of allergies and 'duck itch' from the springtime well water.

Granny, meanwhile, will stay at home with Kai and Zoë, Angus, Patrick and Earl, holding down the fort. Granny will also be riding during the days with the new hired man, meeting liners and trailing out those hundreds of cow-calf pairs. Mother's Day dawns cold, white and windy. I wonder if this Hallmark platitude is wishful thinking for Caiti, or if it will, by day's end, be fact. Hours later, I am still wishing. Please, God, let my grandchild be born soon — safe, healthy, with a tired but very relieved mother. Please, God. Please, just this.

The day is spent going through the motions. There are brutally long hours in the saddle, finished off with cold, wintry chores. All this, while awaiting word from the hospital. The time goes by with the sharing of short texts — early labour for mummy, a pill to induce stronger labour, another pill, harder labour, an epidural, even harder labour. At two-thirty the next morning, granny is up and pacing about the dark house, wondering and fearing what might be going on in that faraway hospital room. Then, just after four-thirty, a message from daddy goes ping on her phone.

"Meet Ruby Lee!" it announces, and with that she is ours.

· 59 ·
ACCEPT CONTACT
AND GO FORWARD

I know exactly the day I began to grow up.

I was forty-two. This one day was made more powerful in that it was the first time I'd had to see something frightening and unknown to me, all the way through, all on my own. My whole life, 'til then, had me skimming from one shallow demand to another. Always, I'd left the really heavy lifting to someone else. But this day was different. I was alone in a strange city, without my belongings or my language. I had only a paper gown in which to wrap myself. I could not swallow or raise my hands. I could not speak.

I was having a stroke, of course, and all the while it was happening, I remember feeling annoyed. Inconvenienced. For God's sake, Lee, don't make a scene. Besides, I have made other plans.

None of my family knew that I'd been sent from where I was teaching a 4-H riding clinic to the local hospital. From there, I'd gone by ambulance to the nearest city and the stroke unit. Somewhere along the way, my purse and clothing had gone astray, left unnoticed in a corner of the busy emergency room. It was a typical Saturday morning. The locals had filled the place after rounds of beer, a few thrown punches. They were getting patched up after a regular Friday night.

The trip to the city had been surreal. The ambulance ride, the calm talk of the paramedics, their pulsing of lights and siren through icy intersections, constantly checking my vitals. Pulse. Blood pressure. Repeat. Breaths in and out. Oxygen levels. A glance at the IV drip in my vein. I began watching in the third person because how on earth could this whole ludicrous episode have anything to do with me? This is a waste of taxpayers' money. I calmed myself with practical thoughts. Why didn't I just go lie down, rather than make a big fuss?

Instead of a rising panic, a feeling of helplessness, I was consumed with a trademark sense of shame.

I tried to downplay the seriousness of my condition, but nothing intelligible came from my lips. The attendant quietly reminded the driver to step on it, that we weren't out of the woods just yet. The rest of that afternoon is a blur to me, waiting in a long hallway with searing lights overhead, raised voices, my stretcher banging into myriad others. I remember trying to joke with a harried triage nurse about those 'vital three hours' that had long since passed. "Time's a-wastin', lady," I wanted to tease, but nothing even close came out.

I woke up in a curtained room, alone on a bed now, but still with my IV and the paper gown.

"Go home! You go home! You have headache, no need to be here!" I tried to open my eyes against the harsh lights and the foreign voice, but the pain in my head was too much. Instead, I vomited. This happened three more times throughout the afternoon until I was able to get myself sat up and my own IV line pulled from my hand. A bustling nurse came through the curtain and seemed surprised to see me.

"You're still here? You're free to go, you know. It's just a migraine," she greeted me, as though I'd planned to be a hanger-on 'til closing time. The dream grew weirder. Nobody seemed to care that I had no way of phoning home for a ride and that I had no clothes to put on. I still had not uttered a recognizable word, nor was I sure that I could actually stand. Worse, I had no way of communicating that I'd never before had headaches, that these symptoms were entirely unknown to me. I grew tearful. My jokes had all dried up. I pulled my gown closed around me and shuffled out to the hallway in my bare feet. I was in the way, bumping into people, confused, too ashamed to make eye contact and try to get help. In the end, a kindly woman mopping the floor came to my rescue. With a series of hand gestures, I showed her my discharge sheet and somehow conveyed that I was to go home.

"Where are your clothes?" she asked. I looked down at my crumpled gown. "Wait here. I'll see what I can find over at the morgue." She came back, cheered by scoring a pair of yoga pants, a fleece hoodie and some cross-trainers. I decided not to push my luck by asking for underwear and, no word of a lie, I ended up wearing the running shoes for several years.

"Do you have any money for the phone?" My saviour put in the quarter and dime, while I tried to remember my home phone number. It wasn't easy. I just couldn't think. We dialled a few wrong ones before I heard my husband's familiar voice on the line. The relief of this one sane thing in the middle of overwhelming chaos meant that I could only sob into the phone. Somehow, somehow, Mike knew I was in trouble. He hung up and headed for the hospital. Some hours later, he found me at the main doors, hugging a cafeteria sandwich to my breast, still unable to speak. Neither of us thinking straight, we failed to ask any questions and began the long drive home to the ranch.

In the end, it had been a comedy of errors. After lying two days in agony, miles from town in my darkened bedroom, one day, a voice on the phone directed me to make my way back to the local hospital, without further ado. With no mention of mistakes made, or blame taken, or apologies given, I realized that a grave error had been made. That the other woman who had shared that curtained room with me had indeed had a migraine, rather than the stroke that had been diagnosed. The mistake had not shown itself until she had undergone a brain scan and the results had been cross-checked with her old roommate's. To her credit, the clerk at the stroke unit had done a fine job of tracking me down.

So began a lonely journey through the land of unwellness. That first day began my new life, far removed from the one I had known. There would be years of learning to focus, to withstand bright lights, noise, colour, movement. Years of staggering nauseous from the crowded aisles of the grocery store, my full cart left behind. Years of learning to swallow, fussing with hearing aids, of walking without tipping over. I struggled with depression and an anger so fierce that it threatened to choke me.

"How on earth did you cope?" I was later asked. Well, the truth is I didn't. Gradually, I turned inward, like a wilting flower. Then, when I'd lost all hope, I turned to my horses. Just knowing them, knowing their responses, became a huge help to me in my eventual recovery. While it is understood that our animals can speed our healing, sometimes we can also take inspiration from how they live life. I have long known that in order to find acceptance and relaxation, I needed to give my will over to a higher power. This mindset is so much like the horse who finds the bit and newly seeks guidance — and then with trust and gentle urging, starts quietly moving forward to whatever lies ahead.

. 60 .

NO SWEAT

Get out there and do. Try. Allow the horse to make mistakes. Correct in fairness. Reward with generosity. Learn. Feel. Theorize. Ask questions. Try again. Raise a sweat. Putz around. Don't ride like you are being judged. Ride like you can't bear not to.

. 61 .

REACHING FOR THE BIT

When we use our good gear, or decide to have lunch on our best dishes, we remember to look for beauty in the everyday. Don't wait for perfection. Choose to celebrate the here and now.

. 62 .

BROTHERLY LOVE

Burrito and Pilot, with yet another lesson we can learn from horses —
dare to love someone who is different. (Kate Berkan Photo)

. 63 .

A DARK HORSE

Cypress is going through a dark night of the soul. This has been brewing for a while now, but I've been busy enough with other horses that the big fellow's problems have been easy for me to ignore. Too easy, looking back to those days when he and I were just building partnership.

With his newest injury taking precedence — a last chance to heal lies in yet more rest for a year or so — quite frankly, my shining star is feeling banished. This sort of thing can easily happen with young or green horses who are turned out or turned away.

The lovely Hanoverian came to me early last summer, after two surgeries and two years of stall rest, following a life-changing injury to a tendon in his front leg. Nothing in Cypress' origins or prior experiences had prepared him for a move to the ranch. Yet, the young horse literally turned his back on all that he knew and said he was ready to try anew.

After a few months of ponying and ground work, I started Cy under saddle in July that first year. By September, it was feeling like home whenever I'd swing my leg over his lofty 17:2 hands. I think both of us thought it was going to be easy, this turnaround from sad story to happy ending. And for a while, it was.

One day, riding away from home at the public arena, I asked Cy to pick up an ordinary trot. Uncharacteristically, the energetic horse did not respond. By the time I'd got him home and unsaddled, he was holding up his front leg, unable to bear any weight on it. Turns out, the original tendon injury was fine. Instead, Cypress had torn both branches of the suspensory ligament, within the same leg.

Who knew that a horse who has stood for two years, immobile and medicated, will be in such an overall weakened state? Well, of course he was. I was thoroughly disgusted with myself. I should have known, but I was too cocky and too impatient to think about anything other than riding him. Our vet didn't sugar-coat his diagnosis. A practical man, he went straight to the bottom line.

"You should have given him a year of free pasture turnout, let him scrabble around and harden up some. You grow your own feed and you're not paying board," he shrugged. "I'd say something very different if you weren't living where you do. If you want to try another year or two of rest, just turn him away. The snow cover and constant slow grazing and movement may be just what this leg needs. He's in nice shape now but don't fret about trying to maintain him too much," the vet warned.

"Just do your best to keep him warm when it gets really cold. He can rustle around and come in for hay as needed. He's going to start looking rough, but that leg doesn't need to be supporting a big, fat horse right now," he added.

With that, Cypress received my guilt-ridden hug and was sent out with our horse herd in the big pastures to fend for himself. Watching him limp over the windswept hillside, I remember thinking, "Lee, let go and let God."

It is coming two years of watching and waiting, now.

The brown gelding has learned to paw through snow for the tough, native grass. Holding his own, he is picking his way along the icy slopes down to the creek, or up to the yard pens for water. On warmer days, I've been going out to pull his rug and let him stretch and roll. When it threatens to drop too far below freezing, or it grows really windy, I trudge out to throw on his winter blanket. He and the other horses also have free-choice homegrown hay. So far, I guardedly feel that this free time and movement have been working. Cypress is going sound, and the look of his front pastern joint is markedly improved.

There has been one other difference, though — a less welcome change. The friendly horse who once sailed down the grassy slopes to meet me, lowering his head into my halter, has gone away. Lately, Cypress has been anti-social, keeping to the far side of the herd. When I do manage to lay my hands on him, he is watchy. Wary. The other day, he said he was plumb scared of me and recognizing that this was a fundamental change that needed me to stop everything and deal with it, I didn't even try to approach him.

When the horses next came up to the corrals, I was ready, and swung closed the gate behind them. Storm clouds were brewing in the west. Southern Alberta was under a cold weather warning, with a promised heavy snowfall that night. The wind was whipping up dust when I walked out with a halter to catch my horse and blanket him, lest he shiver off any more of those precious pounds.

Cypress had other plans. An appointment in town had to be postponed while I stayed out there, working to the bottom of this fault line between us. Weaving in and out of the other horses, Cypress threatened on several passes to jump the corral fence. Bred to be a Grand Prix jumper, he could easily clear the shoulder-height barrier from a slow trot. I was mindful of the pressure I was putting upon him, keeping the big horse moving until he was ready to negotiate, without pushing him up and over the corral rails.

That beleaguered front leg did not need all the churning, cantering and wheeling that Cypress did in an effort to evade me. When finally we stopped and faced up, both of us were winded. Cy was trembling, with whistling snorts and dark, worried eyes. I stopped to mirror his body and made myself look down and take several deep, cleansing breaths. I could not allow his palpable fear to put me on high alert. I could only help him if I stayed calm and quiet myself.

"Cypress, what's going on? You're worried, hey? I think you're wondering if you're beginning to lose your mind." Slowly, slowly, my friend and I edged towards one another, but he would not let me touch him. After close to an hour from closing the corral gate, I was able to rub his neck. But he was head shy and, at first, I was unable to halter him. Finally, I could lay my hand flat upon the big horse's forehead. We stood there, Cypress threatening to wheel away at any hint of falsity and me, silently promising that he was safe.

Words and intentions. I reminded myself that these two things must match, if we are to present our truth.

In the end, after holding an accessible calming acupressure point, with a total disregard for my missed appointment, the threatening storm clouds, rising wind, and the passage of time, my horse decided he no longer wanted to be a stranger. We both sighed and turned to the gate to fetch his winter blanket. That, too, posed a whole new threat. With the wind howling and surcingles flapping, we worked our way through all the reasons why Cypress had grown afraid of me and of his warm winter rug.

That done, I eventually led him over for a long drink, straightened his forelock and said that I was sorry, but that he didn't need to fall apart at the seams. I slipped the halter from his head and stepped back to let him go off with his friends. Cypress looked away and shook his forelock from his eyes. He paused and then gently dipped his muzzle into my open hand. We stood like this for quite a while, until he slowly turned and rejoined the herd.

When life is going well, it is easy to believe in ourselves and have faith in all the good that we might bring into the world. It is when we hit a hard patch that we lose all hope and begin to feed into our deep shame and unsettling doubts.

Horse or human, sometimes we need help to remember who we have always been — and who we will be, once again, when we are healed.

. 64 .

LATE ENTRIES

We need to talk. There's a new group of us in the horse world. We're getting older and wiser. The kids have finally left home. We've quit that job that ground us down for decades. After a lifetime of loving everything about horses, we've decided that it's time to ride.

What are you waiting for? Well, I'll tell you. You're waiting for the right horse. If you're an adult beginning rider of a certain age, now is not the time to take on the young, vigorous horse that 'needs some work', never mind the middle-aged, neglected horse who never got his chance. I'm closing in on five decades spent in the saddle and I'll tell you absolutely, without reservation, that when I want to enjoy myself on the trails with friends, or at the cowboy challenge fun day, or dressed to the nines in the local parade, I'm looking for an old kid's horse.

If you're just starting to ride at fifty, sixty, or seventy years old, I salute you. Find a great teacher and treat yourself kindly. Our ageing bodies take time to move with ease in the saddle and, often, our confidence is easily shaken. This isn't cowardice, folks, this is Nature trying her best to keep us safe.

Please, don't discount the late teens or twenty-something horse with maintenance issues. Sure, his teeth may require extra work, his joints could use supplements, his shoeing might need more care, and winter will be a little more challenging just keeping him warm and well fed. But if he was a good horse, once upon a time, he will take your safety seriously in the future. Cody, my own old standby is hale 'n' hearty and now in his late twenties. Long in the tooth, a little scarred and creaky, he is my go-to guy for days with crowds and microphones, or whenever life is getting too 'lifey'. Just being with him slows my racing heart. Will we have to say goodbye before too long? Sadly, probably. This has only made my time with him all the more bittersweet.

I know there are many of you waiting for old campaigners of your own. Keep looking! Somewhere, out there, are others like Cody, high-mileage horses needing what you have to give.

Here's to the genuine old-timer! He and his tribe, the battered brigade, will allow our hearts to soar.

. 65 .

SIMPLE CHANGES

Our minds and our bodies are funny things. I was reminded of this while teaching a lesson a while ago.

"Move your lower leg forward," I would say. "I think I am," replied my student. "More, more, more," I'd urge. Our perception, when asked to adjust our muscle memory, is that by moving one body part a fraction of an inch, we're moving it a mile. We think we're over-exaggerating, but in reality, we need to, in order for us to change longstanding habits.

When we're being taught, if we hear the teacher repeating the same information, over and over, we can be pretty sure that we're not quite getting the desired result. The answer is to keep dialing up the adjustment until the horse or the teacher deems it good. Many times, the only way to convince a student that change is still required is to video the ride, or to ride in a hall with mirrors.

"Oh, my goodness, I thought I was doing what I was told!" is invariably the student's response. This feeling that 'our bodies know best' is similar to that feeling of knowing the direction we're headed while being blind-folded, or the way that miniscule bit of something caught in our teeth will rule our thoughts. We'll worry this spot with our tongue all day, until such time as we can floss. Lo and behold, a mere speck is all that is stuck there.

Riding — and changing how we ride — is similar. Sometimes, in order to make even a tiny fix, we feel as though we're moving mountains. Feel is one thing. Trusting others to guide us safely is entirely something else.

. 66 .

HEAD SHY

While we like to say that horses always tell the truth, I have learned that the people-pleasers will don social masks, allowing them to sail through life without causing waves. These horses have learned to shut down, to dissociate, rather than risk sharing their opinions. Imagine that.

. 67 .

MARES' TAILS

I had a wonderful time yesterday, just meeting a new friend for lunch.

She has been in the horse business forever and yet until this past summer, we'd never crossed paths. What a discovery it is to find a kindred spirit! Not only is she another hat person, she thinks what she thinks, and does what she does because she has learned the essential skill of being genuine. She too has found that standing for something you believe in sometimes means you'll be walking alone.

We agreed that the high price of being authentic to yourself is even higher, when you are not.

We talked about everything from the culture of fear-mongering to the rise and fall, in our lifetimes, of curb bits; of riding one-handed; of leaving the arena; of using cows to train horses; of hitting the trail with show horses; and of building an entire fashion wardrobe around our ubiquitous boot-cut jeans. We talked about old-time horsemen who trained — really trained — hunters and jumpers and cutting horses. We talked about mentors and the people who shaped us. We talked about women's issues, and alcoholism, and the unspoken toxicity in the horse world. And then we talked about everything current.

We talked of tax audits and the crushing price of fuel to feed our hauling trucks. We talked about our love of homemade music, and the incredibly diversely-talented people hidden among these hills. We admitted to old dreams and some new realities. We talked about learning life lessons and the honour and art in teaching good horsemanship. We agreed that much of day-to-day teaching has little to do with riding. Often, we are providing a getaway from real life and a listening ear. In between these services, we slip in nuggets of instruction on position and technique and feel. We discussed the differences between teaching adults and children, about responsibility, and always, that little unspoken fear of the day something goes sideways.

We reminisced about winning — about winning, at all costs — about what today's industry is doing to all the baby horses. About the technical improvements we see today, in comparison to riding as we knew it when we were kids. Still, I think, if asked, we'd both agree that we were glad we grew up in the saddle back when we did. You know, before helicopter parents and liability issues. Remember, when?

Through it all, we shared knowing glances, a few regrets and guffaws of laughter. I drank an entire pot of tea, speaking of regrets. But on my long drive home, I also learned that I now believe in the rightness of finding a kindred spirit. Was a time, when I was younger, I did not know such joys existed.

. 68 .

HERDBOUND

When Mike and I were first married, he had a red dun colt called Holiday. The horse was perhaps euphemistically named, for he was tough-minded, unpredictable, and prone to episodic bucking. Riding him was about the farthest thing from a vacation that one could bring to mind.

Interestingly, of the thirty head of horses who ran with Holiday, none were friends of the little horse. When they were jingled into the corrals each morning, Mike's colt would lag far behind to avoid any altercations near the water trough. During the day, he would be kept in a nearby but separate spot for his own safety. Often, when we went out to find the horses, Holiday would be several hills over. 'A part of the herd, but always apart', seemed to be his mantra.

The majority of the family ranch horses spent their winter months trailed south to a remote and hilly pasture called Section Two. There, they would drink from the year-round springs, pawing through snow to the tough native grass kept just for this purpose. Surprisingly, after five or six months living the feral life, our horses always came back in the spring in beautifully hard condition, with all the cobwebs blown out. They'd be healthy, full of jam, and ready to tackle another season's hard riding.

One particular winter morning, it was fiercely cold with a lot of snow. While I ladled out porridge to our three preschool children, Mike pulled on his warmest clothes. He was going to fire up the snowmobile and head back to Section Two to check on the horses. Several hours later, we could hear his machine come howling back into the yard.

"They all look fine, but I can't find Holiday," my husband reported. "I'll go back tomorrow and look again. Maybe he got pushed through a fence or something." We looked at each other because the 'or something' meant that the colt was most likely dead. Several more trips by snowmobile failed to turn up the red dun horse.

88

Holiday remained an eccentric character all his days. Remembering him, I can only think that we must be true to ourselves, whether it is convenient or not. (Author's Collection)

Love & RULES

By this point, Mike was looking for a pile of bones, but nothing could be found. It was as though Holiday had vanished into thin air. Rustling was briefly considered, but common sense told us that no stranger would ever be able to lay a hand, or a loop, on this particular horse.

Months later, Mike and I were enjoying a rare night out at the annual calving-time cabaret. A local band was playing while groups of farm and ranch folks were gathered discussing the age-old issues of scours, backward calves, and challenging weather. You could look across the dark room and see men engaged in hard-pull scenarios, mad cow chases, and the like. Mike was deep in conversation along the bar when a voice behind him caught his ear.

"No word of a lie, the muleys were running along the ridge, and a horse was in there with 'em. Wild as the deer, when we spooked the herd, the horse took off running. Jumped a wire fence, too." Mike turned to face the speaker, a rancher from the southern edge of our rural community. His range was quite a distance from our family's and it seemed hard to imagine that Holiday had travelled those many miles. And yet what other horse could it possibly be?

"That wasn't a little red dun you saw, was it?" Mike shouldered his way into the discussion. "I've been missing a horse now for four or five months." A nod from the rancher confirmed Mike's suspicions. Living within the mule deer herd — and now literally wild as a jack-rabbit — the question was, how on earth would he get his young horse back? Several more sightings were reported of Holiday running with the herd of deer.

Just when it seemed hopeless, the gelding turned up one day in a section pasture beside our wintering horses. None the worse for wear, there were no wire cuts on his legs, but he was ragged and wild as could be. Already a lone wolf, Holiday had become very reactive to noise and movement during his winter off.

In the spring, when the horses were all run in, Mike managed to catch the gelding in the alleyway back of the barn. Wild-eyed and snorting, Holiday allowed himself to be brushed and saddled. The hackamore went on and then he was led out to start another working day on the ranch. The half-wild colt, surprisingly, rode off like an ordinary horse. That was Holiday's only year of running with the mule deer.

He spent the rest of his days with the remuda, 'a part of the herd, but always apart'.

. 69 .

LIVING WELL, RIDING BETTER

This is my code, my mantra, the mission statement behind my business. What I want you to know is that this phrase applies to me, yes, but also to my horses.

I believe that with age comes wisdom. I believe that each one of us has the ability to bring something unique and beautiful to the world around us. I believe that we are not our mistakes, our suffering, our sickness or our shameful secrets. I believe that from sharing my stories — the happy ones as well as the humiliations and hard lessons — only good will come.

I believe that my horses are my friends and my teachers. I believe that given the right tools, they will do their best to please me. I believe that my work and training will make them stronger, physically and mentally, as they grow older. I believe that I must strive to add to their quality of life. I believe that to ride well is to ride with ease — both for ourselves and those who, without a voice, must carry us.

I believe in forgiving all the horses and people who are not able to do right by me — and, yes, this one is hard.

I believe in the power of turnout, and of sitting in silence in nature. I believe in recycling and not wasting water. I believe in grass management. I newly believe in the magic of walking, using our bodies, and eating food that supports our wellness. I believe in creating our own art, clearing the junk from our homes, and making time for music. I believe in finding a way to enjoy and dream about that one thing we've loved since childhood. Whether we're watching the stars, learning to dance, to ride a little better, or make a new recipe — I believe we owe it to ourselves to at least try them.

I believe that we are put here to learn and grow, and to serve others. I believe in good manners. I believe that with age can come beauty — in people, dogs, horses, gardens, and homes. I believe in paying forward the ways of the masters who taught me. I believe that when I slip up, I have only to apologize freely, forgive myself wholly, and look for a second chance. I believe in lifelong learning. I believe that our dreams are essential, but they will need to be nurtured with much hard work.

When it comes to living well and riding better, I have learned to believe with all my heart.

· 70 ·

TRICKS OR TREATS?

I'm not one for feeding horses hand treats, as a rule. Blame my background of making performance ponies, but I've always weighed the balance between the fleeting joy of seeing those cute little 'cookie faces' with the knowledge that we can't buy the core values of honesty and regard. There are times, however, when a well-timed cookie can be a boon.

Some years ago, I taught a teen girl a number of western riding lessons so that she could compete at higher levels in 4-H. Her mother phoned to make all the necessary arrangements for our first lesson — and then dropped the bombshell that her daughter suffered from seizures.

"She usually knows when one is coming on, though. Please, don't talk about it at the lesson. She'll be mad that I told you, and she's self-conscious enough." This didn't sit well with me, but I managed to hold their secret close until the opening moments of our first ride. I watched this lovely, delicate girl warm up her horse, Rusty, for a few moments, and then called them over to where the mother and I stood.

"Rusty's wonderful," I said. "You've done a good job with him. What plans have you made so that he can handle your seizures? Does he know how to help you, without becoming afraid?" The girl's cheeks turned pink, she looked down and grew inward. The mother spoke up to tell me that we really shouldn't be talking about this. I could only hold up my hand and ask for a moment.

"Rusty deserves to be a part of the team. He knows there's something wrong, and he's a good, honest horse. He could help." And so we began. The first step was to teach Rusty to stop and wait whenever he felt his rider lose her balance. Every time his girl leaned forward and pressed on his neck, when he stopped quietly and looked back at her, she would feed him a cookie from the saddle. Then, she began to slide off him to the ground, again giving him a food reward when he immediately stopped and watched her. This, of course, took mere minutes. We were about to ramp things up.

"I want you to dismount and do a bit of acting for Rusty," I told her. "You're going to pretend you're having a seizure. You don't want to scare him, but

you're going to show him a little bit of what to expect." Rusty watched with great interest and, you guessed it, he got a cookie. Within minutes, our shy, self-conscious teen was gasping, twitching, and convulsing on the ground amid gales of laughter. Every time she had a bigger 'seizure', Rusty, so long as he stopped and watched calmly, got a food reward.

The mother was amazed at the openness of her child to turn her condition into a learning opportunity for her horse. We added to the drama by hurrying over to the prone girl and giving her 'first aid', all the while being careful to not scare Rusty. When he could lope around, feel her loosen, then stop and concentrate on his seizing rider while we rushed up calling her name, we knew that he now owned this new skill.

Rusty had been given the tools to look out for his rider. What he knew now would help keep her safe while she challenged her own horsemanship. The pride shown on the little sorrel's face brought us all to tears. Rusty had learned all of this by our being honest with him. Then, by breaking a frightening thing down into chunks, we were able to make his ability to cope into a pleasant experience for all concerned.

This horse and rider went on to have other, less unusual riding lessons with me. They competed up to the highest levels in 4-H before Rusty was retired and his girl went on to university. I never knew if he needed to use his newfound skills, or not. It was a wonderful thing, watching him gain mastery, and seeing his shy, troubled girl set down her burden by asking for his help.

Horses can be our best teachers, if we will give them the chance.

· 71 ·
PULLING UP

A horse(wo)man knows when to push the horse, when it can give him, or her, more. A horse(wo)man also knows when the horse has given all that it can, and when to have the grace to be thankful. The trick, of course, is in knowing the degrees of difference.

Today, I had a beautiful ride on a pony I'd not swung a leg over in about six weeks. Why did I turn her out? It seemed the more I camped on her, the worse she got. We had somehow reached something of an impasse. I had tried to teach her, without making headway. She had tried to learn, without feeling good about any of it. Finally, I decided that it was high time to just walk away from each other, to let ourselves find forgiveness and healing.

Whether from soreness, sourness, or overtraining, it always pays to listen.

. 72 .

RIDING IN LIGHTNESS

Repeat after me: Your past is not who you are. It has shaped your story. It has taught you everything you know. It has hurt you and maybe left scars. If your life was a novel, it might well have had a hard beginning, or a hard middle, but you have yet to write the end. Maybe you had a brilliant start right out of the gates. Maybe luck wasn't with you. Maybe you made some poor decisions when you were young and didn't know any better. Or maybe you lost your stride due to things beyond your control. Abuse. Poverty. Addiction. Depression. Divorce. Illness. Grief. Shame. Fear. Broken promises. Broken relationships. Key decisions. That said, there comes a day when we must move forward. Forgiving others is one step; asking their forgiveness is another. Then, we begin the long journey of starting to forgive ourselves.

For myself, I know now that I had an unusual childhood. Shame often wants to step in, to have me downplay these forces that have shaped me. This fascination I've had with energy and intention are light-years from a childhood spent at the livery barn, a place rich with shadowy men, knife fights, and the trafficking of stolen horses. My mentor, the man who soaked this young sponge in so many beliefs, was an old chuckwagon driver who I instinctively feared yet tried to emulate. He was well known for his cruelty, but he had a charm about him that kept one going back for more. Among my mementoes was a whip he'd made me to use upon my balking pony. His bawled command, "Lay it on, Lee!" will be forever burned upon my brain. It wasn't until recently that I was able to throw the damned thing out. Such is the power of mentorship, whether for good or evil. Acknowledging that I loved him, I still walked back to the house, driven to wash my hands.

Later years were spent in a vastly different environment, a classical dressage barn long before the term was so widely used. The horses, highly fed, impeccably managed, were honoured with a religious zeal. They wanted for nothing and grew into heart-stoppingly beautiful creatures, their bodies sculpted with the stretching

and straightening exercises that methodically filled our days. When I close my eyes and recall them, I picture the musical clinking of the bits in their double bridles, the dust motes floating on golden sunbeams. I see only this quiet cathedral, blocking out the daily abuse to the riders and stable help — the whip brought down on the too-slow response; the lungeing lessons that went on with bloodied knees; the hours locked away in a dark and airless bedroom without food, drink or a toilet. This shame is the taproot of my horsemanship.

A lot of water's gone under the bridge. Always, my prow is fixed upon two distant points — one, the point of practical knowledge; and two, the point of the great unknown, the magic I now know is out there. My basest nature and holiest moments have shown themselves in the saddle. For me, horses have always been shadows and light.

· 73 ·
LONG IN THE TOOTH

Cody, high mileage and nearing thirty, is getting worn out. Whenever he walks by, his joints are so creaky one is tempted to yell, "Tim-berrr!" My friend saw him tottering around one day and figured he'd be a good candidate for a well-known brand of pain relief.

"He'll feel so good, you'll swear you're on a three-year-old," she predicted. Skeptical, I decided to inquire about the stuff. Half pills, then quarter pills, I listened to the directions on how to crush them and administer daily with a sinking heart. My aloof and ultra-picky senior equine was not going to be impressed. Again, my friend to the rescue.

"Forget all that," she said. "Take a horse cookie and stick a little pill on top. He'll be lined up for his dose every morning." That sounded easy enough and next trip to town, I made a stop at the feed store for a big bag of treats.

Now, if you've been with me long enough, you'll know how I feel about hand-feeding horses. Blame my background with cookie-monster ponies, but I never understood how one could trade treats for the core values of honour and respect.

Nevertheless, I grabbed the biggest bag of nibblies I could find and headed to the checkout. Sigh. Wouldn't you know it? I stood smack dab in the middle of three of the biggest names in the cowhorse industry, hot trainers who really know their stuff. During our brief hellos, I was painfully aware of their eyes drawn to the huge, lumpy bag I was trying to conceal under my arm.

When I hit the head of the line, the clerk, a jolly local with a booming voice, hollered, "Will that be all for you, Lee? Just the large bag of horse treats?" And then, horror of horrors, he bellowed across the store to a stock boy, "GET THE CODE ON THE LARGE MOLASSES MUNCHIES FOR LEE McLEAN." Awash with embarrassment, I could only think that this rivalled the classic, "Price check on tampons!" at the grocery store.

Meanwhile, the blow to my self-esteem has been worth it. Cody, who now waits for his pill by the gate every morning, has shaved a zero off his age and is truly behaving like a three-year-old. Snorting, shying, ever-so-slightly humpy, I'm toying with cutting his dose. By autumn, I began making his pill pocket cookies inexpensively, instead of buying them. Besides, standing in front of the oven is a nice change of pace, whenever the winds blow cold.

· 74 ·

CODY'S COOKIES

Mix together in a large bowl:
1 cup chopped or crushed apple
1 cup grated carrot or mashed ripe banana
1 cup each of bran and rolled oats
¼ cup molasses, sorghum, maple syrup or honey

Mix well by hand. Roll into 1" balls, or pat into an 11x14"
pan with wet fingers, bake at 325F/160C 'til firm.

Cut into bite-sized pieces. It might need to set up a little, first.

Keep in a sealed container in a cool place. Some horses prefer their cookies a little bit crunchy, while others like them soft. Cody just says to keep 'em coming.

Either way, offer them to your old favourite with love and gratitude.

Even if you're not into feeding hand treats, Cody's Cookies are a caring, affordable way to administer ongoing meds. (Author's Collection)

· 75 ·

PONY UP

For a long time, my horse business was a 'ponies only' enterprise. In my quest to find good kids' ponies with real-life experience, I was on the road a lot, looking at those I had scouted in sales ads. Not all were as they'd been advertised. One particular trip was a flop, so far as buying went, but it provided one of the funniest memories that I can recall. Long before this day, I had learned to never, ever climb aboard a sale pony if the family was balking at riding it. And, yes, I had to learn this the hard way.

"Right, then. Who's going to show me her stuff?" I asked the small crowd after they'd escorted me to the corral. A menacing hairball was pacing back and forth, along the far side of the fence. Quiet descended on the until-now boisterous family, with much scuffling of feet and downcast eyes. Quick as a wink, the youngest brother piped up, "You ride 'er, Randy, I don't feel so good."

Randy, not to be shown a coward, manfully tightened his skater shoes and twisted on his cap. Locked and loaded, he climbed aboard. It was the world's shortest demo ride but, thank goodness, he wasn't hurt. I politely declined mounting this barracuda who'd been advertised as a kids' pony, choosing to hit the long road home with an empty trailer, instead.

"You ride 'er, Randy, I don't feel so good." Years later, in all manner of sticky situations, I'm still quoting that kid.

. 76 .

GO LARGE

Riding and writing publicly has taught me that our inborn fear of failure is what stops so many of us from trying anything new. It's important to learn that disappointing other people is a risk we must take, in order to fully live and grow. Unless we are caregiving for those who rely wholly upon us, keeping other people comfortably satisfied is not our job.

. 77 .

BITS AND PIECES

While so much of our horsemanship seems random and overwhelming — and it's true that we'll never, ever learn it all — most of it is incremental. Piece-by-piece, like building a huge jigsaw puzzle. Often, one little thing that we've been struggling with will improve then, before we know it, everything else about riding a particular horse does as well.

We'll have a horse who is resistant whenever we so much as touch the reins. This is not fun to ride — not for us and, taking a wild guess here, probably not fun for the horse. Every single thing we do with this horse is tinged with tension. Impatience. Maybe even a little fear. Is it him, is he crazy? Is it his teeth? Perhaps the bit is to blame? Or is it us?! We lie awake nights and wrestle with these unanswered questions, along with the prospect of spending more time and money yet again.

How can we canter the perfect circle? Or go on an enjoyable trail ride? Sign up for the clinic? Stand quietly for the vet? Learn to stretch and reach for the bit? Slow down? Bend?

Just when we're ready to quit entirely, to hang up our spurs and take up knitting, we see a glimmer of hope. One day, we pick up a rein and wait quietly. The horse softens and turns his head. We release. We try the other rein, with the same result. This is encouraging! We pick up both reins and slowly, quietly walk the horse ahead — all the while, yearning for some sign that tells us we're on the right track. He softens, so minutely, and we've just found our first corner piece of the puzzle.

We go looking for a piece that will fit in with that one. And we do it again. And again. Over time, we have fit in so many pieces that we've lost count. But we know we're getting somewhere because, suddenly, all we want to do is enjoy working on our puzzle. It feels good under our hand. It looks wonderful, with its pieces lying snug and flat, no missing holes or ones forced in that do not fit.

Our puzzle, that started off with a messy heap when we dumped out the box, is now making sense. The soft and round feeling at the walk becomes shared euphoria for the first time. It becomes a horse who wants to be caught. He stands still for grooming. He is happier to be saddled up. He waits for us at the mounting block. He moves off when we ask, relaxed and stretching. He starts to learn a little bend. The trot grows rhythmic and swingy. We sweat together, from good work now and not so much from nerves.

All of a sudden, our legs mean something beyond 'checking out of Dodge'. We can softly rein back, side pass, and open our own gates. More achievement! Cantering round-and-round or over the trails. Loading in the trailer. Exploring everything, learning always. Joy and partnership. Trust. Just one person and one horse, starting to yearn for this thing called connection, every single time they meet.

So, hang in there. It's all about finding one little piece, then another. Slowly, slowly, our puzzle evolves.

. 78 .

COMMAND CLASS

We humans are linear thinkers. We're all about the goals. We clearly see where we are right now, and where we want to be sometime next week. It looks like a straightforward journey, and so we'll pick, pick, pick at the poor horse until he understands. Or, as is more likely, until he's at his wits' end.

We see this a lot and, if I'm going to be honest with you, I've been at fault as well. I've driven the unfit pony 'just once more, with feeling' to the point that it bolted with the carriage and ran through a wire fence. That was one hugely effective way of getting me to stop. Less dramatic, but just as demanding, I've had the one-sided horse who finally, finally, gave me that right lead. And what did I do? You know it. I asked him to do it, again.

Whether we just get keen, or lack feel and timing, or perhaps we're downright greedy, it doesn't make much difference to the horse.

When we're teaching a new skill or idea, we need to discipline ourselves to 'be happy with the one per cent', as my own mentor says. Just a snick of lightness or improvement is enough, then we'll go on to something else. We'll head out for that outside ride or hack. We'll go to something else the horse already does well. If it's been an especially challenging concept, we might just step down and loosen our cinch, right then and there.

My point here is that we human beings tend to get greedy. We want it all and we want it now. Thank goodness, horsemanship doesn't work that way. We're not on a time continuum, other than the fact that it's hard work learning something new and, for the horse, a few moments is where we'll find the good stuff, if we're really looking. People get confused because we know that 'time and mileage' make good horses. But this concept is found in riding out over varied terrain, leaving the horse alone, and just letting him find his own balance and the working relationship evolve. When we're schooling new concepts, it's different. We first have to learn, ourselves, when enough is enough. Only then, can we effectively — and kindly — teach others.

· 79 ·

THROW YOUR HEART OVER

Those horses we feel we've somehow failed, or did not understand, ones who we've piled such hopes on, only to have our dreams dashed — these are the horses who we will count among our greatest teachers, in the end.

I, too, have memories of such horses and they visit me quietly in the dark hours before dawn. They have told me to savour the bittersweet moments with my elderly horses because, in the blink of an eye, time will pass. Life can, and will, surely change. I am now mindful to smile in amusement at the antics of the young ponies,

rather than give rise to exasperated thoughts. My teacher-horses have taught me to watch and wait, to think instead of the long game. They have taught me to cry, openly, and not be too self-absorbed to smile.

There is now one horse who is here to mentor me on love without payback and on devotion without dreams. With Cypress, there will be no glory, nor financial windfall. Just between us, I wasn't all that sure that I had it in me. Turning one's passion into one's business can make you question your own motives, even with the personalities you love. You can become so scarred from disappointment and too much caring, that you stop before you get hurt again.

Cypress and I are well into the slow season of watchfulness. A second year of waiting, feeling for heat, gauging his movement for those dreaded careful steps. Hoping for a miracle and steeling ourselves for something else entirely. Every day, he strides out to meet me, head high with his tail blowing in the wind. I am happy when he greets me, his long, arching neck pulling me in for the hug. For a while, I am content to let Nature take another day, or weeks, or months, if that is what she needs to work her magic.

Cypress will never carry me forth in competition or pay my bills. I now know this. He is my friend, though, reminding me that this one thing is more than enough.

Today, he travelled with me to farrier day, then practised waiting all alone in the arena until the other ladies and horses could join us for a play date. Cy stretched and snorted happily while he ponied out beside little Tee. He looks good, we had fun, and all the while I was handling him, he proudly said that he remembered how to be a good horse. Yes, just saying this is making me blink.

It was a lesson to me, that to be with a horse such as this one, is more than enough. It is my bliss.

. 80 .

BE THE BOSS HOSS

Why do so many riders think they want the submissive horse? To clarify, I'm not referring to submission as in training. Dirty word that it has become in many circles, I still aim for as much compliance as I can get. Submission, in this case, is where my horse stands in the herd's pecking order.

Love & RULES

Even if our horse is one of the unlucky ones to not have a herd for turnout, he or she will be either dominant or submissive. Trust me. Our horses, by nature, will be either leaders or followers. They are never just neutral beings, taking up random real estate.

So often, when marketing horses, people will say that their animal is submissive with its herd mates. As though this is a selling point. Well, they can't all be The Boss Hoss but here's the thing. The horse who waits an hour-and-a-half outside the corral for a drink isn't just mannerly. The horse who wants to hide in the middle of the trail ride isn't always the safest one. These horses have a little niggle of self-doubt. They usually crave being told what to do.

If I'm a dominant, forward-going rider, I can give this type of horse wings. If I'm bossy and they want leadership, this can be a match made in heaven. If, if, if ... The submissive horse is so often characterized by beautiful ground manners. 'Should I wait now?' 'Do you want to go first?' they seem to say. Unfortunately, this veneer of civility can wear thin when we start to ride. Suddenly, this horse panics if he doesn't have a courageous captain on board. Often, this fear shows itself as herdboundness. Suddenly, our nice, kind horse is a problem.

The domineering fellow, so often pushy in the corral, has no such qualms. Yes, he'll need reminding that he is not to run the show. Because run it he will, if you allow. But this brave horse will be splashing through streams and scaling mountain trails, while you are gripping the saddle with terror. He doesn't need your courage or your convictions to get through life. Of course, as with all rules, there are grey areas. Many a dominant, intelligent horse will shy, or even throw in a little buck, as a means of avoiding work and regaining power. It's up to us to recognize this.

Yes, a submissive horse filled with self-doubt can become a sensitive, beautiful ride after a lot of mileage in sure hands. This horse can become safe for a nervous rider if nothing bad happens, and if there is enough good in the courage account to operate in the black. Generally, however, this takes years of riding and reprogramming. If we're at all nervous, it will be many hours and miles before this horse has enough bravado for us both.

The pushier fellow, not so much. This is the horse who leads the others past the scary construction project on the way in for a drink and some salt. This is the horse who will pin his ears back at almost any herd-mate who dares to try moving his feet. This is the horse who has resolved that he will be the hero in his or her own life.

This is an easy horse with which to get on board.

If you are not big on boundaries, the dominant horse will be a challenge for you from the ground. He will teach you that it is okay, nay, that it is absolutely necessary, to stick up for yourself. The rider who struggles with this concept may recognize this common thread within many of his or her human relationships as well, especially with family and significant others.

Don't discount the dominant horse. He can teach us a lot. When we finally figure him out, we'll have unlimited fun with him. By working this issue through, with help as needed, we can expect the rides of our lives.

. 81 .

LEARNING YOUR PATTERN

It is an interesting exercise to look back and see the pivotal decisions that have affected one's life and, therefore, one's riding. We can clearly see that a lot of what we are doing — or not doing — with our horses has been mapped out by ourselves for years. This gets sad, sometimes, because key decisions we may have made when we were young, vulnerable, hurting or helpless have held huge power in shaping our destinies. We may be able to understand, for the first time, why we are not competing at a level to which we've long aspired. We may remember why we suddenly 'went off' horses, after they'd been childhood passions. We may be able to recognize a turning point where we took a fork in the road that was all to the good. These decisions seem to be either very, very positive, or else, filled with heartbreak. Such are the choices that shape us.

I don't remember not liking horses. Perhaps liking them is too tepid a word. I was drawn to them, mesmerized by them, as though the need was deep in my soul. Even if I was afraid of them — for there was no such thing as a 'kid's horse' in my early years — I still felt a need to touch them and to breathe deeply. So, the decision to read only horse books, think only horse thoughts, talk only about horses was one of my first unconscious moves towards being unhappy in any other environment. First among these, of course, was school. One of my first choices was to ensure that I would be a fish out of water for twelve solid years of my growing, formative life. That I would walk solo and have few, if any, real friendships. That if I wasn't immersed in horses, I would be unable — or unwilling — to thrive.

Many of my early decisions were not mine at all, but rather my older sister's. It was Kerry who wanted to have the ponies at the lake, where we lived in a remote cottage during rich, adventure-filled chunks of each year. And so I voted to have our ponies kept at the cottage too. It was Kerry who wanted to take English riding lessons on one of those 'pancake' saddles after seeing pictures from the Olympics. And so I voted to have English lessons too. It was Kerry who really wanted to go to our first pony show and, well, you know the rest. Lucky for me that my sister was an achieving sort, or I would have peaked with riding bareback to the store for a pop and chips.

The next formative decision was the year I was able to lease Friar Tuck. I was eleven and my excellent childhood pony had just died. Inconsolable and worse, on foot, I went to try out this half-Thoroughbred pony who was definitely not for sale. Tuck was on loan, brought to western Canada from Maryland, solely that he would teach young riders here what it meant to ride a talented horse. It was a generous move by his owners, but it also meant that when I fell in love, it would end sadly. I would have to say goodbye when the lease was up. Afterward, I watched a succession of fellow competitors ride Tuck, riding against me, usually all the way to the win. A little piece of him stayed with me, because I'd finally had a chance to ride a well-schooled, athletic animal who was correctly on the aids. When Friar Tuck left, I was unsure of what it was I craved. I only knew that I wanted more.

Then, the huge decision to quit riding at home and to sign on with Mrs. Boerschmann. At age fourteen, I was immersed wholly in all things dressage. Suddenly, I was taught that I was too unstructured — too emotional, too fat, too Canadian — too much of all the things that I really was. It was then that I made the decision to turn my back on myself and become whatever possibilities she might see in me. For better or worse, the chiselling of my character during these stormy four-and-a-half years made me who I am today. Daily, thoughts of my teacher, her words heard over and over, still pop into my brain. Thirty-five years to forget, and I'll still walk around my horses, going through the motions with one of those cartoon text bubbles over my head. Her words, my actions. The teacher I left behind while I was yet a young woman, in tears and amid hurled accusations, is still my moral compass today.

Oh, the need to rebel! To be heard and allowed to kick sand in the face of all that I'd been taught. A decision to turn my back on what I knew and to join forces with Mike McLean. I was all of nineteen. It was this decision to come to the ranch, to have the last laugh on those who knew best, to live my great adventure, that put an end to any serious riding. I would never get a boot back in the door of that

old world, I would never again catch up. There was an apprenticeship of sorts in this other environment, one of salty characters, people and horses. I was back in a world much like where I started. I'd gone full circle. No more tests to ride the perfect circle, the square halt. I was in a land of staying warm, not getting scared or hurt, riding only to help our extended family make a living. I fell in love with horses again, relying on the good ones to save me, watching them help raise my kids.

My next formative decision was to get involved in the exciting new sport of Combined Driving. The successes of my ranch-raised ponies came rapidly, in lofty circles. It was an inkling that there was a place for me in the horse business. An idea was beginning to form of what I should be or do — and then, ill health. This seems to come up when we're not paying attention, when we're forcing ourselves to keep going, no matter what. We ignore the warning signs of our bodies until something is presented that we can't sidestep. I lived in a dark hole for a long time after this, just licking my wounds and feeling sorry for myself. My kids grew up and left home. I needed to make a decision to thrive, now that my survival was ensured. The decision to get back in the saddle, to learn something new again saved my life. Finally, I had a reason to throw back the covers and greet each new day.

Decisions, decisions. Forks in the road, paths chosen. Right or wrong, these become the maps of who we are.

. 82 .

RUNNING WITH THE HERD

Turn a new pony out and it throws the whole place into a tailspin. A twenty-something gelding turns into the wild stallion of the Cimarron, gathering his harem and threatening to kill all who trespass. Mares slam dunk into season, old ponies gentle enough for children act like they've never known the human hand. Yes, we could keep them separated, newcomers from old-timers, mares from geldings, but why? We've nothing so valuable that we can't afford to let it live like a horse. And until they work out the pecking order, ideally in a roomy pasture, our horses and ponies will never be safe to haul together in the stock trailer, to ride in group lessons, or work with one another on the ranch.

So, we take care and have patience whenever we bring in a new personality. We can never tell how the new one will fit in, or even how the old ones will accept him. Just as disturbed water, sloshing in a bucket, must be given time to regain its stillness, we can't say that a 'quiet' individual has turned aggressive, or harried, or spooky, until the dynamic has played out. Until the herd has found its level. Meanwhile, the chewed hides, squeals, kicks, wide eyes and flared nostrils will eventually pass. Nature is working her little miracles. So have patience. Take care. Stay safe.

Watching my horses sort out their 'pecking order' has primed me for the herd dynamics that play out among new neighbours, budding and waning friendships, regular office politics, and how well we human beings play with others. Sometimes, we settle in as though we're part of a calm and well-balanced herd. Other times, we bare our teeth and pin our ears. You never know what will surface when you start running with the herd.

. 83 .

THINK. FEEL. RIDE.

My working horsemanship, as I have aged, has become clearer in its composition. Daily, I am balancing three components of equal importance to me, like a triangle. Thinking. Feeling. Riding. Neither matters to me, without evidence of the others. Like yin and yang, I pit my passion with technique.

Your triangle may well be different. If so, what balance makes up your horsemanship? What encourages you to grow? What keeps you safe?

. 84 .

CONFORMATION CLASS

I am almost sixty years old. I have achieved modest good in this time, while learning to accept my failures and blown opportunities. I have survived raising three kids and one serious illness. I like to think of myself as having some depth of character, of slowly growing wiser ... and yet.

Why am I still fighting my body? When did I first learn that how I look would be allied to whether or not I am worthy? What one thing happened that told me I am second-rate? Unlike all other self-knowledge, why will it take years — if ever — for me to learn that I am more than my outer packaging? Worse, not content to judge myself thusly, I have been schooled to hold other women to these same

uncomfortable standards. I'll justly rank men on their kindness, honesty, humility, and willingness to help. Women? Well, I'll just say this — it surprises me to realize that I am still thinking about outer beauty, much the same as I did when I was a teenager. Surely not?!

I was always made of sturdy stuff. Large-boned and freckle-faced, I must have come as a shock to my mother, whose youthful claim to fame was a twenty-two-inch waist. Throughout school, my friends were always leggy and slender, tanned like surfer girls. I grew used to shielding their beauty from bothersome boys, taking bullets like a loyal bodyguard. Listening quietly, without deflecting focus, seeing the trials of their full social lives. It occurs to me, only now, that these gorgeous young women needed me, a body who posed no threat, to find security amid their own feelings of worthiness.

Thus, I learned early that we must never be more than, never rise higher than, the women around us — that is, not if we want to be liked.

Despite my longing, I could see that being beautiful came at a price. It wasn't all fun and dates. There was the high school science teacher who traded secret photoshoots into vastly improved grades, and the gym coaches who eyed up these girls as they circled the red cinder track. There was an unspoken code that had some girls stay in an inner circle, the rest of us sent to the outer galaxy, watching and wishing, learning how to behave.

Do we blame our mothers or significant female mentors? Was it while watching them that we first learned to withdraw from life if one felt less than, or too thin, or too fat? Do we blame advertising, magazines, movies or social media? Was it while watching these, that we learned the sexy girl is always the star? Ordinary-looking girls can be loyal, funny, clever, heroic — but they are never the star. I think, though, that this cruel cull we do long predates popular culture. By now, this need to be beautiful in order to count, dwells deep within. It hides quietly, like shame, waiting to pounce.

My saner self says that this judging, like the conformation class in a heifer show, is utter nonsense. And still, even with age spots and varicosities, my heart secretly longs for me to be tan, tall and blonde like my friend back in grade four. She laughs and calls me "her little fatty". I can only smile and swallow my hurt, giving thanks for meriting this beautiful-looking friend.

I see now that I still demean my physical self, just as surely as did the mean girls in school. I have brainwashed myself into believing that if I look better, I can demand better in life. Without losing and gaining these same twenty pounds over and over, how will I be happy? Will people want to know me, just as I am? If only I was beautiful — but not too. If only I was beautiful enough.

. 85 .

PUT THROUGH OUR PACES

Get fit. Not size-six-jeans fit, but as strong, flexible and lean as you can become. Start working out a little, with walking exercise, yoga for flexibility, and some strength training. I, myself, have a few joint issues and now pay particular attention to stretching my hip flexors. I am being more mindful these days about my posture and breathing. I have found that if I work with my body from a health and healing standpoint, this is easier to stick with, than if I am just trying to get into a smaller set of clothes. All this and getting myself to bed on time. Every little bit helps.

. 86 .

TURN ME LOOSE

This thing between us began as pure love. We met and I was knocked sideways by the force of Billy's personality. When I first brought him home, our herd silently parted like a pool of water while the cocky horse waded right through them. The horses recognized something that I did not. Thus, Billy became the boss hoss and, all the while, he was smiling.

Riding Billy was euphoric. A small dynamo, he was as handy as a deep pocket. Full of energy, the little bay could work for hours. Never had I been on such a horse to sort cattle. Sweeping left, then right, a gathering move, heading up a pushy cow, everything was effortless. I grew used to being 'the gate man' no matter where we'd ride. Yes, it felt good to be this ageing ranch wife, handling this horse in a land of Marlboro men. They, who still call the shots, so grudging with their respect.

Mike started hauling Billy to brandings. I'd watch the trailer leave with my new horse, proud and feeling left out, all at once. They'd return home, tired but happy, Billy having worked like a machine and Mike missing very few loops. Then, one night, a change.

"He bucked me off in the branding pen," said my sheepish husband. This, for the uninitiated, is the cardinal sin in a ranch horse. Branding pens are crowded, bustling places for the serious business of vaccinating, castrating and recording the year's calves. People are rushing around on foot, there are ropes sailing out between horses and cattle, along with everything that represents one family's livelihood. Bottom line, bucking is not allowed.

Excuses were made. Perhaps the rope came hard across Billy's hip or goosed him around the hocks. Perhaps he was just sore from a long season. Life went on. I forgave and forgot.

Our immediate family kept a small herd of our own cows separate from those of the main ranch. One June evening, we were down at the pen beside the creek, our cows gathered and bawling, the calves healthy and ready to treat. I remember smiling as my daughter prepared to do the roping on Billy. She would heel the calves while the rest of us would wrestle, brand, castrate, vaccinate, and put in ear tags. We made for a small but efficient crew.

All went well until the last calf. He was duly roped, the dallies were made, and my daughter reined back toward the wrestlers. Without warning, Billy blew apart at the seams. After losing his rider, he bucked overtop my two sons who were down holding another calf, then he knocked over the branding pot that held the fire. At one point, all three of my grown children were lying about the pen, hurt and stunned, while the rest of us raced to stomp out the spreading flames. All of this, while avoiding the violently bucking horse. Luckily, our injuries were minor — bruises noted, tried gingerly, joked about, shaken off.

Excuses were made. Perhaps the rope, perhaps he was sore, perhaps, perhaps ... I made things right by absolving Billy of any blame.

My family began to voice their doubts about my new horse. Discussions were held, though I refused to listen. I felt that Billy was genuinely sorry whenever he lost control. Strangely, he himself was never frightened or upset by his outbursts. It was as if I had two different horses. He'd be lovely for months on end — kind and affectionate and, my word, could he perform. Despite these foibles, I never felt unsafe with him. Rather than focus on problems, my mind would stick resolutely to our good days. And so another year passed, all the seasons made beautiful by riding a top horse.

On our good days, Billy gave me wings. It was easy for me to ignore those seeds of doubt that were growing deep down inside. (Cattle Cait Photo)

One golden evening, Billy and I pulled into our yard after a long day's work at a neighbouring ranch. I greeted him happily as I swung open the stock trailer's door. Usually, my horse would be hauling untied, turned around and watching me from the front, ears up and ready to be asked to unload. But not this time. Billy stood as in a trance, his head to the far corner of the trailer, unmoving. I waited and called out to him.

"Hey, buddy. It's time to go have a roll." Nothing. No blinking, no breathing, a horse carved in stone. Without thinking, I walked in and put my hand on his shoulder. I remember hearing the sound of the trailer door swinging closed behind me, the snick of the latch clicking shut.

Billy woke up. Suddenly, my horse was a stranger, a panicked whirlwind of hooves and flying snot. In his nightmare, he seemed to be drowning. Survival meant climbing onto the only solid thing he could find. Me. As long as I live, I'll not forget the crashing and sparking of his shod hooves on the walls of the trailer. The bouncing of the floor, the banging of his head on the metal roof and the jingling tie rings, as I tried to stay at his hip, away from those lethal front feet.

I made it to the bulkhead of the divider, a mere six inches of aluminum, to escape the worst of his blows. I knew that the big door was firmly shut behind me, a good eight feet from where I stood. Could I make it all the way to the back corner and the door latch? Would my fingers remember how the slammer worked in that last moment before my horse took my life? In the middle of this panic was a calm sense of knowing that I was done for. I was alone with my killer, and nobody would be coming to save me.

I made a rush for the door at the same time Billy landed on his halter shank. It was the two-second pause that I needed. I threw open the door and fell backwards onto the ground, my stomach heaving with the sickness that comes after the adrenaline's rush.

There was silence in the trailer, some heavy breathing, one quiet footstep, and then another. Billy's sweet face peered out at me, a hank of black hair shading his eyes.

"What are you doing down there?" he plainly asked. With a shock, I realized that once again, he had dissociated from the whole nightmare. To Billy, he was asking permission to unload after a great day together, to go have a drink and a roll, then tuck into his supper. The deadly switch had clicked off, again. This was my moment

of reckoning. On my back in the gravel, gulping down air and relief, and the sour taste of shame, Billy and I had reached the end of our trail.

I have long wondered how this generous, sparkling, sunlit force of life could be crossed with such shadow. Had it always been in him? Was it how he was raised? What he'd endured, whether abuse or injury? Perhaps, a tumour or some imbalance in his brain? None of it mattered, once I realized that each of these questions lay outside of me. None of the answers were mine.

Whenever I hear of a woman who finds herself, somehow, mired down in a bad relationship, I remember Billy. I think of how exciting he was, the highs he gave me on those good days. The joy that came from being with him, instead of wishing that I wasn't still looking for a partner. Still alone. I think of the unholy terror that eventually forced me to see him for what he was. I have learned that always, always, my horsemanship mirrors real life.

I have ridden that horse. I have trusted that man.

. 87 .

GOING KINDLY

We understand the healing power of forgiveness and yet it can be so hard. Forgiving a person who has wronged us seems as though we're just letting them off the hook. Instead, it took a counsellor to explain to me that carrying this burden of being wronged was like toting around someone else's heavy suitcase and never ever being able to put it down. If only we found the forgiving and setting healthy boundaries as straightforward as do our horses — but, of course, we do not. Still, I have never been able to find forgiveness as fully as did Sugar.

I first laid eyes on Sugar Showgirl when I was sixteen. She was the first horse I'd seen where my eyes bugged out and the world stopped. An iridescent sorrel, it has been my observation that those really metallic ones always seem to be a cut above. Sugar's body moved like a cat's as she paced back and forth, back and forth, along our neighbour's rail fence. Simply put, I loved her at first sight. Mr. Lyons owned a handful of very nice Quarter Horses. His focus was all about quality, rather than quantity. When he issued an open invitation for me to go and help with his horses, I was over there like a shot. The man must have sensed my longing towards the sorrel mare because his only mention of her was to stay well away.

"She's mean. I don't want you going in that paddock ever," he sternly warned. I avoided his gaze, but understood that he wanted only to get a foal or two out of her, due to her bloodlines. She was not to be turned into a saddle horse. The seven-year-old mare had been on the track, which explained her physique. By Diamond Bar Dee, who was by Sugar Bars and out of a mare by the beautiful Quincy Dan, she oozed quality. I wanted her all the more.

I waited for the day that Mr. Lyons' truck was gone from his yard and the lights not on in his house. I went over to make acquaintance with his still-pacing mare. Her head shot up and she swivelled around to face me. I leaned on the fence and called to her, "Hey, Sugar. Come and say hello." With that, the horse snorted, pinned her ears and came straight at me, on the dead run. That should have been the end of this love affair, but of course, it was only the start. In the coming months, I never grew bold enough to leave the fence, but I would still call out to Sugar. She would wheel and charge, often hitting the fence beside me but never knocking me off. Several times, with bared teeth, she would make as though to bite me, but she never quite did. No matter how many times she charged the fence, I would still go after school to visit.

Eventually, something happened. The mare started to trot over, still looking cranky, but she would stop short of me, just out of reach. She would stand while I chattered away, but we had an unspoken agreement that I was not to go into the paddock, nor to try and touch her. I had only to look at her expression and I understood that a boundary had been set. This was a line I was not to cross. My father was on friendly terms with Mr. Lyons, and it took only a little whining from me before he'd asked our neighbour if I could have help catching the horse, maybe to groom her? With some difficulty, Mr. Lyons got a halter on Sugar and held her while I straightened her mane and smoothed the beautiful, metallic coat. She snapped at him several times, but he was an unruffled sort of man and just spoke quietly. I learned that not all racehorses have wonderful lives on the track. Some find it hell and it changes them. Sugar had an iron will and retaining her pride was a hill that she was prepared to die on. I only loved her all the more.

Sugar and I became friends. I could 'catch' her if I stood still, holding the halter open while she reached in with her head. If I grew impatient, wanting to throw my rope over her neck and halter her in the ordinary way, she would go on the fight. While she never once bit me, she snapped at me many times. I learned to respect her and yet I was unafraid. Before too long, I was saddling her and riding in the corrals. The mare was 'track broke' only and proved to be a handful. I, however, was young and had read *The Black Stallion* twice. Unsuitable horses don't hurt wishful children, do they? Somehow, somehow, we made it work. By the time I was in high school, Sugar had moved over to our place. A confirmed weaver, in a state of perpetual motion, I skirted the issue by teaching her to ground tie, while I worked around her. Sugar could go all day, effortlessly like a wildcat, and her lope ate up the miles. She'd made an amazing transformation to please me. Only now, am I able to realize how generous her heart was, to trust and try again.

My hours with Sugar were the antidote to a stressful situation with my full-time teacher at the dressage barn. My real riding was practically killing me and Sugar, somehow, saved my soul. She kept me in love with horses. Arrangements were made for my father to buy her. I was over the moon. With blind faith, I entered my former racing Quarter Horse in local shows. She was brave and honest, and nobody could touch her in Trail. Sugar was so beautiful, such an effortless mover, that she somehow won two huge Western Pleasure classes, going one-handed in the silver bit and romals I'd bought with my babysitting money. I have her show trophies, still. I was the only person who could walk out and catch her, though. Sugar was still calling the shots.

Then, more and more often, my brave-heart started taking the odd bad step. A little off on the front, ever-so-slightly bobbing her head. Back then, we didn't know about veterinary specialists, massage therapists, or equine chiropractors. It was decided that Sugar would go back to Mr. Lyons, to give him those foals he so badly wanted. My stock saddle went up on its high rack in the tack room, while I went back to the dressage barn.

I never rode Sugar again. For years after, whenever I would visit my parents, I would see her across the road, swishing flies and nursing her beautiful babies. I went to visit Sugar a few times, but while she said she knew me, she always warned me off. I still loved her, but this time I heard what she had to say.

. 88 .

GETTING OFF MY HIGH HORSE

One of the worst pieces of advice for any of us working with horses is the old adage, 'practice makes perfect'. Oh, the woeful number of times I can recall asking for something just one more time, wanting more effort because we were so close to achieving my goal. Shame on me. The poor horse, already doing his level best, had no option but to worsen. From his point of view — and perhaps, the only one that mattered — his last effort must have been wrong because here we were, asking all over again.

"Once more, with feeling," our music teachers used to say. Nope, schooling our horses is nothing like learning to play the piano.

As a person who is bothered by her own mistakes, I've had a hard time learning that 'perfect' doesn't really exist, at least, not in my riding world. Even more liberating, I'm starting to figure out that there isn't a single one of us who has to be perfect, in order to be a success.

I'm remembering Ali, the Arabian gelding I was given when I was about fourteen. He was looking for a home because he had reared over backwards on his former rider, injuring her badly. My father, a man with an eye for a bargain, heard about the troubled horse and took him on for me. We were an unlikely pair, for I have always harboured a temperamental and impatient vein. Ali, on the other hand, was totally ill-equipped for the demands of ordinary life. Unable to cope with the pressures of being schooled or ridden out, Ali could scarcely stand being focused on by the human eye. However, being young, I did not know that we were ill-suited, and so we began.

I can remember one ride, where I had used up every available ounce of my energy to get Ali away from home. By the time I was physically and emotionally spent, ready to turn back, he had literally frozen in place. We were marooned, miles from home. When I finally dismounted to try and lead him, the panicked gelding started racing backwards, ever farther away, towing me along by his reins. At this point, my free horse was proving to be a poor bargain. Clearly, I needed help.

I began lessons with a riding coach who had gained much wisdom over her decades of teaching. She explained that my low expectations were still too heavy to bear in the eyes of my extra-sensitive horse. What we would need to do was break his training down into steps. Then, we would need to break these down into even tinier steps, always chunking things down until the horse could cope. This sort of rationale is rare in the horse world, and it is only now, forty years later, that I realize I learned more from this one troubled horse, than just about any other that has come into my hands. Working with Ali was like reading all the way through a training book, except that he required us to painstakingly put it into new language, one word at a time.

I wonder, would I have the patience to do this now? Knowing that there are so many horses in the world who would be more happily able to serve me, would I now take on such a monumental training job? I honestly don't know the answer.

Building Ali's new life was interminably slow. One step forward, two or three steps back. A long pause. Some sideways leaps and then we'd take that tentative step, again. As happens with so many highly-strung horses, we weren't dealing simply with training issues. We were needing to rebuild Ali's body. With horses, mind and body are never far removed from one another — and so it proved with the little Arabian horse.

If the head and tail are in the air, then it is logical that the back will be the horse's low point. Such a posture is the least efficient way for a horse to carry a rider. First tension and then pain builds and settles in various points along the horse's top line, reinforcing the cycle of rushed, taut movement with no relaxation in sight. We started small, with walk and trot steps on the lunge, asking the horse to move forward and stretch. For a long time, it felt like I was talking to myself. When he started being able to swing and chew, even while I was standing in the centre of the lunge circle, not making eye contact, not pushing him on too strongly, I began to make plans for us to ride.

Back we went to the heads up, tense horse. Unable to handle so much as an exasperated thought from me, Ali responded to my carrying a small paperback book whenever I rode him. He'd threaten to fly off the rails and my teacher would command me to sit, quietly pretending to read, until he'd calm down enough to go on. Good boy. But even our spoken words of praise felt like demands to him. Instead, we would offer a piece of carrot whenever he'd come close to doing right. Many times, Ali was too tense to open his jaws and accept our gifts.

We kept on. The riding at a walk turned into little jaunts on a loose rein, out over the pastures. Always keeping him safe, never getting too emotional, even in my joy. We would ride for a minute or so, asking for softness, then I would invite Ali to stretch his head down toward the ground. Only in this way was the horse able to process the training, mull it over, and shed his fear. With a stern warning to not count the months, Ali walked and stretched and eventually, said he was ready to try a trot. When that seemed safe enough, he suggested a canter. Such a small, ordinary moment, but I was riding through tears of joy. Strangely, his canter was anticlimactic. All our major work had been done in the time before.

It's a humbling thing to train a horse for whom nothing is hoped. We learn to train for the sake of sharing our knowledge, for celebrating the tiniest moments of improvement. Ali taught me that while love and belief are huge components when it comes to training any horse, ambition can be the thing that kills progress.

Just when I think I have learned that there is no perfection in my horsemanship, I will forget, because I am only human. As long as I am riding, I know that another horse will come along to teach me this hard lesson in humility, again and again.

. 89 .

SADDLE SORES

Mike came up the walkway, lugging his old saddle. With the passing of his father, he's feeling nostalgic. Both of us are at that point in our lives where we still feel sort of young, but we look decidedly old — and the good old days seem like a whole other lifetime.

The saddle was a Christmas gift. He'd just turned fourteen. In an old album, there's a yellowing print of Mike, a serious dark-haired boy, kneeling in front of the tinselled tree and behind a new Eamor saddle. This was actually a trophy saddle won by his famous bronc riding uncle, Tom Bews. The words '1974 Cloverdale Rodeo' are carved on the fenders, 'All-Around Champion Cowboy'. It was a cool gift for a young teen.

Mike lifted the saddle onto the verandah railing. It was grey with dust and mould. "I should clean it up before I bring it into the house." For once, I did not argue. Doing sums in my head, I reckoned that the saddle had sat in the old barn at his parents' place for close to thirty years, a long time without being on a horse. By the mid-eighties, both Mike and I'd switched to riding custom-built rigs. The old Eamor went up on its high saddle stand, to be pulled down every-so-often for guests.

Mike scrubbed away with warm water and a brush, with little effect. This job was going to need bigger guns. A little Dawn drizzled on the stiff bristles started to make inroads on the grime. The carving began to grow clearer, the saddle's dints and bruises sparking forgotten tales. Once his saddle was stripped and clean, Mike brought it into the house.

The old front cinch and latigos were cut off, to make way for new. Mike looked at the spur tracks all along the back cinch. This was unbuckled and the billets removed

from the rear rigging rings, for cleaning. Back cinches, usually of carved leather that is hidden under feedlot muck and horse sweat, have a hard life. He pulled off the old rubber horn wrap, from his days of *Roping with Jake and Clay,* an old classic published by Western Horseman. With a smile, Mike rubbed the dented silver horn cap, a souvenir of his first colt project. This was the saddle's first wreck.

Both stirrups were removed for cleaning, their unevenness noted, and a new set of holes put in the left stirrup leather. This will so often stretch, after decades of mounting and dismounting from the near side. Then, the leathers got a good dousing of Skidmore's dressing, before being pulled back and forth over the bars. "I've ridden how many miles in this saddle?" he wondered. "It took a long time to get these heavy leathers turned." Back in the old days, we didn't see many stock saddles with a 'Texas twist' to turn the stirrups. Instead, we'd wet our new leathers, turn them hard and run a broomstick through them. Eamors, known for their bulk, often had to be hung upside-down by their wetted-and-turned stirrups before they'd set. Only when they were made more submissive would we saddle up and ride.

Mike began working the beeswax dressing into the top and bottom sides of the leather. The saddle was thirsty and drank deeply. "What happened here?" I asked, pointing to a big crater along the cantle and part of the seat. I've learned to recognize a good story when I see one.

"Oh, that was Holiday. I saddled him up, ground-tied in the barn alley, then turned to get my bridle off the rack. For whatever reason, he came unglued. The saddle was loose enough to turn under his belly and tight enough, he couldn't kick free." Mike winced as he remembered. "The blue stain on the seat was from a Navajo blanket. Cimarron and I got caught out in a hard rain, when it was new. I made sure I laid the wet blanket out on top of my saddle to dry. Yeah. The dye leached out of the blanket and into the saddle permanently. Nothing known to man would remove it."

"I wonder what happened to your cantle plate?" I fingered the dark mark where it had sat for years, two holes drilled through the back of the seat to take the screws. What a shame it was lost, as the old silver had been beautiful. Mike smiled, dug in his back pocket and pulled out the tarnished piece. His nameplate had been sitting, mysteriously, on the windowsill of the tack room, among old jars of Furacin and dead flies.

"And these?" I held up the mangled rear saddle strings. Obviously, they'd been well-masticated by a bored and unsupervised horse.

"That happened going in with the big trailer to the Little Britches Parade. We had eight or ten horses on, all saddled and tied head-to-tail. You can squeeze more on, than if you face them all the same way," he explained. Unfortunately, they can also chew on one another's saddles if they're not tied really short. Mike was trying to figure out which of the geldings might have done the deed, most likely a lifelong joker called Robin. Such a crime could hardly be blamed on a dignified, working ranch mare! By this time, the old Eamor was gleaming. Mike started to buff her up with a scrap of sheepskin.

"Are you going to patch things up or leave them be?" I wondered. He stopped and looked at his old saddle for a moment.

"I'm gonna leave 'em. They might look rough, but every scar tells a story," he declared. I looked from the trail-worn saddle to my sixty-year-old husband, and I smiled. Indeed, they do.

· 90 ·
PITCHING HAY

Mike and I are spending the day at a farm sale with our son, Iain.

There is always something heartbreaking and forlorn about three generations of one family's hopes, dreams and harsh realities parked in a few neat rows. Neighbours and tire-kickers gather, hands in pockets, nudging old harrow sections with booted feet. Shaking their heads over aged and rusting Mayrath augers, straw bunchers and old square balers that haven't turned a wheel in thirty, nay, fifty years.

Sunburned faces smile greetings at old-timers who've made a day trip from town. Since the drought-stricken '80s when the banks turned turtle on so many families, I find farm sales a hard sell. Good thing there's coffee and pie.

They can't get a bid on the combines. I grow weirdly tearful when the boys running the show fire up a row of obsolete three-tons. Idling, throaty, these trucks have a sound unlike any other. Those of you who've hauled grain in the dust and shimmering harvest heat will understand.

A row of John Deere tractors comes on the block. An old fellow standing beside me starts into a nostalgic and winding tale of haying with a 4020. The bidding is fitful, and for the family hosting the sale, done all too soon. But the winning bids on two

of the tractors are put forth by a neighbour's son and Iain. Youngbloods. Boom! Boom! Down goes the gavel and these fifth-generation farm 'n' ranch boys are the proud new owners of old iron. Their late grandfathers will be smiling.

I have watched the dream of farming and ranching die slowly but surely in the hearts of first my husband, and then in turn, my thirty-something sons. Raised to be honest, good employees, they all have gone on to the hard slog of the working man, though their hearts have never been in it. Then, two years ago, a change began to take root in my younger son.

Iain has been watching the local sales and online auctions. He has done his research about the tractors and equipment that, no matter their advancing years, can still be relied upon. Because his grandfather farmed with green, our truck yard has become home to first an old John Deere 4020 and now a 4430. These classics are joined by a tired-looking haybine, an even older rake, and a small square baler. A large round baler has been added to the ranks, along with an early-model stackliner for bringing in and hauling small bales.

Slowly, but surely, Iain has been preparing to live out his dream.

Without a shop of any sort, weekends have passed with my son and his father working together, tinkering away at the puzzle of how to get these odd bits and pieces up and doing their jobs. Oh, the cursed, howling wind! Still, my men are out in their coveralls with wrenches, parts, and old manuals spewed about, the discontinued bits and pieces ordered, as they've been found online. Our oldest son, service manager at a big dealership to the south, sources out obsolete parts and sends a heads-up whenever fluids are on special. Duncan has also provided a beautiful toolbox filled with the necessities to service Iain's old iron.

Mike, for the first time in years, is talking about haying time. It is good to see my guys share something in common for a change, something positive, rather than the usual griping about the current news and ordinary vexations at work.

Mike and I have talked it over, hot-wiring off twenty acres of pasture to start Iain's enterprise. Sadly, Mother Nature hasn't read the memo, and our area, usually a lush growing zone with thigh-high grass, has gone the spring and summer with precious little rain. The grass is burned off and beginning to brown. Record highs are set with temps to 40C/105F. Iain knows, going in, that it will be a long drive between bales.

Those 'new' green tractors are running like tops. Each piece of equipment appears to have been parked for at least one generation of farming and it takes tender loving care to get them into the swing again. The machinery whines and grinds, jumps and thumps, shaking off decades of inertia, but slowly and surely it gets the job done. Our native grass hay makes it safely into the old chicken house before the arrival of an unexpected, but very welcome, thunderstorm. The moisture is too little, too late. The pasture's yield is heartbreakingly scant.

Yet, even at a distance, I feel the lightness of their duties as my men are doing what they've been bred to do for generations. You can take the boy from the farm but, no, you'll never quite take the farm boy out of the man.

This winter, I'll still be feeding my herd with large round bales obtained from a neighbouring farmer. But at shows and during trailer hauls, my horses will be munching contentedly on Iain's homegrown hay, baled with all the love and tenacity of a lifelong dream. That's powerful fodder.

I have asked Iain if he is feeling discouraged by his poor first harvest. He only smiles, already making plans to tweak his equipment over the coming months. He is asking his father about a piece of tired and weedy ground that should, just maybe, be torn up and planted to hay land. Still talking about next year, as have countless farmers before him.

. 91 .

RIDING IN CIRCLES

It can be tempting to ride under instruction that never changes. As if the needle is stuck in the same groove of the record, as if it were Groundhog Day.

While a certain amount of repetition is needed to get into this thick skull of mine, I want to know what is needed to make me effective, in my own right. It is my responsibility, not my teacher's, to become in myself an autonomous state. Knowing the 'how' is one thing. But knowing the 'why' and the 'when' to do things, all on my own, has become the next great goal in my riding. This is what will turn us into horse(wo)men, yet.

· 92 ·

ANGELS ON HORSEBACK

People often ask where I find these old sidesaddles that are now so much a part of my life. They seemingly come to me, to be lovingly repaired or restored, and then sent on their way again. They will be of use once more, for women who seek to keep the art of riding aside alive. Only half-jokingly, I say that they fall into my arms, straight out of the blue.

One Christmas Eve, the phone rang. It rang and it rang, and it just wouldn't quit. I hate saying this, but I was growing more than a tad testy, up on a wobbly stepladder, tweaking some lights along the back porch.

"Aargh, why can't I be left alone?!" I stumbled off the ladder and barged through the door, tripping over the dog, the melting snow puddling on our kitchen floor.

"Hello?" My greeting sounded more like a challenge to a duel. Then, when the caller identified himself and the reason for contacting me, all my angst was forgotten. You see, a long time ago, about twenty-five years back, Mike and I were having a hard time. We weren't making much of a wage, all the while trying to raise three kids. Bills were due and no money was coming in. I realized that in order to make ends meet, I would have to sell my saddle.

I consigned her to a local auction one sad and dreary day. I stood at the back of the sales room, tearful yet amazed at the frenzied bidding. Glowing with glycerine soap atop the honest wear of many miles, she went under the hammer for four thousand dollars. That was a lot of money for a saddle in those days. Surely, I'd been blessed.

The money may have saved us, but as time passed, I never quite forgave myself this treachery. It was highly unlikely that I would ever again see this particular saddle, let alone have the chance to buy it back. Worse, the Mayhew had been given to my sister and I as children, by Winnie Harvey, the queen of sidesaddle mentors. In the years since I'd sold her, there'd been glimpses of her carrying other riders, even with a famous Hollywood actress in a period film. More recently, I had heard a rumour that she'd been sold or stolen. It seemed that my saddle was gone for good.

Winnifred Harvey showed that women can compete handily with the men, looking elegant while doing so. This, the only surviving photograph of my mentor, shows Mrs. Harvey with Red, her favourite, just prior to his death at age thirty-four. (Harvey Family Collection)

The voice on the phone brought me back to the here and now. Would I be at all interested in the sidesaddle that he'd purchased from me, twenty-five years ago? The price was right. Before either one of us could change our minds, I grabbed my purse and raced for the car.

At our meeting place, I went and called at the shop door. No answer. It wasn't locked, so I quietly entered the shadowy building. In the half-light, a row of old sidesaddles lay along a bench. My heart sank as I failed to recognize the Mayhew. Then, at the far end, there she was. A quick glance under the nearside flap showed the unusual buttons and keyholes that fastened the girths, along with traces of a yellow stick-on daisy with which I'd defiled her when I was a kid. This was Mrs. Harvey's saddle, all right.

Sadly, the years have not been kind to her. But these decades apart have also been a time of learning. Only now do I know how to restore her youthful good looks.

With any luck, soon she will be gracing one of my horses. Meanwhile, as I wrote out the cheque through misty eyes, I realized how fortunate I was to be given this second chance. As the saying goes, when we know better, we can do better. Sitting here, holding place of honour in my tack room, this saddle is finally here to stay.

There is a bit more to the story of my sidesaddle riding mentor. In her younger years, Winnie Harvey showed, a lone woman with Canada's military jumping team, all across North America. In a brief, glamorous time after the First World War and before the Great Depression, the horses and riders travelled, with their tack trunks and army grooms, by rail. In newspaper clippings of my well-known mentor, she is shown riding in either a hard black bowler, or an ordinary 1920s wool felt hat. The latter was like a soft-brimmed cloche, a more casual look to top her black riding habit, which she gave to our family, along with her bowler hat and Mayhew sidesaddle.

A few years ago, a co-worker approached me, asking if I would like to have an old black hat for my collection of riding togs. I thanked her but I didn't get too excited after she'd described it. An ordinary felt, it didn't seem to be anything special. Yet, something strange happened when I was handed the red plastic bag containing the old hat. A shiver went up and down my spine. My hands started shaking and I turned cold. I knew, even without looking, to whom this hat had belonged. I pulled the soft felt from the bag and looked into the sweat band. In an old-fashioned, very faded and spidery script was written, 'Winnifred Harvey'. Yes, it was her signature. Somehow, somehow, I'd ended up with my heroine's hat.

We don't always agree on the design by which this world is guided, but what I do know for sure, is this — mystery and magic are all around us, and they are far beyond our understanding or control.

· 93 ·

SUNLIGHT AND SHADOWS

Some people lie awake at night and worry about money. I tend to fret during the dark hours, about horses I've ruined along the way. Some I wrecked because of my ignorance. Some were simply too much horse and I was afraid. Some I set up for failure by wanting too much, too soon. Some I fiddled around with homemade remedies when I should have sooner called the vet. Too many of them, God help me, were no strangers to my short fuse.

I'm recalling horses that were totally unsuited to what I was trying to make of them — and still, they did their best. Was I grateful enough? Encouraging enough? Hardly. I'm recalling both long gone and recent horses that, after a time, I just gave up on. I wonder, did I cash in my chips too soon? I'm remembering ones that I never even came close to understanding and, looking back, I know they tried. The failure to connect was never theirs.

The ones I rode in bits I liked, even though they didn't — and ill-fitting saddles that I insisted upon, because show-ring trends did not favour the saddles that did. The teeth that were never fixed, the sore spots that were camped on. Days when things went so well, I kept asking, long after I should have quit. Days when things were going so badly, I should have asked for helpful guidance.

I become all the sadder, for I know that I am still figuring things out, still peppering poor decisions among the good. I might be alone in saying so, but when I see the horses who have somehow worked out, in spite of me, honesty compels me to admit that there is another herd of forgotten souls who have paid the price to teach me. I must remember them and apologize, for only this keeps their time in my hands from being entirely in vain.

What has helped, in a small way, is to write of these characters. To share openly of their stories, all the chapters and the parts that I played. This does not absolve me. May these words serve as a reminder to me, along with the hope that they will allow others to know that they are not alone in these dark moments. May my own admissions of wrongdoing and ignorance allow us to learn, to vow to do better, and then to finally give ourselves permission to set down our shame.

A life spent among horses has shown me that no one of us is all good, no one of us is all evil. Sunlight and shadows. No matter the faces we present to the world, our horses know us the best.

· 94 ·

GOOD-MINDED

Sarcee, my little wildie, has had much to teach me. One of the most poignant lessons, from this latest in a long line of training-horses, is one that I would like to share with you.

There is a reserve, a 'deep waters' aspect to this horse that is at once appealing and mysterious. Even people who do not know horses can recognize that something about Sarcee is different. While no horse in any way resembles the shrieking, slobbering hot messes portrayed by Hollywood, most horses are more vocal, engaged and easily distracted than is this little cayuse.

I find myself dialing down and matching my breathing to his when I am with him. Unconsciously, it has had a profound effect on my own behaviour, both around other horses and humans.

At the public arena, Sarcee observes a group of people who have been isolated in the pandemic and starved for human interaction. They are laughing and calling loudly to each other. He stiffens. His neck is locked in that 'up periscope' position that harkens back to his days in the wild. Instantly, he is on guard. I watch his breathing quicken and his eyes deepen to onyx. He is waiting on these strangers to soften, to trust in their own energy and ability to recognize safe harbour, without the shrill noise and constant movement that we chattering, happy women so often share.

I watch and wonder if I can bring him back down with my own silent grounding. Breathing in, feeling the pause … breathing out, feeling the pause … and again. I soften my gaze and begin to think of love, of quietude, of slowness, of support, of courage, of trust, of grace. I keep slowing my breathing as I draw upon these thoughts. My horse swallows and without pause, lowers his head. He shakes his damp, curling forelock over his now soft eyes. He and I are, again, sharing space.

In the short time that I have known Sarcee, within mere months, I have learned to rely upon this communion with my horse, without words and without touch. This does not mean that I don't tell him when he has done a good job. This does not mean that he doesn't enjoy that special grooming spot, once he is unsaddled. But this mindful calming has become an oft-used tool in my toolbox, a thing to bring myself into quiet stillness when my horse is losing his own. I am always able to settle him, to reinforce his waning courage by simply breathing slowly and deeply, simply being quiet and still. In my mind, I have only to picture the horse that I want.

Simple, yes, but not always easy. My recent practices of yoga and meditation have done much to support this theory. It also excites me to learn that at my age, I am still learning and still getting closer to that place in my horsemanship where I have long yearned to go. Yes. To be still. To be quiet. To be counted upon. These are my personal goals.

THE DIAMOND HITCH

You gals will understand why my head was turned by Mike McLean! A man whose love language lies in acts of service, rather than in diamonds, we have been blessed with many a good laugh, as we embark on our fourth shared decade. (Author's Collection)

I have a soft spot for all the ol' married folks. You know, the wrinkly ones who annoy each other and still know how to share a laugh. From riding over rough spots to skating down slippery slopes, they get up every morning and mend their fences. Mike and I are no exception. While we knew of each other from childhood, as both our families showed ponies for many years, we didn't actually meet, as individuals, until I was in my last year of high school.

Before that, Mike was a division ahead of me at the shows — a very mature youth rider in the oldest youth age group, mounted upon a beautiful palomino called Cimarron. I, squarely-built and freckle-faced, was chugging along on my little Welsh Pony, Peter, with the kids under age twelve. These two groups are far-flung galaxies with kids. We'd never actually spoken a word.

Fast-forward five years to a summer day in the park in town, where I was having a bag lunch on a bench near the deserted baseball diamond. I'd just fetched a parcel at the post office. With bated breath, I opened it, for I knew that it was a picture ordered at a recent horse show. Long before the days of digital cameras and having our photographs taken constantly, this was a huge deal. At the time, my heartthrob horse was a towering Thoroughbred gelding called Eclipse. I saw nothing but beauty in this fellow and as he'd just won the ridden championship at our last big show, I was certain that his worth was plain for all to see. Suddenly, a shadow fell across the image. I looked up and it was Mike McLean.

"That horse has a huge head!" were the very first words my beloved said to me. Of course, I was quick to anger. I don't even remember my reply. Eventually, Mike would ask me out on a date, albeit to prove only to his younger brother that I would be fine to ask to the upcoming Christmas ball at the high school. Mike likes to say that he wanted to train me, himself, instead. Our love blossomed, despite its seeds being sown on such rocky ground. We would end up marrying when I was nineteen and Mike a grizzled twenty-three. Much as I can look back on those early years and the subsequent arrival of three little ones to our household, I don't know if I'd want to go back in time, even if I could. We had a lot of growing up to do and a short while in which to do it.

There are many ups and downs when two lives intersect, but as Mike said to me not all that long ago, "If I had to grow old and grumpy with anybody, I'd still want it to be with you." I ask, if that's not true love, then what is? Seriously, though, we learned that life-altering change — and something good and long-lasting — can come from the humblest of starts.

· 96 ·
HIGH-HEADED

Rockytop Shadow was a birthday gift to me from my new family, the McLeans.

The solid black Paint was a green four-year-old and, as a young wife and mother, I was only sixteen years her senior. Until her death, when she headed across the late-night highway and was killed by a drunk driver winding his way home, Shadow lived large. She was always a presence.

She was the first horse I'd known with 'the look of eagles'. An old-timey aphorism that so brilliantly describes horses with an unquenchable spirit, Shadow would be scanning the far horizons all the while more mundane things were going on around her. Those people who say that 'the horse's mind is a little bird that should be kept in your hand' have never known such a horse, I don't think. There is no caging this bird.

That said, I never did wholly understand Shadow. We made many miles over our twenty-one years together and I can only think, in retrospect, that the way she said goodbye was probably the most fitting way she could have left me. Shadow, quite simply, was not meant to grow old and frail.

No matter how many hours in the saddle, I don't remember her ever giving evidence of being tired. Hot and sweaty, yes, but never worn down. I used to plan my babies' naps around getting out there and long trotting her for miles, knowing that if I didn't, I'd have a really hard time handling her the next day. She was honest, though, and never pulled a fast one on anybody. You see, despite her training, mileage and dignity, Shadow was never really what I'd call tame. She always kept something back, something that would not be mastered.

The mare ranched, long and hard, all week. Weekends were spent at local shows, competing in just about every event we could muster.

Like most warrior princesses, Shadow was a brave-heart, a Trail machine, back when these classes were more about steady nerves under pressure — and not about counted trot poles and lope-overs. As you can imagine, this horse was not meant for Western Pleasure, although I tried my best to mash my square peg into that round hole. The show where she finally, finally, could not be beaten was, in fact, the day before she came down with a near-fatal attack of strangles. She'd been so sick that, finally, she'd put her head down and just showed. Shadow, I was sorrier about that than you ever knew.

An uncommonly pretty horse, Shadow had a huge talent for ignoring rider error. This made her a hot commodity in the movie business — *Legends of the Fall, Black Fox, Little Women, The Scarlet Letter*. Through much of the '90s, it was Shadow who made our mortgage payment. This mare helped make possible the purchase of the beautiful place where Keystone is based today.

In her twilight years, as she started to slow down, I drove Shadow over pleasant miles in an antique high-wheeled McLaughlin sulky. Her need to make tracks was met with the sound of her shoes ringing out over the miles of highway. These

hours are among my happiest memories of a long and passionate relationship. Ours was an unlikely marriage between two iron-willed and unrelenting souls. 'Lee and Shadow', 'Shadow and Lee' — for two decades, the one name was seldom mentioned without the other.

She gave me one foal, a filly by then national champion cutting horse, No More Mr. Nice Guy, who was unusual in that he was a Paint. I remember coming into the house after discovering the newborn baby, in tears and unable to speak. Mike was making pancakes in an apron that read, 'Kiss the cook'.

"Is the colt dead?" he asked, quite reasonably. "No, it's white!" I wailed. I suppose I'd been hoping for a carbon copy of Shadow and the small, loudly-coloured filly she presented to me was almost translucent, too delicate, too different. Or so I'd thought.

Chilcotin grew to be a mighty personality, all 13:3 hands, in her own right. She served my son with the same ironclad loyalty as did her mother, albeit during a too-short life. Chilco was, frankly, my last stab at wanting to be a horse breeder. I somehow knew that there would be no replacing my black horse — an oddity, a one-off, a legend.

Shadow flew through her teens and into her twenties, still straightening the curves and flattening the hills, seemingly ageless, still fighting our traditional rules with every step. She was fearless in dicey situations, only losing her nerve once, after a belligerent Charolais bull knocked her off her feet one desperate afternoon down at the river. For the first time, doubt began creeping in, an inkling that her invincibility would not go on forever.

One glowing evening, the kind where the birds are singing and the grass all sparkling emeralds, Shadow came to me, cresting the long hill that comes up to the yard. Something was different. My lion-heart was tentative, somehow, and it took a closer look to realize that one side of her face was hanging, slack, along with a tipped-over ear. By all appearances, she'd had a stroke.

"Shad, what am I going to do with you?" I can remember tearfully asking, as I straightened and fussed with her forelock.

I think that's when she and the universe together planned that midnight foray onto the highway, working together to spare me the heavy decisions. Within the year, I too would suffer a stroke of my own — one more mysterious force that bound me, in life and death, to this horse.

Shadow was a wild heart and entirely trustworthy, all at once. We thought she was ours and we, hers. And yet she belonged to no one. I have often wondered, in the years since, if she and I would have had a different relationship, had it happened in another time. Would I have been more understanding, more patient, more skilled, if she had come into my life now that I'm an older woman? Or were we meant to be as we were, back then?

We were a pair, she and I, young and strong and fearless.

Much to my dismay, my two-year-old demands a ride just before a public sidesaddle demonstration with Shadow. In the end, this wonderful moment, shared with Caiti and her harmonica, reminds me how fleeting is our time with small children. (Author's Collection)

· 97 ·

SHOWMANSHIP

Word was, a new series was being filmed in our area, a spin-off from a hugely popular western movie. Some of the original cast was involved, but no matter which way they sliced it, that TV series was going to be a hard sell. It had none of the star power, grit, charm, or good writing of the original. It was, however, an absolute godsend when it came to employing the pool of local cowboy talent. I, for one, was keen to sign up and be involved.

The set was crawling with friends and neighbours — men who were hired for their ability to ride anything with hair, to rope runaways, to look after the stars a-horseback, to hitch and drive teams. I got the call one night to join my mother-in-law as 'special skilled extras' to double for the female leads. When we arrived on set early the next morning, we were told that they really only needed one rider, after all — a woman to sedately go up and down the main street. My mother-in-law had brought her own sidesaddle, so was a shoo-in for the riding part. Disappointed, I hung around the wardrobe trailer, while they laced me into a period corset, restyled my hair and penciled in a pair of formidable eyebrows. Just when it seemed that my stylists' efforts were all for nought, came the call to action.

A stuntwoman was needed to drive a buggy horse. Well, I like driving, so how hard could it be? I signed the lengthy safety release and headed over to where the movie horses were milling. I do remember the difficulty I had with walking in the yards of homespun fabric that made up my prairie skirt. At one point, I stepped out in front of a passing horse when I crossed the street blindly, due to my poke bonnet. I hastily folded back the brim. This get-up was going to take some getting used to.

I introduced myself to the buggy horse, a raw-boned sorrel who went by the name of Rooster. He'd had a long season by the time I showed up and was little interested in either me or my small talk. Rooster was already harnessed and hitched to a decrepit doctor's buggy, tied to a corral post by a rope around his neck. I figured the best thing to do was stay near him until we were called up by the director. It wasn't long before we were summoned.

I had a heck of a time climbing into the buggy, due to its huge, steel-rimmed wheels, my tight-laced corset and the voluminous skirt and petticoats. With a little reticule looped over one wrist, I fingered the worn, dry lines. Rooster's harness appeared to be from the turn-of-the-century, with very little care evident in its authentically dust-filled cracks and numerous fixes. We backed out onto the street and wound our way around thick electrical cables and dust fans, over to the film set. Two mounted horse wranglers materialized on either side of us. Looking back, they seemed very intent on my horse staying at a slow walk. I also remember noting that Rooster and I didn't seem to have much in the way of steering.

I waved demurely to my husband, whom I spotted among a loitering band of men made up as horse bandits. They were laughing and joking, having the time of their lives. It was hardly work for them, paid to be galloping around on half-broke horses, shooting blanks from their long guns, scaring the good townsfolk. Movie work was the next best thing to cowboy heaven.

Meanwhile, back in the buggy. The director met me over at an old steam engine, hissing and puffing on the railway track that encircled the set. Rooster showed little interest in the one-hundred-and-twenty-ton locomotive, which emboldened me, considerably. I listened intently as the director set up the scene. I was to go to the very outskirts of the historic village and wait behind a copse of trees. The engine would build up a head of steam and get going along the two-mile circuit. As it passed me at full throttle, I was to yell "Hyah!" to Rooster, overtake the engine and cut in front of it at a flat crossing.

The first two takes, Rooster was merely hard-mouthed and headstrong. But the biggest shock was finding that the level crossing we were to take in front of the train quickly turned into a dead-end downward ramp. This was the loading dock of an old paddle-wheeler that made leisurely excursions around the city reservoir. I had to somehow get the runaway horse stopped before he ran out of loading dock and landed us both in the deep water!

By our final takes, however, Rooster was no longer seeking management. He would bolt straight ahead as the train was approaching. Sparks shot off our steel-rimmed buggy wheels as the rattly equipage fishtailed down the dirt road, crossing in front of the smoking train and down the ramp, toward the water. At one point, while pulling up — my feet braced against the buggy dash, me hauling back on rein-wrapped hands with all my might — one of the ancient and crumbling breeching straps broke. There was nothing to hold the old buggy from slamming into my horse, and the mounted men waiting to rope Rooster at the pier had a dicey time getting him stopped.

"We need one more take!" crackled the director on the two-way radio. "The horse is still crossing too far in front of the train. Tell the lady that it's got to be a nearer miss!" I was receiving further instruction, all the while a wrangler quickly repaired my life-saving breeching strap with a roll of electrical tape. By this point, I was shocky enough that I would have driven the horse off a cliff, had they told me. Instead, I piloted the wide-eyed Rooster back to the start, turned him around and again waited for the train. As you can imagine, it was quite a length of time, setting up the steam train, actors and extras between takes. The sun was almost setting, and the dusty sorrel was on his hind legs, snatching at the bit, when we heard the steam engine picking up speed. Rooster shot off, on the dead run. We were on two wheels as we inched past the cow-catcher on the locomotive. Clattering down the hill to the pier, all hands on deck were yelling, "Whoa!" and bravely waving their arms in an effort to flag down the horse.

We made it out alive. With my overtime and special skills' action, I went home with my unibrow and a pay chit for close to three hundred dollars. Not bad for one day's work. Despite my cash windfall, however, I remember making some vague excuses the next time I was 'called up' to the front. In the end, I don't believe that our big chase scene was used in the final production. Rooster and I, for all our valiant effort, had ended up on the cutting room floor. Such is the glamour of show business.

. 98 .

THE WILD 'N' WOOLLY WEST

I had a bit of a scare yesterday — with a coyote, of all things.

Wildlife is a part of living where we do. Coyotes are always on the periphery of our day-to-day lives. I've grown to love falling asleep to their haunting music, to seeing them silhouetted on the windblown hills. We've never had any trouble with these wild canines at calving time, unlike others who so claim. Perhaps the routine of making sure someone was out there regularly on horseback, 'up close and personal', was reason for our coyotes minding their manners and staying away?

Walking out in the blowing snow yesterday, I was on my way to catch a horse when I had the feeling that my dog Glen and I were not alone. His hackles rose up and he wheeled around, snarling. When I turned, we were an arm's reach from a big male coyote who showed no sign of backing off. He had eyes only for my dog. I figured if I yelled at him, he'd snap out of his trance and leave us alone. Nope. He snarled and then turned on me as well.

Long story short, it was a strangely exhilarating but frightening walk, backwards, the long hill towards home. I tripped over a big caragana branch that had somehow travelled from the yard a good distance down towards the creek. Thank goodness. This, I was able to pick up and brandish at our aggressor until we finally made it, with Glen still in one piece, to the corral gate. Anyone within five miles of our place probably heard me screaming bloody murder the whole while. Yes, Glen was the underlying problem, but this coyote is on warning. We'll call it a first offence, and if it happens again, there will not be another.

Mike and I take seriously this living in harmony with nature around us. Regularly, we see bears along the creek and cougar tracks in the snow. For the most part, they live their separate lives, and we try our best to leave a light footprint, to not disturb this fine balance. Sometimes, though, our worlds collide.

Years ago, when the kids were young, I used to 'run away from home' by harnessing up one of the ponies and going for a head-clearing drive. The wind would dry my tears while I'd gnash my teeth and cry out loud without anyone knowing, save the poor pony.

On this particular day, I was trotting up the deserted road from the creek, with Piper in the little cart. The grade rose steeply from the creek bank and carved its way through a bushy area of silver willow.

Suddenly, without warning, a tawny flash came through the brush and out onto the road. It was a cougar in full stride. Before either the pony or I could react, he had leapt out of the ditch and right into Piper's side. We'd been T-boned, like two cars at an intersection. The cougar bounced off and ran back the way he came. Of course, we ran off, too, and it was quite a chore getting the spooked pony stopped. Luckily, the road was a steep enough climb that Piper ran out of steam before we'd made level ground.

It was another walk on the wild side. Sometimes these encounters scare me, but most of the time, I try to settle down and feel blessed. If we believe in animal spirits and totems, we can usually find meaning in the wild animals we encounter. Cougar teaches us how to find our inner ferocity and innate psychic awareness. Old Man Coyote is telling me to stop taking myself so seriously, to be open to change and risk. A middle-aged worrier by nature, I can only vow to give them my best shot.

CHANGING REIN

People will say, "I thought my horse would like this sport but he's not very good at it." Or "We tried that once, but my horse freaked out!"

Making a change in disciplines doesn't mean you have to win — it just means giving your horse a break from his routine. It means working a different part of his body than what you usually do. It means giving him another skill to share with you, another thing of which to be proud. That said, not all horses, or people, embrace change. Sometimes, we have to help one another out.

I am remembering Winchester. A brave, happy, workmanlike pony, Win came from a busy hunting outfit up north. The little gelding thought nothing of packing out meat from the bush. This business of partnering me, he said, was stressful. Our first trip to town saw Win and me in the large well-lit public arena. People were loping around us and there were children running in the stands. Win saw none of it because he stood, transfixed, staring up at the overhead lights. It was as though he'd seen angels on high. I could only sit there and wait, amid helpless laughter. A moose in the bush was one thing, obviously, but electric lighting was something else.

Weeks later, helping out at a neighbour's branding, Win again struggled with change.

Windblown, wide-open spaces set the stage for a morning's gather of four-hundred cow-calf pairs. As the herd poured from the hills and toward the corrals for sorting, the din of the bawling mothers and babies grew deafening. My new pony thought we were under attack. Suddenly, my plans for the day were changed. Seemingly confident with grazing cows in little groups, Win panicked when the scattered pairs grew into one seething, bawling mass. It took an hour or so, just getting him to remember the aids, all the little things we'd been working on. Then, it took quite a while to have him understand that my simple demands needed to be met.

Watch the cows. Follow the cows. Stand still when you're told. Lucky for me, Mike was on a rock-solid horse. We tucked in alongside them for a while, just for the mentorship. Later on, we were good on our own. If we hadn't devoted the day to building Win's courage, I might have said that he was too scared to ride out on the ranch. Like most horses and ponies, however, he grew to love working cows.

One would think that a day of fresh air and sunshine would be a nice change for a horse. The job might be cross-country jumping, or gathering cattle, maybe going to the mountains. We forget that if this isn't something he's used to, he will need our help to figure it out.

Change can be liberating and joyful. Change can be scary as heck.

. IOO .
TACKING UP

I open the trailer door to unload our newest horse. Today brings our sixth lesson together. Our downward transitions and halts do not go well. All the long way home, I roll them around in my mind. A retired racehorse, Pamela has yet to seek the reward of softly slowing or quitting this forging ahead. So, she stiffens, drops various body parts, braces herself and hits the ground like a lawn dart. This is not comfortable for either one of us. As yet, her default is in leaning upon a strong pull. We have moments of beauty and softness, broken with moments of sheer habit. She looks so kind standing here, that I pause. Smiling, I softly stroke her forehead.

"It's not all bad, Pamela. You're doing a heck of a lot right."

I keep a series of riding diaries that are now fifty years old. Since age eight, almost every lesson and horse show have had a notation made of what I know for sure, and what I do not. My recent rides with Pamela are at the end of the latest notebook.

So far, she stands still for saddling on cold, dark mornings; loads alone onto the trailer and waits while standing tied; hauls down the busy highway; goes into a crowded public arena and gets straight to work; sidles up to the mounting block; stands still for mounting; opens and shuts the metal gate; does a one-rein stop at the walk and trot; backs up softly; walks on a free rein and in collection; occasionally does her upward and downward transitions with a soft feel; side-passes both left and right; jogs along and also knows a working trot, done in roundness and while 'stretching'. She is trying to understand leg-yielding at the trot and reining back, while circling both ways. She can lope beautiful circles and diamonds; extends the canter down the long side and collects around the end; waits quietly while tied amongst strange horses. Every day, knowing Pamela is becoming more of a pleasure.

Today, she gives me two clean flying changes. That is a lot to learn in new hands in only six lessons. Going over Pamela's recent accomplishments, I realize that our

challenges are but little bumps in a long and winding road. Every ride, we will take one more thing and work to make it just a bit better.

I straighten Pamela's forelock and she gives a happy snort. Feeling unstoppable now — which is way different than focusing on not stopping well — together, we step out of the trailer.

. 101 .

FINDING MY STRIDE

Sometimes, despite our mothers' best efforts, we did not turn out in the way that was expected of us. I know this feeling all too well as, I suspect, does my mum. Surely, we are not alone in this?

So, I say, here's to the mothers of girls who love horses.

From the very beginning, she was different from other girls. And while you would have loved your daughter to be pretty in ruffles, she danced to a different beat. Games with other children always turned into jumper rounds and skipping rope chariot races. And every single night when you tucked her in, she prayed for a pony. Finally, you relented.

"Get it out of her system," friends said. If anything, she grew worse, and horses were all she could think of. School teachers praised her storytelling and artwork, but God help her math and home economics!

Soon, you were working two jobs to get her into lessons with the best teacher, the one who saw brilliance where others saw nothing much. Lessons, board, a new saddle, show entries, a nicer coat, a more talented horse ... you were never done.

Horse blankets in your washing machine, paying the vet, volunteering at shows, learning to haul through strange cities, packing lunches for the road. You were never done. Weekends spent walking hots, nursing concussions, doctoring wire cuts, pulling boots, drying tears, eating bad hamburgers, sleeping in the back of the truck to save money. You were never done.

And then, one day, you were.

Sometime after wondering what you were going to do with this tomboy with unbelievably bad fingernails and a farmer's tan, she was ready to go. You were free, finally, left with empty corrals and a spare bedroom of wall-to-wall ribbons. Every single one with a story. Somewhere along the way, you grew proud of her, of how she was different. Looking back, you wouldn't change a thing. Please know that neither would she.

Here's to the mothers of girls who love horses! Everything of which we've dreamed, you've somehow made sure it came true.

. 102 .

SOFT HANDS

I was walking in the pasture today, when suddenly I felt I wasn't alone. I turned and there she was — Doll had left the others and followed me. I spoke her name and she walked carefully up, lowering her head with a big sigh into the front of my coat. I smiled and did what she was asking of me, for it has been a long process getting the respect and affection of this complex, many-layered personality.

We have a routine — she stands with eyes closed, while I literally groom her all over with just my hands. I feel the old lumps, and sometimes new ones, and have grown to know these places where she most wants my touch.

The process is like I'm painting her all over with slow, light, measured strokes. There is no teasing, no scratching or tickling. It is a meditation. One-by-one, I've watched the defensive actions she has shown in certain areas melt away — first an area along her left ribs, then both ears, a thickened hind fetlock, and now the relaxation of her tail. Rather than think of her earlier crankiness as disobedience, I was guided to wait and listen to what she had to say.

I knew that each of these out-of-bounds areas had a story, a memory that she needed to share with me. The reward, if I must have one, has been her complete trust. There is much chewing and yawning while we do this grooming ritual, and it has surprised me to find that it relaxes and pleases me every bit as much as it does my mare.

Twelve seasons have rolled by since the time I needed to be careful with her, never quite knowing whether her warnings were for real or just bluffs. Not all that long ago, I would have 'got after her' for these shows of defiance, but something has

made me wait it out. I'm glad I did, because these things she has taught me are now routine with all my horses, including the new ones who come here.

Doll's way is now my way. It is one of making friends and softening boundaries, just as surely as if the horses and I could smile and shake hands. While no substitute for wet saddle blankets, or working at our schooling, it is my way of honouring them, of showing my genuine love.

. 103 .

THE LARGE, FAST CIRCLE

I'm remembering a beautiful first day of spring. Several years ago, I took a steaming cup of coffee, one Border Collie and two mewling cats, then walked over the hill pasture in search of early crocuses. Sure enough, they shyly said hello. Poignant now, as I've neither the crocuses nor the horses I visited that day. Today, the pasture is empty, still deep in slumber beneath a blanket of snow.

The horses I mention were firm friends — the fourteen-year-old Appy, the three-year-old Quarter Horse — and we had nothing on our minds but the promise of happy trails. By summer's end, both Riel and July would be gone, each giving in to a serious illness that would not be denied. I'm thinking of this never-ending cycle as I look out over the snow-capped Rockies. Spring's rebirth, autumn's goodbyes. Even though it hurts sometimes, isn't it all just beautiful? You know, we're going to make it through another one. Raise a cup to blessed spring!

. 104 .

SILVER BITS

Do I believe that our horses get a little better or a little worse, every single time we handle them? Most times, yes. But I try my darnedest to make any changes small ones. Baby steps, baby steps. When it comes to the long haul, I've learned to avoid leaps and bounds. Every so often, I require myself to sit quietly with my secret demons. One of these is riding from a place of confrontation.

When we deal with tough situations, tough horses, or tough people — anything that has us surviving by staying alert, reactive and using our wits — we run the risk of becoming embattled ourselves. Like soldiers. In order to cope, we forget how to soften. We stay guarded. Braced. This is why it is so important, if we are hired to be heroes or enforcers — or if we regularly fix 'problem' horses — to be gentle with ourselves and to continue to ride the soft, quiet ones. With their help, we are reminded that there is always a place for gratitude and love. We remember how to ride with less, rather than always looking for more. Seeking goodness and beauty will remind us to be kinder, gentler people.

Today's challenge? Go out and find beauty. See something that stops you and brings such gladness that tears come to your eyes. I have this chance on every ordinary walk out to check the horses. It made me wonder. How many times have I been too busy, too self-absorbed, too embattled to really notice?

Today, I will look for the good.

. 105 .

LET 'ER BUCK!

My daughter Cait on the lovely, fierce, unique, sweet, salty, and utterly fearless pony, Doll.
Actually, these words pretty much describe either one of them, on any day. (Author's Collection)

The sidesaddle seen here was built around 1885. Rescued from a dumpster, the nearly one-hundred-and-forty-year-old saddle is somehow mighty, too. It is a survivor. For many years, these ladies' saddles, representing generations of feisty, pioneering women, were not well-respected by horsemen or those entrusted with their well-being or 'repairs'.

Times are changing in that regard, but I always feel sad that so many of the old sidesaddles were thrown away. They represented such beautiful workmanship and the largely untold story of Woman and the Horse.

Untold generations and the fleeting spans of our lives ... Who rode these saddles? What were these women's lives really like? How did so many of their saddles end up in lonely western Canadian grain bins and farm sheds, so far away from their riders' roots? Did they come because of a man, a war or a great adventure? I will always wonder.

Having just welcomed my first grandchild, I saw this picture and it stopped me. It has me wondering anew about the generations of mighty women in all our stories. The mighty women within me ... and the mighty women within you.

. 106 .
ROUGH RIDER

We admire the rider who can get the job done with ease and smoothness. Their horses respond to quiet aids and one of the hallmarks of a beautiful rider is the impression they give of making it seem effortless, as though anyone could do what they do. We recognize this same quality in the trained movements of skiers, skaters and dancers who have been well taught.

How does one join their ranks? Beyond time, mileage, more body control, more knowledge? If you recognize yourself as unpolished, perhaps this is the year to stop 'riding madly off in all directions'. I'd say the first step is realizing that one is not where we want to be, quite yet. There is power in feeling the need for change. So, we recognize that we are maybe too busy, too active, too rough around the edges. Then we give ourselves permission to move on. Quietly, we vow to somehow improve.

Interestingly, I've found that many unschooled riders say they like a jazzed-up sort of horse. They say such a horse best suits their riding. That they don't want to ride any 'dead-heads'. It has been my observation that when we feel that way, we have yet to ride enough highly-educated horses. We just don't know any different. Those trained on a thought or a touch, with the willingness and ability to exactly match our required energy and intentions — their flame rising and falling to mirror our own — bring to us precious moments that we may relive again and again. Such horses teach us to move sparely, to breathe deeply, to use ourselves effectively, to hold ourselves with poise and yet be relaxed.

I have learned that subtlety in our riding is a powerful drug that, taken just once, will have us wanting more. If we decide that we want to change our riding by becoming quieter, by doing less in the saddle, we can start by finding a mentor who will inspire this. We are looking for a teacher who believes in classical horsemanship. Good horses, themselves, can school us almost as surely as can any human. Watching and learning from those who've been correctly finished, both horses and teachers, are necessary for learning refinement — and still, people deride the 'push button' horse, as though he is a terrible thing. Oh, God grant me the horse who has been ridden so correctly, so consistently, that he is well and truly in understanding of the aids. To ride effectively but less noticeably is to ride classically — fluidly, with a firm seat, small aids, still legs, and slow hands, our eyes up to match the forward gaze of our horses.

Becoming subtle — yet clearly understood — is a worthy goal in anyone's life, let alone in our horsemanship. Less is more. Less is more.

. 107 .

AN ADVANCED-LEVEL HORSE

Silly, old, anthropomorphic me. I should know by now that 'horses aren't as smart as people, because they are unable to reason'. Or so says science.

I listen to such arguments with a grain of salt. Could my horses pass a test in science or mathematics? Well no, but then again, neither could I. By definition, reason means 'the ability of the mind to think, understand, and form judgments by a process of rational logic'. With a scientific explanation of the word in front of me, it frees up my mind to make a decision as to whether or not our horses can reason, without being influenced by my heart.

Any of you who've relied on a horse to help you in times of stress, to help you make an honest living, are already laughing at the pomposity of our even questioning the ability of horses to use logic. I've seen horses drag loaded calf sleds through gates and into barn alleys, all the while unmounted, knowing enough to go slowly, steadily, taking the turns wide so the sled doesn't bang off the gate posts. All the while they are doing so, their so-called rider is on foot two corrals over, sorting the cows while manning the gates. I've seen horses refuse to go through two trees because they were close enough together that the rider's knees would be bumped. My son's childhood horse, Playgirl, stopped and went around the clothesline in the yard, because she knew that if she held course, he would be scraped off.

I've known extraordinary horses who would go like gentle kittens with babies on board, only to become efficient war horses when it was time to rope up a cow. Nobody needed to explain to them that one job involved precious cargo, while the other needed solid and brave help. They just knew.

I remember Cowgirl, who was Playgirl's daughter. The young ranch mare stood alone on a knoll in a blizzard, until someone set out from the home yard to check on her, only to find the lone newborn calf she sheltered. My own horses have long been trusted to know — and then to communicate — when they want their turnout rugs put on or taken off. It is not unusual for those who have been somehow hurt to leave the herd and come to us when they need human intervention.

Right now, I'm sitting here at my dining table, looking out at a fresh fall of snow blanketing the countryside. Mike — Chore Boy to my Horse Woman (as he has taken pains to point out) — is out in the top field, unrolling some hay to the hungry, wet horses. They are gathered, milling impatiently, in the lower pasture closest to the yard. In order to join Mike and partake of breakfast, they will have to lope a quarter-mile away from the feed truck, to an open gate in the wire fenceline. Worse, this gate is far away from the safety of the yard and involves navigating two coulees and passing a large, scary rock.

I get up from my post at my laptop to get a better view. This interests me because, in my experience, not all horses are clever enough — or brave enough — to solve this puzzle on their own. Except Chickadee. I should've known.

Today, I've watched her spy the feed truck in the top field and then, with ears up, wheel sharply around and lope far away to the open gate in the distance. She takes the corner, easily, lightly, even on the slippery ground. At a run, heels up and head tossing, she races to Mike and the feed. She stops, puts her head down and begins to eat. But she, alone, has done this. The others are still milling around, waiting for

Mike to come and let them through the yard. Chickadee whinnies encouragement but they only frantically call back to her.

Then, as I've seen with only the truly independent thinkers, Chickadee takes one more mouthful of feed — an on-the-go-snack — and resolutely turns back to that open gate a quarter mile away. She is now leaving Mike, the feed, and the milling horses on her own, to go help her friends. She is not herdbound, wanting to get back to them, as we might expect. Oh, no.

At the open gate, I see her silhouetted on the far hilltop, the wind whipping the snow around her. She stops at the gate and calls to the other horses. One-by-one, they leave the yard and run to her. Pilot and Henry pass by her on the lope, racing to be 'first' to the waiting feed. Chickadee does not leave her station until old man Cody has trotted by; then Betty, Harry and Sanchez; then finally, the two yearling colts. Only then does she wheel around and lope back to the rolled-out hay.

I've seen this application of equine logic to solving puzzles many times, usually masterminded by my cleverest ponies, or a few of the more mature mares. Their thinking goes beyond rote and memory work, beyond running with the gang. There is no food reward or human intervention, no reliance on intuition or feeding off energy. No instant payoff, no drills or conditioned response. As always, it fascinates me to watch this little-known equine ability to problem solve.

And yet science does not support such findings, despite the magic I have just witnessed within my own herd. How do you feel about this? Are horses able to reason, or do they simply rely on drills and repetitious learning to navigate through life?

. 108 .

HOBBY HORSES

My work with horses is something of a balancing act. You know, that ol' 'love and rules' thing again.

I realize that no two of us perceive horsemanship quite the same. My experience or feelings will not necessarily be shared by others. You're not wrong. I'm not right. We're just different.

Riding is about maintaining a constantly-shifting balance, giving equal merit to the intuitive and physical aspects of horsemanship. It reminds me of trying to do my yoga on one of those big exercise balls — it is always part feel and softness, part core firmness and resolve. Our very best work comes when we recognize that, if we are to improve ourselves, to raise our horsemanship, one cannot exist without the other.

Where this gets challenging is that the riders who dwell in the softness camp often struggle with firmness, and those bristling with resolve often don't cotton on to the 'feel' that must be nurtured from within.

The trick, for me, is in recognizing when I am leaning one way or the other.

I'm constantly learning how to correct my course and captain myself through calm or choppy waters. For me, the challenge lies in recognizing when I am spoiling for some sort of argument or release, and then resetting myself. Or, when I'm being too soft to allow for clear leadership. When in doubt, my horses always tell me.

This fine balance is the crux of safe and effective horsemanship. Is it doable? Oh, yes. Is it easy? Never.

. 109 .
FEELING BETTER

To me, feel is equal parts body control, intuition, and understanding of how a horse thinks and reacts. It is that place where my own riding discipline meets my horse's softness and understanding.

. 110 .
REINING BACK

It's a strange déjà vu, catching, grooming and saddling a horse whom I've once owned and schooled. I well remember riding Brown Betty six years ago, but now, despite the years spent in good hands, she feels something of a stranger to me. My bridle still has faint marks at the holes where Betty once wore it. She, too, says that the bit feels weirdly familiar. All through the day, she and I bounce off one another and then softly, tentatively, reconnect. All through the day, loading, tying, warming up, then working ... Like this? Not quite? Hmmm. How 'bout now?

"Just move forward, Betty. Now, do it with a soft feel." Is it you who has changed, or have I? Most likely, it is both of us. In the small window between getting started and running out of horse, Betty and I make big strides towards moving back into partnership. You know those friends we all have, who we haven't talked to in years, and then one day we think of them? How it doesn't even really surprise us when the phone rings and there they are? We'll start out with tentative small talk. How's life? Are you staying busy? How've you been?

Next thing you know, an hour's gone by, and we are back laughing at all the shared jokes and little stories that link us. That's how it has been with me and Betty. We're awkward, perhaps, but not so much that we can't remember our shared history. Walking out, warm steam rising up from the cooler, I can only put my hand on her neck and say, "Welcome back, my old friend."

. III .

TAKE A RIDE ON THE WILD SIDE

Like all of folklore, home cooking, and music, the art of sidesaddle riding is handed down through the generations, reverently, hands-on and by word of mouth. While riding aside is perhaps anachronistic in light of equality of the sexes and in today's horsemanship, it is a branch of my family tree and a root of all modern riding culture, come to think of it. Woman to woman to woman to woman. For this reason, I receive the knowledge respectfully and pass it forward, vowing solemnly to never forget.

. 112 .

WORKING THE FLAG

It is my great honour to be asked to sing *O Canada* when the RCMP Musical Ride makes a special appearance in our small town. After wrestling with my personal demons for a few days, namely, self-doubt and a fear of proving myself unworthy, I settle upon saddling old Cody for the occasion.

At the time of this public appearance, my horse is in his late twenties. My right-hand man, my go-to guy, is looking old. I have the good fortune of having several younger, willing horses who would happily do the job of playing a supporting role for me.

Lee M<small>C</small>LEAN

It was a huge honour to sing the national anthem when the RCMP Musical Ride came to town. I can't imagine sharing this solemn moment with anyone other than Cody, even if the old rascal upstaged me in the end. (Loree Photography)

I have decided, however, that it takes a special horse to arrive alone, amid a sea of family cars in the overflow parking of the rodeo grounds. To tack up and carry the sidesaddle rider to the back entrance, through the golf course waterworks, past the clanging machine shop. To wind through a bewildering maze of chutes and pens, navigating numerous gates with a 'one-legged' rider. To squeeze past a fire truck, waiting alone in the crowd, while being petted by horse-starved children. Then, on cue, to jog into the arena, to stop, stand and wait while your rider sings on a live and crackling microphone.

In planning my special day, I have wondered. Will I look ridiculous on the creaky old horse with the sunken eyes? Will I appear a better horsewoman, seated upon a horse with an arching neck and more topline? No doubt.

But as I shampoo these familiar snowy stockings, wipe this dear face with my rag and brush out the wavy copper tail, I feel a flush of love for him. On his trustworthy back goes my sidesaddle, a relic from 1885. I slip the beautiful pencil-thin bosalita over his wise head. I tie the horsehair mecate in the traditional bowline knot known to all western horsemen.

Cody lowers his head and accepts the spade, a treasure made by Gutierrez in the 1920s. He rolls the cricket as have countless horses before him, slowly and contentedly, like a breath mint, while I fasten the old and delicate romal reins. He tells me that he is ready.

I climb up the side of my trailer, as Cody sidesteps over to pick me up. There is no debate, negotiation or repeated asking. I simply clamber aboard, arrange my split skirt and remember instantly why I love this old horse.

Cody carries me with pride amid the crowd's commotion. We shall not speak of his upstaging my efforts by drowning me out with a good, long pee, along with his audible groan of relief when he is done. Is it my imagination, or does he bask in the crowd's appreciative whistles and laughter? In my memories, it is just he and me, alone in the arena.

I sing my heart out — for my horse, my community and my country.

. 113 .

LEARNING TO LEAD

I once went to a clinic that came to our town, keen to observe a well-known horseman. I sat poised, ready to take notes. Being open to new ideas is something that many of us who have been riders for decades sometimes forget. Excited at the rare day out with like-minded people, I cringed only slightly when asked to fork over the hefty auditing fee.

"An education is never free," my mother's words came to mind.

The famous clinician entered the arena after a long-winded intro and build-up. The very first thing he did was to bear down on each of his students' horses with a flag, a hand-held whip with a plastic pennant attached. Without any warning, or so much as a howdy-do, he snapped and shook the flag at the heads of each of these horses. The results were spectacular.

A few of the horses stood still and overlooked this lack of good manners. Most of them promptly wheeled around and laid tracks. An interesting few stood their ground, however. When provoked further, they advanced on the rock star, more than ready to use their front feet. The clinician then explained that these 'on the fight' horses were dangerously spoiled, as they were without boundaries and did not know their rightful spots.

Though I am what many of you would tag a terminal traditionalist, I disagreed mightily for several reasons.

In my eyes, the whole experiment reeked more of showmanship than of horsemanship. I knew of too many good, safely-reliable, dignified horses who would not have accepted this flagging if they had not previously been introduced to such a tool. Many of the working ranch horses and brilliant show-ring campaigners I have known personally would have not. They, brave-hearts who sail through life, wholly prepared to stand tall in the face of life's trials, would have most likely stood and launched a challenge.

I learned a lot at this clinic, though admittedly, it wasn't what I'd bargained for. I looked at the packed house around me, hoping to see a pair of acknowledging eyes in the crowd of rapt followers.

I learned that when we approach any methodology with a sycophantic belief, often using the words 'always' and 'never', that we are failing to honour individual lives with their own stories, doubts and possibilities. We are rebuffing all other practices that may well work — in some places, with some horses, in some hands. We are saying no to seeing with our own eyes and to thinking our own thoughts.

The best part of the day was when I gave up my seat to go find a good restaurant. Ever since, I've asked myself these questions when it comes to my education. What does the teacher gain, if and when I believe? Does this align with my personal compass? Does this newfound knowledge feel right in my heart? Ultimately, will it help or hurt my horse?

. 114 .

ON THE WRONG LEAD

If asked, most of us would say that having fun was why we got involved with horses in the first place. If riding is no longer fun for you, I'm sorry. Please take time to reflect and really find out what is going on. Whatever the reason — fear, guilt, boredom, health, frustration, burnout, money woes — are you ripe for a change? I'll admit to feeling any of the above at different times in my life and my riding has evolved because of this. A serious health scare, subsequent job loss, ageing, then watching friends and family members get hurt with horses, all have taken their toll. I've accepted that certain horse sports and certain types of horses will never be a comfortable fit for me. Finally, I have realized that we have nothing to prove, and you know what? It's okay.

. 115 .

AS LITTLE AS POSSIBLE, AS MUCH AS NECESSARY

I believe in mentorship. I also believe in lifelong learning.

This takes the form of carefully curating my horsemanship library and DVDs, of watching and following only the people who open my eyes to possibilities, and of auditing clinics and attending lectures during times when I'm afoot. I've ridden for half a century now and it's made me very careful about where I gather new information. A lot of 'sure things' have come and gone over five decades. I've learned that sound, classical horsemanship is here to stay.

I'm fortunate that a certain percentage of my ready cash can go towards my riding. For me, personally, this means regular lessons with a knowledgeable pair of eyes from the ground. Every week, I haul one of my horses on a two-hour round trip, to go and learn something good.

My study has morphed beyond being coached constantly. I know what to do and when, trusting myself to put in the correct feel and method to achieve the desired result. I've ridden weekly with this one trainer for ten years now. What keeps it all fresh and forward-thinking is the fact that I ride a variety of green horses, of all different breeds, sizes, ages and scope. Often, I'll ride for an hour with very few spoken words directed my way, merely suggestions, sometimes only the odd observation.

I've learned that silence from my teacher means that I'm doing good work. That is, most days.

"I think I'll sit this one out," I announced when it was time to work the flag recently. This is a method of teaching stock horses how to stop and turn effectively, without

using a cow. "My mare is getting crankier each session." My teacher only raised his eyebrows. He knows that I've parented three kids and somehow survived their teens. The notion that I would back down from anyone getting moody brought a quiet snort of laughter.

"If my horse gives me attitude, I need to find out why," he then said. "I'm going to figure out how to get the point across. Maybe I'm in her way. Maybe I'm using too much leg or spur. Is she sore? Or maybe she'll just have to accept that we're going to get the job done, whether or not she approves."

I felt like a fool because all of this was common sense. In my quest to honour the little mare's dignity, I'd lost sight of the fact that she is healthy and in shape. Her gear fits. I am kind and fair. I never ask her to do the impossible. For twenty-three hours of every day, she does exactly what she pleases. Spending five minutes working this flag, perfecting her stops and turns, upping her ability to focus and mirror the mechanical 'cow', would not kill her. We all have to do a little drudgery in this life. It is not all shits 'n' giggles for any one of us.

I've been aware for some time that when I put any amount of 'leg' on this horse, she sucks back and pins her ears. I've made darned sure that I don't use leg and hand together, that my aids are clear and that I'm using less leg all the time. No matter. She's still calling me out and the flag has become the hill she's prepared to die on.

My teacher explained that I might wish to use no leg whatsoever for a while, but rather to instill 'forward' with the end of my romal.

Whack! Whack! Just once behind my right leg and then once behind my left. With a singular over 'n' under, the mare sprang forward and became a different horse. Amazingly, she worked her best ever, with enthusiasm and drive, and with her ears up! In my quest to be empathetic, I'd gone over the tipping point to be a doormat. The caution here is in knowing where the balance lies. Whenever we decide we need to up our leadership, we can move too far into forcefulness. So, I'd shifted the other way, into ineffectual nagging. Golly, why is it so easy to turn into an old hag?

"Do as little as possible, and as much as necessary," my mentor reminded me. Good advice for riding, or parenting, I've been mulling this over ever since.

. 116 .

GOOD GROUND

Be quick and don't overthink it — name three good things that you are grateful for right now. Say them out loud, to wholly enjoy the feel of them on your tongue. Old jeans. A hot bath. My friend.

. 117 .

MOVE IT, OR LOSE IT

I ride under the premise that every single thing I do with my horses, mentally and physically, either breaks them down or builds them up. Yes, this unpalatable truth is at the bottom of all horsemanship.

Because bearing all manner of mankind is not a natural state for the horse, I must do my best to help him resemble the strong span of a bridge. I must help him straighten so that certain body parts don't wear out from stress or overuse. Only then will he serve decades without arthritic joints from unyielding movement, or concussion. Only then can he serve without developing a swaying back, or hollow posture, from this heavy burden for which the horse was not made.

Worse, few horses live a 'natural' existence anymore, wandering for twenty or more miles a day, browsing, relaxing, finding friendship. So, we must make sure that our time with them most approximates this, and that our training teaches them ease and relaxation. Too few training programs do this, and so this is why I write.

My own riding has zero to do with competitive goals because I feel that modern competition, with its repetitive moves, has put so much stress on ourselves and our horses. Hence the need for ongoing joint injections, ulcer meds, and chiro — no matter our equestrian disciplines.

Simple, joyful approaches to riding are felt by the horses too, and I make note that the moment we feel as though we are being finicky, working hard or 'micro-managing', we are straying from riding with ease. If I progress along time-honoured, classical lines, my horses will strengthen, straighten, and grow healthier over the course of their lives. This generally means riding roundly and riding with stretching, in equal parts. This means riding mindfully over the course of years, rather than for months.

For those who honestly, genuinely question the 'nit-pickiness' of schooling horses correctly, I say this — while horses theoretically know how to look after themselves without us, it is with us that they most need help, if we truly mean to have our horses thrive as they are ridden. I've purchased many older horses who've been worked 'naturally', and our next years must be spent with chiro, mindful stretching, and correct riding, rebuilding their worn-out bodies back to a healthier state.

Human beings can also move ergonomically and efficiently, or we can shlep along without caring for our own long-term wellness. It's a choice I've been thinking of, more so as I age.

. 118 .

MENTORS OR INFLUENCERS?

"Who is the horsewoman you most admire?" asked Ayesha, my publisher. She wanted me to inscribe one copy of *Horse Woman,* my first book, and then she would send it to this person as a gesture of my gratitude.

What a hard question! There are so many women who inspire me in their horsemanship, whether they have overcome huge odds, or they have taught many people, or they have achieved lofty heights in competition. So many women ... and then it came to me.

It was the Queen.

Her service, her fortitude, her ceremony — all are forgotten when Queen Elizabeth's face softens in the presence of the horse.

Her incredible steadfastness, riding sidesaddle when the gun went off in the crowd surrounding her beloved black horse, Burmese. Pictures of her leading her children, grandchildren, and great-grandchildren on their dear ponies. Mother and grandmother of international event riders. Happiest outdoors, and always, always surrounded by her dogs.

More recent glimpses of our Queen, now in her nineties, riding her Fell pony in Windsor Great Park. Riding beautifully, sitting quietly, correctly, in the Hermes scarves that drive today's safety police so loudly mad. I will forever remember heart-rending images of Her Majesty, stooped and alone, sitting in the chapel after Prince Philip's death. He, too, has long been a guiding light for those of us who love carriage driving. His book on the subject has earned a permanent place on my library shelf.

While her children have dropped the ball too many times to count, I thought that as another mother, I wouldn't hold any of that against her. We've all done our best. Surely, we've all tried.

And so I inscribed a copy of my book. "For Her Majesty, the most inspiring horsewoman among us. From your humble and obedient servant, Lee McLean."

An official reply arrived in our shot-gunned and wind-blown mailbox some weeks later. Signed by the Queen's lady-in-waiting, it was a thrill to have royal mail come to rural Pekisko, all the long way from Sandringham House.

. 119 .

RIDING OFF INTO BATTLE

I asked Whoever was listening that might I please cross paths with a wonderful pony? The Universe, with its trademark sense of humour, sent Montcalm.

I had just come off a one-year lease with Friar Tuck. A household name in the pony hunter world, the bay gelding literally changed my riding. For the first time, I knew what it was to ride into the ring without any doubt. I learned that there was a formula to logical riding and competing — that one clear wish, combined with one correct aid, would garner one predictable result. Until Tucker, I had not tasted of this elixir, and it was heady stuff.

Going back to my homemade horsemanship was going to be a rocky road.

Sitting in the stands at the bustling All Pony Show, still unmounted for the summer, I was idly watching an afternoon of hunter rounds when Montcalm strode in. A chestnut Thoroughbred standing only 14:1, this fellow had a lot of the same sheer ego that drew one's eye to Tuck. He seemed impervious to distraction and his canter flowed like water. Monty's answer to an awkward distance in the handy hunters was to land and immediately take off again. By leaving out the tight one-stride, Monty appeared to fly the in-and-out like a bird, rather than get in too tight by playing it safe.

Fond memory has me smiling at Monty's indomitable spirit — ears up, eyes sparkling, all a-quiver for the next challenge in life. I still have the trophy from the win we pulled off in a strong class of show hacks, riding before a late-great among judges. (Author's Collection)

The effortless, bold fellow won, of course. In that moment, I got a glimpse of how the chestnut — who was for sale — attacked life.

A trial ride was arranged. I rode him and did not have the experience to realize that my aids were being anticipated, rather than obeyed. Monty had a 'hold my beer' attitude that was, at once, endearing and alarming. What made him biddable was that he was hauling and competing in both the hunter and jumper divisions at the All Pony Show, the City of Calgary Show, and the Alberta Light Horse Show during the two weeks that he was in our province. All this, after hauling in from the east.

Monty was thriving under a gruelling schedule that would have exhausted most horses. It was a telling point that we somehow missed.

We went home to think about him, armed with a list of his show wins that was four pages, all single-spaced. These were major competitions over a period of several years. What we didn't realize was that for every big win, there was a disastrous round not mentioned. Asking around, people knew Montcalm's name, all right. "Talented. Scopey. Tough." We heard the words we wanted to hear and ignored all others. Arrangements were made for Monty to stay on.

I'll never forget the trip our family made in to Calgary to pick up our new 'pony' from the grounds after the City of Calgary Show. Earlier that day, I had crushed my father's hand with the draw-bar of the tractor, as we'd been pulling posts. In agony while my mother drove the truck and trailer, dad's hand was wrapped and swollen, resting on a bag of ice. Like so many of my memories of Monty, this one has stayed charged with negative thoughts.

Fresh from the show barn, always stabled and blanketed, Monty arrived at our home with its mixed herd and a life of turnout. A warrior at heart, he was always battle-scarred and chewed-upon from that day forward. The herd boss was challenged daily by this new upstart and I'm not sure if they ever really sorted it out. Our family started calling him Super Pony because he reminded us of a caped crusader — fighting, running, leaping about, always with a glint in his eye. Oh, to convince him to use his considerable powers for good!

One thing was for certain, my new show pony had sparkle.

My first ride on him, at home, was an eye-opener. Forty-five minutes later, I'd still not got him down from the canter. Finally, out of desperation, I'd run him into the arena wall, just to get stopped. White foam rolled off his neck where the reins lay. Raw blisters behind my ring fingers stung with our combined sweat. My breeches were welded to my knees with blood. A trip was made to The Tack Shop in Calgary for a pelham bit, along with laced reins. A desperate phone call was made to my teacher. More lessons. More riding. More blood and sweat. More tears!

The more I rode him, the fitter Monty got. My riding changed subtly, a shift from softer classical methods, to learning such coping skills as a defensive seat and pulley-rein stops. I kept showing, learning also that for every trophy, there would be an elimination. My smile of joy became the set jaw of sheer resolve. He had cost a lot

of money. He was from a well-known, successful show barn. He was athletic. I just needed to learn to ride.

My three years showing Montcalm were my last as a junior competitor. We were eventually improved with many lessons on the flat, concentrating on our dressage and the concept of softening. Lessons spent on the lunge, in an effort to improve my seat, usually ended with me bailing off out of sheer exhaustion. He had no bottom, no limit. It was my first experience with an animal that, despite his training, remained unmastered. Monty, I think, could have run until his heart burst, had only he been given the chance.

At the time we were showing, I was also interested in riding western at the open shows. Monty did his best for me, eventually learning to neck-rein and ride one-handed in romals. His heart, however, was not in jogging and loping slower than his stock horse counterparts. This was the era of swapping out horses in equitation. I would sit, in greedy anticipation, wondering who would be asked to switch with me. The poor soul, for I would be granted a lovely, smooth trip on their horse, while they would struggle through trying to pattern my own. It seldom went well for my hapless competitors, as Monty's trademark move when faced with unfamiliar riders was to 'confuse' the standard lope aid as a cue to buck. More than once, he would bronc his way back into line, my erstwhile competition hanging miserably from Monty's neck.

I grew to love him despite our tempestuous relationship. Monty was brave and had a keen sense of humour. He lived life largely by the motto, 'no guts, no glory'. My confidence grew by leaps and bounds in learning to stick up for myself. Oh, the blood, sweat and tears that were poured on this talented blackguard, who was either going Champion, or stopping at the first fence and sending me home in shame.

It was a hard day when he miscalculated while jumping a solid fence, flipping and landing on top of me. Neither of us ever jumped again. I went on to study with my life's mentor, an elderly dressage teacher. Monty went on to ride the mountains with a retired forest warden on fire watch. I tear up, writing this, for it was his true calling. My warrior prince, so embattled, always at odds with what life required of him, finally had found his niche. For the first time, he was admired for being brave, for never quitting, slowing down or faltering. Finally, Monty was being lauded as the little horse with the big heart.

ADVANCE AND RETREAT

"I'll see you past the gander," is something I remember my grandpa saying, at the end of each visit. He had learned the saying from his own mother, the words harkening back to a time when fowl were roaming every farmyard and the fact that geese can be territorial thugs. Like all such old saws, you don't entirely reckon their truth until the day that you find out for yourself.

I'd taken Tee out for a nice lope along a cultivated row that Mike had started, opening up the oat field. There's nothing like a mile or so of freshly farmed ground to straighten out a horse and improve his third gear. Spirits high, away we went. Springtime is a blessed relief to those of us who have just made it through seven or eight months of winter. The creek is newly flowing, the very air is filled with birdsong, and dotted about the landscape are pairs of nesting Canada Geese.

As we loped up a little rise, I could see a gentleman and lady goose, checking out the real estate. They looked exactly like a couple on an open house home tour, discussing such things as location and the view from the kitchen window. Now, I'm no expert on reading the facial expressions of geese but, all of a sudden, these two seemed to undergo a change. They looked as though they were expecting to be evicted for drunk and disorderly behaviour. They also looked as though they weren't going anywhere without putting up a fight.

Tee began to falter. I quickly decided that it wouldn't do to act afraid of two silly old geese. I mean, what would I be teaching my horse? As captain, I boldly issued the command for Tee to maintain his bearing and continue full steam ahead. Mistake! The first goose snaked his head out and came at us a lot quicker than Tee could wheel and run. He is not the fastest horse at the best of times, and I could hear those geese flapping and hissing behind us for quite a few jumps before we began to gain any ground. In the midst of all this excitement, I had the presence of mind to note that these things were, in fact, very large when viewed up close and personal. They are not little birds — standing about the height of a kitchen counter, their wings make a surprising span as the geese half-run, half-fly in hot pursuit. We finally pulled up at a good distance and I could feel Tee's heart hammering away against my leg — as was my own heart, pounding and threatening to burst. It took the two of us quite a few minutes to catch our collective breath and settle down.

"I'll see you past the gander." Thanks, Grandpa. As God is my witness, Tee and I will never allow ourselves to get goosed again.

.121.

ON PARTNERSHIP

Yesterday, I was witness to a young woman changing her life. It began as a regular riding lesson with a new student — a person of unusual empathy and 'feel' — on a horse with an unusual level of tension and self-preservation. Three of us, including me, their teacher, mirroring one another's damaged pasts.

In fact, in the beginning, I could not look directly at this horse while he was working as it would set him off. He would feel my gaze — or, from his perspective, my judging eye — and proceed to throw up his head and check out of Dodge.

Dial yourself back, Lee. Dial yourself back.

We began on the lunge. Softness, softness, don't pressure him quite yet. Ask him for more, back off, ask him to stretch. It's okay, regroup. Nobody died, just change through the circle. Tell him he's smart and good, ask him to stretch. Ask him to stretch. Ask him to stretch. This enlightenment on the horse's part transformed him, body and soul. Reaching down, lightly mouthing his bit. His back growing round, shoulders sweeping, arcing. The tail swinging, the happy snorts. Suddenly, he was telling us that it was time to ride.

There is so much honour and responsibility to be found in teaching. The ancient understanding within the young woman was magical. I watched her soften as tension was replaced with a silent conversation. 'Would you like to stay and hang out with me? Share a few laughs, kick back and escape all the worries of the day? May I get to know you?' Her horse said yes.

Again, I was shown how our relationships with horses echo the ones in our personal lives. Do we come to each day bearing — protecting — the hurts of the past? Do we encourage the people around us to display the same old patterns of addiction and dependency? Are we quick to anger because we are carrying the horrible burden of shame? Do we speak in a plain, honest, authentic language, or are we hiding our own truths?

There is magic in changing how we view life, how we ride, how we enter the world of our horses. While teaching, I was given a gift. I was witness to a young woman choosing her path at a fork in the road. She will never again ride quite the same. That ordinary day, I saw the powerful, gentle forces of good. The awe in one holy moment. Now, more than ever, I want to learn to see and believe.

In one ordinary moment, we can see our lives and patterns in a new light. We can see that our horses, as well as people, can struggle with addiction and enabling. Along with mindfully choosing to teach our horses to cope with stress, calm themselves, and think on their feet, there is something else that comes into our work within all horsemanship. It involves our own basic need to be needed.

I ride mostly alone now. For years, though, I boarded my one show horse at a popular barn. This environment became my social network. These people, so similar to me, became my friends. This was healthy for me, lone wolf that I was, and I basked in their company. There was a dark undercurrent to life at the barn, however. It became a contest of sorts, to see whose horse needed her most. We'd get talking, laughing, comparing stories.

"Oh, yeah? You should see him if there's a fake stone wall!" one rider would say of her hunter. Another would top that with how badly her horse reacted to wind, or adjusting to any other rider, or being left alone in the wash rack.

Nobody was saying, "Oh, my horse doesn't worry. He figures things out. Beyond feeding and scratching him, I wonder if he needs me at all." To have a horse like that might mean that we weren't true horse people — empathetic, loving, able to manage 'difficult' horses, or worse, that we were only along for the ride. To own an uncomplicated horse might mean that we lacked some essential skill.

Many of these horses were unwittingly encouraged to bang on stall doors before being 'shushed' with attention. They'd be goaded into acting fried and frazzled while their owners sat them, smugly confident, soothing them all the way. They'd be allowed to circle endlessly because 'their thing' was that they could not stand.

If we find ourselves falling into this pattern, it might help to remember that what we visualize generally comes to pass. If we get our personal pay-off from having the difficult, needy, neurotic horse, the laws of the universe will give us exactly that for which we ask. Some of us might even recognize our need to be needed by buying only what are termed 'problem' horses.

This needy behaviour is not restricted to women and their horses, by the way. We'll speak this way of our own husband or children — the man who can't get his own supper, or the children who 'need' us to do it all, the conversations with friends, comparing how incredibly busy we are.

Men may go on about handling the cow that took such skill and courage, the loud know-it-all who talks at us instead of to us, the fellow whose horses buck at the start of every single ride. These are signs of not wanting to be in a relationship, so much as needing a fix from each and every relationship we're in. There's a difference.

If we recognize this innate need to be needed, if the unheard child within us longs to be thought clever or brave or emotionally-gifted, it may be time for a change.

. 122 .

DON'T SAY WHOA
IN A TIGHT SPOT

I just got off the phone. I'm a bit deaf and a lot cranky and, you know, I almost didn't answer it. I'm glad that I did. Turns out, the caller was a lady whose sister has just had a stroke. She wanted to talk to me, to get some insights into how her sister might be feeling and coping. Kindly, she wanted to know some first-hand opinions on what she could best do to help. I grew teary listening to her, because it's been twelve years now since I had my own stroke. Suddenly, a host of jumbled memories came tumbling back to me.

My life is good now but, yes, it is different.

There are still days when I grow desperate, wishing that the buzzing 'fax noises' would magically shut off in my head. I often wish that I could hear with my left ear, that I didn't need to wonder where I'd left my hearing aid or pay attention to running out of batteries. I wish that I didn't sound drunk and slurry after supper, although friends and family often find this amusing. Well, it is sort of funny, when I think of it. I wish that my face didn't sag, that I didn't have to think about swallowing, and when I do so, to manage without a big choke or a loud click.

There are still days that I wish I could hear people talking without having to see their lips move, where I could walk without keeping my eyes to the ground, where I didn't somehow fade away shortly after supper. But that's all just stuff.

I'm still here, and let's hope a little wiser. This getting sick and somehow being awarded a second chance is what it means to be called a survivor. We sit with that a while and then, taking it one step further, we learn how to thrive. Yes, we can do this. For those of you who are just now handling life's latest curve balls, this is easier said than done. I know and I'm sorry. I remember.

So, here's to surviving all these things that clutter our paths. We did not plan on them and here they are, rudely demanding every scrap of our energy. They will make us strong and wise and, dare I say, better able to appreciate the sunshine? If we haven't managed already, here's to making peace with ourselves.

. 123 .

HEELS DOWN

Singing. Painting. Writing. Riding. As an artist, which is more important, our 'feel' or our technique?

'Feel' is a very big thing in horsemanship circles nowadays — without it, nothing else seems to matter. I'm going to share with you my thoughts on this notion. In doing so, I might be swimming against the current of popular thought. Nonetheless, here goes.

Feel is the ability to sense the try, reaction, or response of the horse, and reward it with the appropriate amount of release or reinforcement. It allows the 'art' in what is otherwise a craft. All of this, with just the right timing. Without feel, horsemanship loses its soul and artistry. It is very like music in this regard. And, like music, I think much of it is instinctive, an ancient knowledge that is randomly handed down at birth.

That said, with the right horses and human mentors, a great deal of feel — of refinement — can be learned.

'Equitation' is the study of correct position and technique. In many circles, it has gone by the wayside in favour of feel. Why worry about where our legs and hands are, when we need only listen to the response of the horse? Why? Because the study of equitation is our acceptance of responsibility, our commitment to be worthy partners in this relationship between human and horse. Let me explain.

If I worry about my core and the quality of my seat, I will be easier to carry. If I study keeping my leg still with a soft ankle and a lowered heel, I will have some control over my leg aids. If I learn to control where my hands are, teaching them to be slow and quiet — both independently and in concert with one another — my horse will have the opportunity to trust my connection to his mouth. If I require myself to look up and away from the back of my horse's head, I am aware of my place in the bigger picture and I'm proving that I, too, can trust. One sure goal of a horseman is to strive to become a lesser burden.

Our study of equitation removes the onus of our ridden achievements from sitting solely upon the horse.

Now, we can get so caught up in our correct position that we become 'fixed' — braced in the saddle, unaware of when to soften or when to increase the forward urge. We can get so caught up in our equitation that we are not effective in the saddle, 'sitting pretty', so to speak. But like playing the piano, our riding is improved if our technique is sound — if we've done our classical scales and fingering before launching into the boogie-woogie.

I am aware that many riders of exquisite feel and timing have never taken a lesson in their lives. They are like proud banjo players who boast of not having had enough coaching to ruin their music. I think perhaps that they are the exception, these natural-born horsemen, many of whom might be even better if they knew how much their quirks and crookednesses affected the horse.

I have always been an inherently feely rider. But where would I be now, without those formative and hugely-difficult years of being lunged without reins or stirrups? As both student and teacher, I know how hard it is to erase the bad habits of yesterday. Better we learn well, early on.

Yes, feel puts the art and magic into our horsemanship. It is the sublime in what is otherwise a mode of transportation. But without position — body control and muscle memory — we're asking a lot of our horses.

We're asking them for perfection when we don't ask the same of ourselves.

There is a current move away from classical horsemanship, the lessons that teach the how and the why of riding, in favour of sheer performance. We have put more importance on our goals than our fundamental journey. No matter the discipline, I think that to turn our backs on classical position is a mistake. Equitation is the here and now. With the right horses and teachers, improved feel can come. People harbour this belief that improving ourselves makes it somehow less fun for ourselves and for our horses. I wonder. Correctness and intuitive riding do not need to be exclusive states. One does not need to come at the expense of the other, as we like to console ourselves whenever things get hard.

To call it horsemanship, one must strive, always, to do better. To be a better person. By caring about something other than ourselves and our own comfort, we aim to do no harm to those we love.

. 124 .

GOOD GIRL

Our willingness to love — and pay the bills — on animals that frighten us is often rooted deeply in a desperate need to be good, to assume the blame, to try and rise above. I believe it's the same feeling of guilty responsibility that comes with keeping secrets about alcoholic parents, or creepy uncles, or abusive partners. It's all the same and, for many of us, it is how we were raised. No matter what, we were told to be good.

The magic of horses can surprise us. Invariably, they pick off the scabs that cover old wounds. You know, those little secrets we think we're better off trying to hide.

. 125 .

HOME ON THE RANGE

When you ride mainly green horses, you get used to riding only green horses. This means that nothing is guaranteed, and that the simplest things will bear repeating. That is, until the horse finds the correct response.

Even when the new kid is trying hard, he is usually falling short of the mark. He's maybe upset when you go out to catch him because, for the first time, you've worn your chaps. Maybe when it's time to tie him to the hitching rail, the wind comes up and the trees start making scary noises. You'll have to remind him that everything he knows for sure, up until now, is still going to be his truth.

The green horse is constantly having to learn that outside circumstances don't change any of the good stuff that he holds within his head and heart.

You will teach your green horse to load and haul calmly on the trailer, and to be confident upon arrival, even if the trip means a whirlwind ride down the rush-hour four-lane highway. The only way this lesson can be learned is to keep on keepin' on until it becomes second nature. It means that there will be weeks of unloading a wild-eyed youngster and proceeding to mount up and get to work, as though nothing is amiss. The young horse will spend the next hour worrying about that strange dog, or the unknown horses that come too close, or that rider who is just a bit too loud, or the slicker that snaps and flaps in the wind.

Riding out is only one-half of the equation, so the rest of your time will be spent schooling the colt — installing buttons and cruise control, power steering and a good set of brakes. He needs to build the muscle memory that will one day allow him to work in a 'state of grace'. For this, we will need equal parts time and knowledge.

The green horse who understands how to go forward maybe struggles mightily with stopping or relaxing and standing still. The horse who is chilled out and willing to stop is maybe tentative with moving boldly out, or perhaps he has a hard time keeping his shoulder up through the turns. Maybe he's good with all these things at home, but a strange arena with kids running around, or the humming Coke machine at the entrance has made him forget. You smile, and with two hands on the reins, you send a firm but gentle reminder to go forward and to concentrate.

So much time is spent trying and then trying again. This will go on for weeks, then months, and on the really challenging horses, maybe years. You are waiting for that one day when you'll reach for the stirrup, swing up, and it feels like you've come home. One ordinary day that should be just like all the others, but it isn't. One tiny shift in energy that means more will be remembered than is forgotten, a shift where the horse's mind and muscles are united and working as one.

I don't know what happens to bring the green horse suddenly, on one ordinary day, into partnership. Time and mileage, certainly, but there's something more. Your trust in the horse, along with his trust in you?

I don't know what to call this thing, other than magic.

Yesterday, when I put my leg back on Chickadee and she rose into the most effortless, educated canter, I knew we'd turned a corner. Around we rocked, collecting into the turns, then carrying herself on the straightaways. When I changed legs to prepare for the struggle of a green horse's lead change, the mare quietly answered my aid with conviction and confidence. I gasped in astonishment. She knew that I knew that she knew — and it was sweet.

When we ride green horses, we're waiting for that 'home sweet home' feeling that all good horses instill. After weeks and months of searching, this one defining moment is what keeps me coming back for more.

. 126 .

MUCKING OUT

I have one of those knees. Injured a few years ago, it never quite went back to 'the way we were'. Some days, it's well-behaved and I pretty much forget about it. Other days, it demands to be heard.

A big gust of wind woke me from a deep sleep last night. As I rolled over and settled in, my mind automatically asked, "How's my knee doing?" In the same moment I acknowledged that there was no pain, suddenly, there was.

"Gotcha!" said my body. It reminded me that we have no trouble becoming what we're thinking. If we've been unwell for a while, we begin to think of ourselves as unwell people. As in, 'I'm no longer Lee. I'm sick'.

If I start a walking or yoga program, I begin to think of myself as a person who seeks fitness. If I pay any attention to my friends' political rantings, I begin to think of myself as either one of the enlightened, or outnumbered and misunderstood. If I read the late Thich Nhat Hanh, I think about peace and beauty. Our minds are our secret power. We become what we think.

This, of course, holds true with our marriages and friendships, along with our dogs and horses. My husband bangs around in the night, long after I've gone to bed. This can grind my gears, until I choose to remember that he will have made the coffee that is waiting ready for me each morning. This means that I have had to teach myself to stop referring to my shallow flake of a gelding as a 'little shit'. Yes. In so doing, I was actually steering him down the wrong path. Instead — and it took a friend of mine to point this out — I began to think of him in different terms. I began to thank him for bringing much-needed fun and adventure into my life. In all my adulting and being a killjoy, he alone made me smile. Suddenly, the horse who was known to be silly and over-the-top became a boon, my very own ray of sunshine.

I've seen this play out time and again. We have many different theories and names for this phenomenon, with books, podcasts, and whole movements that follow the precept of manifestation. Call it what we like, we are what we think. There is huge power within the mind. In horsemanship and in life, let's choose to use this in a way that does some good.

. 127 .

BRIDLE WISE

Everyone thinks they want a smart horse. Not me. I can stay ahead of those unimaginative fellows just a little easier — but perhaps this only points to my own mental shortfall.

Dumb horses get a bad rap because people think they either explode over little things, or they're always getting hurt. I disagree. Explosive horses are reactive horses. They take a little bit of pressure and respond in a big way, which to me has very little to do with intelligence. Horses that are accident-prone are not so much dumb, but rather fearless. These fellows have a knack for putting their noses and feet in places they don't belong, because their curiosity outweighs their self-preservation. And so, they get hurt.

I've ridden both smart horses and slower-thinkers. The smart horses learn everything the first time they do it. Congratulations, you are riding an equine Einstein! That means the pressure is on. You've got one time — and one time only — to show them what you need them to know. One time to have them do it right or they'll forever be trying to outsmart you. This is why mules and ponies take a little more thought and resolve to train. This is why so many of their people end up running amok.

Smart horses are forever figuring out ways to do what they already know 'mo' betta'. These are the ones who learn the dressage test in one go, who learn how to unfasten all the gates and let the horses out for a run down the highway. They learn how to flip their heads so their bridles come off. They learn how to anticipate stops and lead changes. I could go on. In other words, if you're not careful, your horse is going to be way smarter than you. Smart horses have a way of keeping us on our toes. If we don't up our game, we'll soon be up the creek.

My daughter has a wonderfully steadfast fellow called Cinnabar. They have been partners ever since the sorrel gelding was weaned from his mother, so they know one another inside and out. No specialist superstar, Cinny is a jack of all trades. He can do so many things just well enough to be safe and allow Cait to have fun. This works well for Cinnabar, who is not overly excited at the prospect of toiling all the way to excellence. As he has aged, however, a new problem has opened up, one to which few horse people will give credence.

In recent years, as he sets out to ride away from the corrals for a few hours of ranch work, Cinnabar is showing up lame. Bobbing his head and favouring what seems to be either front leg, the soreness 'works out' the minute he is turned back towards home to be unsaddled and turned out. Surely not. But there it is again when you rein him back away from home.

Cait and her ranching husband have finally figured out how to get around Cinny's mystery 'lameness'. They haul him out to the farthest reaches of their range, checking cows and doctoring calves as they ride towards home. Knowing this character, however, it is only a matter of time before something else comes up. Cinnabar, while appearing biddable and willing, is always more or less in charge.

Slow-witted horses are different. They might take being taught the same thing over and over again, but once they've got it, they've got it carved in stone. Their minds are not always trying to come up with something 'new and improved'. Like goldfish in a bowl, they are happy to see the same thing coming around, again and again. This type of horse is far easier to keep fresh for the show ring because he is not always three steps ahead of you. He is not always thinking that he has seen and done it all before.

Less-intelligent horses are usually happy to wait for our guidance. They are content to breathe in and out and wait for us to tell them how it's done. These fellows don't usually have as much imagination, and they don't seem to get as readily bored. They are content to bond with us and let us be in charge. While they're lacking in cleverness, they generally make up for it in reliable service with a smile.

The next time somebody tries to sell you on a real smart cookie, just remember this. If it's going to work — you've got to be smarter than the horse.

. 128 .
PICKING PENS

Getting bundled up for another blustery day of chores and frozen water lines, I had something of an epiphany. You can be warm, or you can be sexy. What hit me is that, once upon a time, this might have been a difficult choice.

. 129 .
SOFT EYES

I'm thinking a lot about being more mindful these days, both with my horses and in my own personal space.

It is morning. I am sitting in the dark comfort of the kitchen, sipping my first coffee. I challenge myself to notice something — anything — of beauty. This is an exercise in mental wellness as, God knows, I don't want to do the running, sweating kind.

What came to me was the unhurried, almost-stopping sound of the nearly two-hundred-year-old grandfather clock standing behind me. Tick. Tock. Tick. Tock. I try to imagine what on earth this clock has seen. It never falters, never speeds up, and subconsciously I start breathing more deeply.

This feel-good mental exercise is also useful when it comes to our horses.

I will go out to them, greeting each one in turn, thanking them for bringing something beautiful into my life. I am careful not to mention physical beauty because I think that all of us, whether women or horses, have so much more to offer than just a pretty face. But I will stroke one's forelock and thank him or her for being safe and honest. Another one will be thanked for being such a keen student, or a much-needed dose of joy in my life, and so on.

I don't take treats because I want my horses and ponies to feel the benefit of my gratitude and to not be sidetracked by grub. Each horse has something beautiful they bring to our relationship and, if they do not, I need to work on that and find it. So many people find themselves taking care of horses that they do not like. This is such a shame, and it is something that we can change if we so choose. This one thing has had a profound effect on how I see these horses and they, in turn, feel valued. Of course, once they have been called beautiful in some way, they try hard to make it stick. It interests me to note that certain horses — and people — will deflect this mindful loving, as though they do not as yet feel worthy. I understand, for I have also been challenged by praise.

I urge you to play with this exercise that uses the power of our intentions.

. 130 .

STRAIGHT UP THE CENTRE

Writing and sharing it is both gratifying and terrifying. My struggles with fitness, finances, ageing, iffy health, weather, courage, self-doubt, relationships, troubled horses and so on — these have struck a chord with many of you. Despite age, discipline, and geography, we're all in this together. Often, you tell me that my stories have come at just the right time. You will say that, somehow, I have told your own stories with my words.

This can be powerful medicine for me too. Even though I've kept a riding diary for close to fifty years, I've had to remind myself to concentrate on what I feel and then just get it down. Writing for one's eyes only is very different from writing for publication. Writing, knowing that others will read it, tends to become what we think other people would like us to say.

I've learned that if I'm honest and speak my truth, it will usually be received kindly. I've also learned that, sometimes, when we speak with candour, certain friends and relations will turn their backs on us. Being heard can come at a price. Somewhere along the way, I have come to the realization that while horsemanship is something that many of us think about constantly, it is not what defines us as human beings. No. Each of us is so much more.

Each of us has a unique way in which to serve.

Some of us are meant to be supportive adult children and/or parents of our own children. Some of us are artists or musicians, social workers or mechanics, bus drivers or beauticians. Some of us are meant to help with bookkeeping and the law, to administer drugs to ease suffering, to check groceries through the till. Some of us are meant to nurture young clean slates or troubled souls and, somehow, get them to believe in themselves as learners. Some of us are meant to train service dogs or

other peoples' horses. Some of us are meant to tell our stories about all manner of lifestyles, of failing, of picking ourselves up, and of trying again.

I suspect that we are all just doing our best to get by and do no harm along the way. You and I both long to arrive at the end of this journey with wisdom and some sort of wholeness of spirit, to know that we have somehow left this world a better place.

More and more, I believe that to learn about horsemanship is to learn about life.

. 131 .
LETTING GO

Late spring is always a sad reminder for me, an anniversary of a time when I really, really let someone down. I have always started and trained my own horses and ponies, if they've come into my life as colts. My method isn't flashy. There is no microphoned guru, no large round pen, no flagging or roping of feet. There are no colts running around saddled in groups, no bronc rides. No flipping of halter ropes from one side to the other while the colts lope along on their first go. No, there is none of this.

I watch the slow-handed cowboys who do so. They move like flowing water, and I feel nothing but shame about my ageing body and old-fashioned methods. Why is this?

My colts are trained in a very ordinary, backyard sort of way. They are brushed, tied up, taught to lunge, ground driven, ponied out. Then, when they seem pretty gentle, I lie across them. I'll shimmy until I'm sitting on them and, if that goes well, we'll start to ride, often with the help of an experienced pony horse. Eventually, without too much fuss or fanfare, they are cruising along in all three gears, indoors and out. We make the odd mistake and, in doing so, both the colts and I grow wiser. This ordinary mucking around has stood me in good stead — until a few years ago, when I decided that I, a fifty-something farm wife, was not enough.

So there's more to this sad story than horsemanship. There's a boatload of second-guessing myself and feeling inadequate in my own skin. It became my burning desire to send a beautiful metallic bay gelding out to a colt starter who was making a name for himself. One of the last colts by a well-known stallion, July Johnson — if he could be judged by his brains, sparkly personality and neat conformation — might even be a keeper for my own enjoyment. I've always wanted such a horse.

The young trainer came and picked up my colt one glowing May evening. I'd brushed him out and his blood bay coat resonated against the vibrant green of our yard. July stood calmly and confidently at the hitching rail waiting for his ride. There was to be a colt starting clinic with a celebrated clinician that weekend and July was set to take part, with the young apprentice. I was honoured that my colt had been selected. The day of the clinic, however, was stormy. A cold sleet blew in sideways from the north.

Cody and I lead July across the creek, back when the colt had his whole life before him. July would become the horse who paid dearly for my education, forcing me to face up to a lifetime of insecurity and self-doubt. I will never forget him. (Author's Collection)

I made the drive down to the clinic at a nearby arena. Hot coffee in hand, I enjoyed watching the day's proceedings for the most part. My colt was a little rattled. He wanted to buck some, at first, but he tried hard. Part of me recognized the 'flooding' aspect of the clinic, the shutting down of these colts in order to cope. 'Many roads to Rome,' I thought, and before I left, I made myself feel better by taking a quilted blanket out to the back pens. July was standing, trembling in the vile weather, with a dozen or so others. The pipe corrals were out-of-doors in a muddy corner of the parking lot. I, like an old mother hen, did not want my stressed colt to get sick.

I didn't count on the reaction of the men hanging out there at the end of the day. They were enjoying a beer and reliving the previous hours with laughter and stories.

They were friendly, as I knew many of them well, but there was a hectoring aspect to their response when I showed up with the waterproof turnout rug.

"He doesn't need that coddling," the headliner clinician told me. "One of the problems with most horses today is that you women spoil them." Chastened, embarrassed, ashamed, I said a silent 'so long' to my young horse and put the blanket back in my truck. I drove home in the rain, the wipers struggling to keep the windshield bare. It was the last time I would see my colt as he was.

After the two-day clinic, July went home with the young trainer to continue on with his start. I figured no news was good news, but after about two weeks, curiosity got the better of me and I gave him a call.

"He's got a bit of a cough," said the trainer. "Do you want me to turn him out for a while or send him home?" I thought on it for a moment and decided that he'd be best turned out to grass where he was, until his cold cleared up. I had a high-dollar sale-horse at home and I didn't want to risk him getting sick as well.

I've regretted my off-hand, money-based decision ever since.

Little did we know that this wasn't just a cold. Little did we know. I can only think that the stress of the colt-starting clinic, the foul nights spent in the muddy corral among a dozen strange horses, the fact that my colt had come from a closed herd to the training barn — all played a part in the debilitating fever and sickness that descended upon July like a heavy, black cloud. Weeks later, when he was still unwell and after my sale-horse had gone, I made the trip to pick him up. I'd nurse him back to better health here at home.

The horse I saw was unrecognizable. I looked at his brand to ensure this was indeed my colt. July's breath was rasping through flaring nostrils. His fever had him on the fight, and one look at those eyes of black glass, I knew we were in trouble. The trainer and I got him onto my trailer with a fair bit of difficulty, for the colt was ill to the point of being out of his mind. Once the truck hit the highway, I was dialing my vet with one hand while holding the steering wheel with the other. All the while I was making the emergency appointment, in the back of my mind, I knew the outcome was not going to be good.

I left July lying peacefully in a corner of the vet clinic parking lot, underneath a blue plastic tarp.

When presented with the facts about his vitals, his extreme temperature, his slim chance of recovery, the course of treatments that we could try, I knew that this was the only kind decision left to me. One last act of decency that would never make up for all the ways I had let this young horse down. I didn't order a post-mortem. I knew there was no scientific explanation for dying of a broken heart.

May and June are beautiful months of growth and rebirth. While I am always going to love this time of year, there will remain a part of me that mourns the memory of July. He was the one colt I sent away in order to have a real chance at becoming something good.

Like all sad stories, this one has a moral, a lesson to be learned. The responsibility for July falls to me, for I was the decision-maker, and he was my horse. In the end, though, I finally saw that while my ways may be different, that I mightn't be handy or filled with youthful courage, I needed to trust myself. That I was, in fact, enough. July, thank you for this lesson — and, yes, I will always be filled with regrets.

Horses are my victory, and they are my heartbreak. Seldom is there a middle ground.

. 132 .

THE BASIC SEAT

I don't look at a compliant horse as having his spirit broken or his will taken away. This doesn't sit right given my goal of striving, caring horsemanship. Let me better explain. When I ask the softly-receiving, yielding, accepting, amenable horse a question, his response to me is never, 'Why?!' Nope. I will be looking for an 'okie dokie' or a 'yes, ma'am'.

I've heard this best described as how a server can make or break one's night out at a restaurant. The food may be great, but if the waiter is surly and disinterested, so much enjoyment is lost. How much better is our experience if the waiter is engaged, doing his best job, and has decided he is willing to play his part.

Now, being served by a caring, happy waiter doesn't mean that I've been a bully to get good service. Rather, it means that my waiter takes pride in his or her job. It means that he is willing to be guided by my wishes. It means that I respect his craft enough to treat him with decency. (By the way, it is true that you can learn a lot about me by how I treat and interact with those who serve).

Acceptance, lightness and relaxation remain my three pillars of effective, ethical horsemanship. If ever my horse's willingness to serve is missing, no matter how convincingly I may tell myself that it doesn't really matter, I can't get around the fact that it does.

· 133 ·

MUSICAL FREESTYLE

Turns out, riding is a lot like playing the piano. Some of us are content, all our lives, with hammering out *Chopsticks,* while others long to play something beautiful that is always just a bit beyond us. We all start somewhere. We will all end somewhere. The music in which we choose to lose ourselves is almost impossible to explain to others. And yet it behooves us to try.

· 134 ·

SWISHING FLIES IN THE BROODMARE BAND

Girlfriends. They are "the women who know and love us — and love us despite what they know about us," says one of my favourite authors, Anna Quindlen.

I spent so many of my younger years feeling lonely. Trying to be a good daughter. A good wife. A good mother. (I didn't do so well at any of these, if you want to know). I coped with my shortfalls in personal relationships by really striving to be a good employee. Getting the gold star. Always surrounded by people and yet always feeling alone.

There is a stage in our womanhood where so much is in front of us, that it's overwhelming.

We're to keep the house in order, the accounts straight, food in the pantry and on the table, the kids in school, and remember those appointments at the orthodontist. We have to figure out how to pay the orthodontist too, so the pressures at work begin to equal those at home. A child is in trouble. Our partner is acting out somewhat childishly, perhaps feeling neglected? We vow to think about that later. Then, when we can stand nothing more, the dog gets really sick, or the transmission goes out of the car.

All the while we're coping, we're being told to look and act a certain way. This, we have been schooled on since childhood.

We collect stuff to make us feel a little better, get excited about something again. We join a book club so that we'll read those things we're supposed to read, to improve our minds and not stagnate. I would do all these things and still I would feel lonely. I don't know whether it's the same if you live in the city or the country, but I do remember thinking recently that if I could be in my twenties again, I wouldn't do it on a bet. Those proving years are hard.

Decades go past and then you're in your fifties, sixties, and beyond. If you're lucky, there's more time to do those things of which you, as a young girl, once dreamed. You have a big garage sale and clear out all your once-precious stuff. You maybe swear a little more than you used to and enjoy huge belly laughs. Sometimes there's wine at lunch. If you're lucky, you start finding your people. One, two, three women who seemingly understand you and are not threatened by who you are.

Horses have opened so many doors for me. Of these, I love the door that has opened to friendship. Comfortable, pithy, wise, funny, capable of withstanding so much pain and hardship — these women make me see what a wild 'n' woolly trip it is, this learning to age gracefully, after withstanding so much pressure for us all to be the same.

· 135 ·
FREE LESSONS

My mentors — and I've had maybe three or four in my lifetime — are not usually found among my friends. They are paid professionals, people who have long been in their chosen industry. We exchange their truths and knowledge for my money.

I don't expect something that has taken another horseman years to learn to be given to me for nothing. That would not be fair. I am very careful to keep friendship and mentorship separate states. Both are highly valued and worthy of recognition.

When we pay to learn, we can expect to receive kindness, yes, but also bluntness. We are wanting guidance or a second opinion to balance out our preconceived ideas or bad habits. There is no room for hurt feelings or bruised egos. We can disagree, but we must be honest with ourselves about why we do so. We can also outgrow our mentors, especially when the focus of our horsemanship has changed.

That said, I'm very careful when I start veering away from someone whose opinion has been a guiding light. Am I growing my own wings or am I steering clear of inconvenient truths? Am I actually going astray? Good mentorship forces us to dig deep. It holds us accountable.

Free advice is often given by people who have no platform on which to stand. Be mindful of this.

Is your advisor someone you trust because you've seen him or her in action? This is why there is such a danger in learning online — yes, Keystone Equine included. Ask yourself, what is this person gaining by sharing this information with me? Is it a hook to reel me in to buy something? This, my friends, is why I still pay for lessons. Secondly, mentorship can mean many things. It might help you with your riding, and it might help you grow into a better, kinder, wiser person.

I got into horses because I didn't like 'dealing with people'. This is comical because everything we do in life has some aspect of coping with our fellow man. The horse industry has some of the most intense, colourful, convoluted, damaged personalities we might ever find. My mentors have had to teach me how to navigate these murky waters. I've had to learn how to keep good books, make a paper trail, survive a two-year-long tax audit, cope with depression and the losing of close friends, create a training program that aligns with my own morals and beliefs, buy horses wisely and sell horses honestly — all with the help of both voluntary and paid mentors.

No matter where I end up in life, I will stand by the notion of mentorship. No matter how old or know-it-all I become, I shall seek the person who knows my weaknesses, all the while wishing well for me. I shall seek the teacher who requires me to be a better person.

. 136 .

WET SADDLE BLANKETS

More and more, I'm openly showing myself as a 'recovering perfectionist'. This isn't easy. As adult children, homemakers, parents, employees, and riders, we've grown used to comparing ourselves to someone else's ideal. Being online reminds us daily of an impossible standard of airbrushed excellence. But this mindset can be damaging to our souls and it's something of a cop-out.

The need to be 'my best', 'your best', 'the best' kills our equestrian dreams more surely than anything else. What this does for many of us, rather than push us on to betterment, is to tell ourselves to quit before we fail. To wait until things are 'just right'. To put it off until next year. All of these are symptoms of 'paralysis by analysis'. Today instead let's join forces to wish one another a day of 'Happy Imperfection'. Smile. Stay safe. Here's to trying with gusto. Here's to us!

· 137 ·

STRAIGHT FROM THE HORSE'S MOUTH

As riders, we want answers. We ask the experts and, many times, the so-called 'experts' talk down to us about how to fix our four-footed friends.

How do we get them to stand still for mounting? How do we get them to better load into the trailer? How do we stop them from shying? How do we make them change leads on the back end? How do we cure our horses from pulling back? These are some common questions. Because we are who we are, they all slant towards the assumption that we are in control. But I ask you something instead.

What if we stopped looking for help in finding the answers and, instead, went to the horse with the questions? This one step is a sign of evolution in our own horsemanship. It takes us from a place of wanting to be right, to a place of feeling what is right. Rather than asking for help — "How do I get my horse to stand for mounting?" — we ignore all the going advice and shift our attention to the horse:

"Why will you, my dear horse, not stand?"

If we run through all the possible reasons, and then teach ourselves to look for these with open hearts and minds, it can change our horsemanship. The correct answer is usually apparent, if we care to pay attention, and then the training method is right there in front of us. So instead of the old way of making him stand still before we move off — or else — we ask ourselves:

Have I ever taken the time to teach my horse how to stand still and relax from the ground? Does he fidget at other times I'm handling him or just when I'm trying to mount? Is my saddle a good fit? Is he needing to move his feet more before I get on? Is he worried about me jamming my boot into his elbow, every single time I swing up? Is he afraid of my weight slamming down in the saddle because I've not bothered to perfect my technique? Has he learned to love the mounting block? Do I always ride ahead and go straight into the trot or lope? Is he tense through the mouth and back when I ride him? Is he worried because he is herdbound? Is he young and green, or so small that I actually pull him over when I step up? Or am I actually too heavy for this particular horse? These are hard questions, but good ones to be asking.

When we approach any training problem from asking the horse the question — rather than asking other riders the answer — we delve into the fascinating world of being able to really understand our methods and then get the point across. We suddenly understand that behind every technique, there's a why.

We begin to realize that we don't have a mounting problem. We maybe have a horse whose mass is unable to hold our sideways pull when we mount, and so he has to make a few desperate steps to keep his balance. So, we learn to 'lock' his front legs into a tripod by rocking the saddle back and forth before we get on. Or we see that his back is tense because we flop down heavily when we take our seat. Once the horse trusts that we will do better — and this may take many times to prove it — he will be able to relax and stand still. Maybe if we dismounted at the mounting block, just as often as we used it for mounting, our horse would learn to trust it more?

Sometimes, we have a hard time getting honest with ourselves and we need the help of a pair of knowledgeable eyes from the ground, or the video taken by a friend. Whether we have poor driving habits; a hot and claustrophobic trailer; a bullying horse in the next slot; whether our horse could change leads behind if we rode him more forward or taught him how to calmly yield to our legs — good training is not usually a great mystery. I am learning that most times our horses know just what is needed. That is, if we're not too proud to ask.

. 138 .
AND THE WINNER IS ...

We are out at the barn, visiting horses and sweeping the aisle, just eight days after the birth of my granddaughter. It is a poignant moment, when my daughter takes Ruby in her arms to meet Cinnabar, a horse who was a gift from Cait's grandparents when she was sweet sixteen. I smile remembering the hopes, hard work, and dashed dreams that come with a teenager's first colt project.

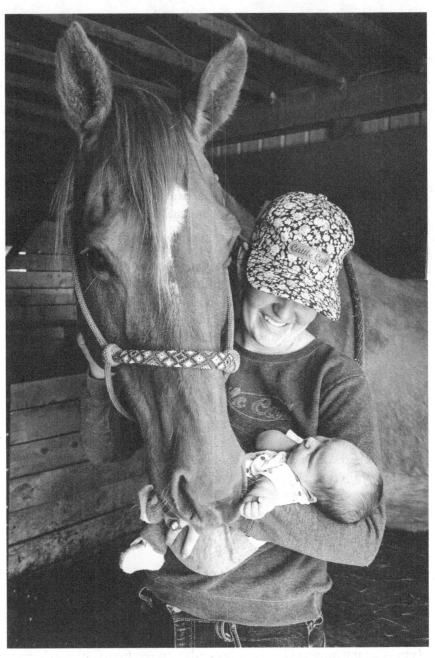

It strikes me just how quickly I have gone from young motherhood with a babe in my own arms, to becoming a grandmother. Again, just one horse and a little girl. And so it begins. (Author's Collection)

Cinnabar was going to be the best horse ever, and he might well have been, had only he read the manual. He did not, of course, and the quirky, skeptical gelding defied much of his young trainer's lofty ambitions. He loathed the monotony of showing in any sort of event. Nor did he necessarily want the excitement of running barrels or jumping. Instead, Cinny followed an independent line of thought, often shying out and occasionally bucking. At the same time, he could be maddeningly lazy. He was his own man. What Cinnabar did eventually shape into, however, was a steadfast partner and friend. He alone knows more about what makes Cait tick than do most of her people. A loyal ranch horse, the tag end of generations of a working bloodline bred by Ruby's great-great-grandparents, Cinnabar turned into exactly the sort of workaday horse needed by a young ranch woman. Not a show horse. Not a particularly fast runner or a high jumper. Just a stand-up sort of guy, one who is broke pretty well, can rope and work a cow, and is safe enough.

I snapped Cait and Ruby's picture with the sorrel gelding. I couldn't help but wonder about the animals who will one day make Ruby into a horsewoman. Chances are, Cinnabar will rank among them. In our family, there could be no higher honour for a horse.

· 139 ·

DRY WORK

"Work harder," screamed the clinician. "It's not supposed to be easy. You should be working as hard as the horse." I had saved my money and bought myself a slot at a weekend clinic that featured an honest-to-goodness dressage god. The man was a legend. But either he was having a very bad day, or he was just a nasty human being. During my lesson with him, I struggled to stuff down every single thing that felt wrong. Willing myself to get tough and not tearful, I obediently followed directions.

I began to exert even more than my poor horse who, God knows, was no longer enjoying himself. I drove him up with my legs. I pushed him into my hands to make him rounder. I brought him back so that he wasn't 'escaping out the front door'. I was riding the fabled 'push-me-pull-you'. When the nightmare was finally over, I stepped down from my generous horse and apologized profusely. I knew that I'd done him wrong.

Not long afterward, one of our horses injured herself, falling down a steep bank while going for a drink to the creek. Mike and I found the dear mare, lying in scattered rubble at the bottom of a cliff. It was obvious Cisco had gone down in a landslide. Several hours were needed to coax her to her feet, then back up to the yard and onto the trailer for a trip to the vet.

It was a weekend. Our trusted caregiver was on holidays and a young graduate just out of school was left in charge. I explained the situation as best I could and then stood, dumbfounded, as the new professional struggled with using hoof testers on a horse unable to stand on three legs. Despite my explanation of what had happened, the diagnosis was grass founder. Yes, poor Cisco was lame and stiff, but this was ridiculous. I stood there, holding the mare silently because I was no health expert. I stayed silent. I knew that despite a scolding to keep her off grass and a gross misdiagnosis, the horse and I would be sent home with some much-needed pain meds.

These two events, though seemingly unrelated, share a common theme. In each instance, my knowing was not enough. I was the one who knew the most of anyone present about my own horses, and yet all I could do was swallow my insecurity and feed my growing doubts.

So how do we learn to trust ourselves? If we have ridden long enough, this question is probably one with which we have struggled. That old 'the more we learn, the less we know' saying holds a pile of truth. Insecurity can freeze any one of us, even if armed with a wealth of practical knowledge. We may know the answer to a horsemanship question but are simply afraid of doing it wrongly. When our horses are involved, we have learned to fear the making of mistakes.

Problem is, this self-doubt is not a healthy way to live.

Have we been immersed in good teaching for years, to the point of knowing what we'd be told in a given situation? Do we know the techniques or practice drills that might help? Do we have a better 'read' on our own horse than the expensive clinician or greenhorn vet? Will we buy into what we're being told, even when we know it's not true? Do we get talked into dicey situations, even when we know better? Do we see or hear something and then change our lifelong programs after a ten-minute read? Do we find ourselves panicked and swayed in the warm-up ring at shows because nobody else seems to be schooling or riding like we are?

Do we have so much insecurity of self that we'll go with just about any consensus other than our own?

One of the biggest hurdles in making or maintaining our own horses is the inability to 'settle in'. By this, I mean having the courage of our convictions to stick with one solid program, teacher or method long enough for it to 'stick'. When we jump from ship-to-ship, going to multiple clinics and lessons by different coaches, we ultimately confuse both our horses and ourselves. There are many, many roads to Rome. Don't forget that. If someone sees you loading your horse 'wrongly' and tells you so, I want you to stop and think before you change it up. Does your horse get on calmly, willingly and safely every single time you ask? If so, you're doing fine.

Your sweet horse maybe doesn't need round penning, or hobble breaking, or flagging to give of his best. He maybe just needs more time and mileage in your current system in order to gel. Those lead changes you struggle with? Pick what feels right between you and your horse and stick with it until they come. Because come they will. Trust yourself enough to know that you can steer your craft through choppy waters.

Now, for the tricky bit. We have to be willing to delve into why we feel insecure about our own horsemanship. Do we really know, or have we stalled out along the road to learning? If we've been riding long enough to know how to fix some of our own problems, why are we dumbing ourselves down? Do we fear wrecking our horses or are we hooked on avoiding any responsibility? This is where being brutally honest with ourselves and having one trusted mentor is key.

I've got to the point now that unless I am riding with my one trusted mentor, getting only his advice, I am best left on my own! Yes. This means unfollowing all of the online groups and training emails out there, scrolling by all the forums and clickbait videos, learning to trust my own inner voice. In the end, I've learned that if flitting from one program to another is hard on my self-confidence, it's especially hard on my horse. I believe, somewhat ironically, that the wealth of free information now at our fingertips has come at the expense of many horses. We have lost a lot of the decisiveness that came, once upon a time, when we were on our own.

If we are lifelong horse(wo)men, still telling ourselves that our own knowledge and intuition isn't 'good enough', we are thinking toxic thoughts. It's why the hardest question in a job interview is the old classic, "Tell us about yourself." We're nice people. We don't want to blow our own horns, so we dismiss our personal truths and gut feelings. If this is us, if this is the soundtrack we play in our heads, pay attention. Yes, we can still learn, we can still be open to new ways, but be it resolved — this is the year we decide we are enough.

. 140 .

LOSING CONTROL

The concept of 'controlling' our fear is an interesting one. Keeping it simple, managing fear depends very much on what is causing it. If my fear is of an intimidating jump or learning a new skill, even trying a new horse, then acknowledging the risks and using coping techniques is healthy and doable. But if I am harbouring an ongoing fear of my horse, then this anxiety is telling me that I am unsafe. This fear doesn't need to be managed, or in any way worked around. This gut feeling needs for us to listen.

The notion of 'not riding scared' is not about telling people they should breathe deeply or show no fear. No, it is time to tell ourselves to stop settling, because only a safe horse or a safe teacher can put back what an unsafe horse or situation has taken away from us. By the way, this question of authenticity isn't only a core truth in our horsemanship. It is a truth that shows up in so many other key relationships as well.

. 141 .

CROSS COUNTRY

After a long day of waiting, we got the call. I walked out to Betty, who'd been grazing in the yard at the ready. There was something about those last slanting rays of the setting sun, the golden heads of the brome grass waving, the green hill rising behind, a few of the cows who'd brought their fat calves up to see what was going on — it was as though Alberta had put on her best face, just to say goodbye.

Betty loaded onto our trailer trustingly, without pause, as she always does. We drove for an hour to meet the commercial transporter who would take her over the mountains, across another province, and over the water to her new island home. Standing in the parking lot of the busy truck stop, the driver had some standard questions.

"Does she have any hauling issues we should be aware of?" No. "No halter pulling? No kicking the trailer? No scrambling? Does she panic if she's first on or last off? Is she a fussy eater or drinker? Is she aggressive with other horses? Has she had any cough or cold in the last while?" No.

Before 'those who knew best' told us what we could not do, we believed anything was possible. Meeting Betty, who achieved despite a late start and physical limitations, changed me somehow. I began to see that if she could try it, so could anyone. (Author's Collection)

"Are there any special instructions?" Yes. Her name is Betty, and she is very, very good. Look after her because, while my heart is heavy, there is another at the end of your journey who is finding healing and happiness for the first time in a long time, because of her. Go safely, because she is precious to us. I said none of these things, of course, because I am a grown woman, a professional who is in this business to sell the horses that I love. Instead, I said only that she was very easy to handle and would cause no problems at all.

I loaded Betty, clipped her tie strap and watched her tuck into the familiar hay we'd brought from home. With a half-smile, I straightened the forelock that is always, always flying uncontrollably in the wind. I looked into the deep pools of her eyes. Go well, Betty, don't forget who you are and remember that you're repping the brand. I have loved you, even when you were new and balky, even when you used to strike me hard across the knees! Then, with eighteen-wheelers roaring past us, their coloured lights all aglow, the driver fired up his rig and they were gone.

Mike and I drove home in silence. Beyond the lights of town and then the thinning suburbs, we headed toward the purple hills. I wondered where Betty would be when we woke up in the morning. I thought of the new projects I have here, all four of them, who I will try my darnedest to make half as good as that one little mare. Yes. Tomorrow, I will start again.

. 142 .

JOINING THE HERD

It can take a long time, this finding your circle. The horse world is like any other — there are all manner of characters — some kind and giving, others maybe not so much. Rest assured that there is room here for all of us. We sometimes forget that horses are only half the equation in our pursuit of their magic. The other half lies with the people who surround them. Modern life, with its worldwide outreach at the click of a button, has changed the horse business.

Gone are the days where we were mentored solely by the closest neighbour. Years where we rode and showed in the one style that was seen in our neck of the woods. Nowadays, we can research different avenues in training and healthcare. We can get instant feedback on judges and industry leaders. We can know what to expect before we haul to the other side of the continent to buy, learn or compete. The wide world of horsemanship has suddenly become very small.

Each one of us — that's you and I — have a part to play in this larger society. We not only buy and sell our unused gear on the sales sites, but we attend conferences, scout out feed, hire vets and farriers, enter competitions, take lessons, pay board, and shop for new horses. You and I are good for the industry.

Yes, you and I are movers and shakers. Every single one of us, from newcomer to lifelong pro, are important to the horse business. We have a vote that we cast every single time we take part — in how our horses will be treated; in how we'll expect them to work; in who stays in this business and who does not. We all have our voices. We get to decide who is cool this year and who isn't. We find out just who is kind and who, not so much. We learn who knows their stuff and who is riding on the coattails of the latest fad. We learn — often, the hard way — who builds us up and who tears us down. We learn who to follow closely and who it is best to avoid. This learning about the horse business is indeed an education.

Educations are never free. When we make mistakes, when we get into the wrong crowd, when we follow the wrong people, we do not feel good inside. We can go on

for a long time, ignoring our inner voice, just keeping up, before we get courageous enough to pay attention. This, too, is part of our learning. It's part of honing our own brand of horsemanship. We figure out how to manifest the support we really need. Horses and horse people matter hugely because they affect our hearts, our homes and our wallets. No wonder they seep into our very beings.

Our human herd will either make life harder for us or it will lift us up. If you are surrounded by the right people, it can change everything about your horsemanship. If you are not yet in a positive group, keep searching. Fear not. Your people are out there waiting.

· 143 ·
EARNING OUR SPURS

Vivid memories are coming across my newsfeed these days. The whirlwind of being one of the original sidesaddle racers is, all at once, still fresh and from another lifetime.

Overnight, we eight women were put upon the worldwide stage. I became accustomed to answering phone messages from journalists around the globe. Surprisingly, the reactions from other women ranged from uplifting all the way to upsetting. There was no mistaking, for better or worse, we gals were in the news.

A lot of folks applauded our bravado, our sheer gutsiness at doing something as dangerous as did the old-time rodeo cowgirls. I mean, what could possibly go wrong riding racehorses in saddles that were up to one hundred and thirty years old? One misstep, one bump, one broken girth strap and it would have been disaster. Yet we smiled and waved, curled our hair, put on our lipstick, and then we rode.

People would ask, "Did you have fun?" I never knew quite what to say to that.

In many ways, the series of four sidesaddle races that culminated in battling it out before forty-five thousand screaming fans at the Calgary Stampede left me with some sort of unnamed trauma. I would wake up nights, for months after, sweating and alarmed at the force of my pumping heart. But there was camaraderie among us, and I still tear up when I think of the gallantry of those horses.

I did not ride my own mounts and relied upon the generosity of others. Ritz, who carried me down a sloppy homestretch in a neck-and-neck drive to the wire; Elvis, who was so pumped at his race that he was prepared to go around again; Brooks, who bore me so safely and surely and then went right back to his workaday job as a rodeo pick-up horse.

My daughter's buckskin gelding remains an inspiration. Jack was 'just a ranch horse', and an aged one at that, before he went to the big smoke for the first time. He hit his stride in Calgary, finishing fourth both nights. Jack and all the other horses that were fast enough to race hard, but safe enough to carry us aside, will stand among my heroes.

Riding this way, racing, appearing on the Stampede stage with my daughter, and appearing on television and radio with her will be something I'll never forget. We laughed, we cried, and we gripped hands oh-so-hard whenever we were scared. That's powerful stuff for any mother and daughter to share. I remember clearly praying that if either myself, my daughter, or these other young women were to get hurt, please God, let it be me. Neither Cait nor I were able to come back the following year and do it again. If I'm going to be honest here, not only was it because I'd blown my knee apart during the first race, but also, I knew that I was left with something inside me that did not honour who I am. But did we have fun? Many times, yes.

My overall memory of being a sidesaddle racer is one of pride that we all got through it, along with gratitude that we could stalwartly represent the brave women who went before us. Yet I'm also left with something else. Something that I've finally been able to name, given the buffer of time.

For me, the experience is shadowed with some shame. I think I was hard on these horses and my horsemanship suffered just in getting the job done. I've learned that for me, personally, how I ride and interact with my horse is more important than how fast we can run. I've learned that the history and equitation that make up the art of sidesaddle — indeed of any equestrian sport — can be tarnished once we turn it into a competitive thing. It has been good for me to learn that I, too, am not above being swayed by such pressure.

I'm ashamed of the overwhelming fatigue that had me riding so poorly on the final night, it almost ended in disaster. Every time I see another photo with me in that turquoise shirt, nails biting into my saddle, trying to stay with my galloping horse, I

am humbled. I had committed to this grand adventure, and in the end, was found wanting. Injured in the first race, physically- mentally- and emotionally-exhausted at the last, I just ran out of steam.

When I cheer for these international women who are riding, racing and jumping sidesaddle, I will do so with my whole heart. I will want them to make lifelong memories, to uphold good horsemanship, to stay safe, and to thrill those huge crowds, wherever they may be. Most of all, I will be cheering for their bravery because I know that each one of them, behind her smiling beauty, will have dug so very deep.

· 144 ·

NO VICES

To anyone watching, he is just an ordinary horse being vetted for insurance purposes. To me, however, it is an emotional sight, watching how he copes with it all. I am on hand to witness Sarcee's exam, all the standard checks that go into applying for coverage. He stands, a horse alone, with a small crowd of bystanders gathered to wish his new owner well. The vet asks his name, age and breeding.

"Sarcee ... and beyond that, who really knows?" we say, only half-jokingly. His age is confirmed at ten to twelve years, and to fresh eyes, he might seem to favour a Belgian grandmother, with myriad other genetics thrown in. We settle on 'Cayuse' as the official term, before the vet continues on with the form. He checks pulse and respiration, listening to the heart and lungs. Sarcee's eyes widen with friendly interest, but he doesn't move a muscle as the vet reaches out to check the ears, eyes and teeth. At one point, a hand is put upon his poll to steady him and quietly the gelding lowers his head. There was once a day that this particular horse would not have allowed it. But today, that seems very long ago.

Next, Sarcee's limbs, shoulders, spine and hips are palpated. His feet are pinched with hoof testers, then the little horse is asked to walk and trot straight out and back. He is lunged briefly, both ways, before the vet begins the dreaded flexion tests. We collectively hold our breath. Those beautifully big-boned legs pass with flying colours, and not once does the little wildie pull his feet away as they are bent in contortions and held. Not once. Finally, the vet concludes his report that this horse has an 'exemplary disposition and manners'. I quickly blink back tears as I remember how very far he has come.

An old friend catches my eye and smiles. She, of all people, understands. "Do you remember when you first brought him to meet me? I walked up just to say hello, and he struck out and almost parted my hair!" she says. We laugh in remembrance, as the horse before us would never do anything so ungentlemanly now.

With that, it is time for me to proffer my branding iron, as per his buyer's wishes, the last stage in this changing of hands. Based on the gelding's hair coat and red roan colouring, the vet prepares Sarcee for an eighteen-second freeze brand. A sedative is administered to the horse, that he will feel no pain. A small area on his near thigh is closely clipped, as the iron cools in a tub of liquid nitrogen. A squirt of alcohol soaks the spot where the brand will be applied. This old Keystone iron will forever mark Sarcee as one of my best. Some very good horses have worn this brand and I blink again as I think of them. In moments it is done, and still the little horse stands proud.

With that, Sarcee is a Keystone pony. Today, finally, he belongs.

· 145 ·

DROPPING OUR IRONS

It has taken me most of my life, through seasons of depression and dread, to truly understand myself. I have learned that while spring, summer and autumn are for my horses — winter is just for me.

My country is a land of blasting wind and inhospitable temperatures from early November until late April. It is not unheard of to experience snowfall in every month of the year. Today, I have watched the sun climb reluctantly over our big hill at nine-thirty this morning and disappear again behind the Rockies, a few short hours later, at four-thirty in the afternoon. With temps reaching below the minus thirties, skin freezes instantly. Our faces burn and our eyes feel dry. It becomes difficult to focus. I have not always done well in this environment.

I have had to make peace with the fact that, for many months, my horses' schooling and fitness will suffer. Instead of saying that I am falling behind, I now call it 'turnout'. This is the time for them to recharge and remember the spirit in which God made them. I have had to remind myself that my garden, too, needs time to replenish her roots and get ready for her coming splendour.

I have had to learn that all of my passions do not begin and end with warm weather. This one has been hard for, in fact, they secretly do. But I am learning to love taking short snow-blown walks with cavorting dogs. I have even embraced a new sport, by trying traditional skijoring behind my quietest and most accommodating horses. I cannot and never have been able to ski, but no matter. It has surprised me to find that I can still be silly and have fun. In adulting responsibly, I had somehow forgotten how.

I have learned that there is satisfaction in the doing of the day's chores, of thawing frozen water lines, of getting the cold truck started for the icy trip to town. Oh, that I may never forget the satisfaction of horses feeding after opening a beautiful, homegrown bale of hay.

I have learned that much of my depression has been the by-product of today's modern diet. Processed foods relying on chemicals, added sugars, and all manner of unpronounceable ingredients have had me reliant on other means to cope with the fallout of eating things that do not promote life. So much of what I have swallowed has fostered unwellness.

I have lived too many years thinking that I would do anything to lose weight — except look after myself.

I have learned that this dark, long season is the one where I take long baths, make wholesome soups and stews brimful with root vegetables, do some mending or making. I remember that wellness lies in creating and resting, in looking after myself for a change. I organize neglected closets and old photos, taking the time to order some prints to frame. I can gaze at these happy moments from summers past and when I do, I allow myself to dream. I stop shaming myself about wanting, and then taking, the nap.

I turn off the things with screens and I read. Real books with covers to crack open and pages to turn. Some of us have forgotten along the way about the quiet meditation of reading.

Every winter, I try to repaint a room. This is not a chore to cross off a long list, but a fun way to try on a colour I hadn't thought of, to brighten my horizons, to have me see my home with fresh eyes. I fill boxes with things I no longer cherish, sending them on to the charity shop for others to enjoy. This one simple act of service is a powerful antidepressant on days when my hope is flagging.

Winter is the time when I make the dental and medical appointments to head off the bad surprises that threaten us as we age. With chin held high, I resolutely make my way to the free screening clinics where I am squished, squeezed, poked and prodded in the hopes of an all-clear. I find that during the hurly-burly of warm weather, I can't spare the time or be bothered to do this essential act of self-care. It can be an exhausting thing, worrying through the night that I may be harbouring another illness. I am learning to do better, promising myself that, above all, I deserve to know what's going on.

Seasons and reasons. They remind me that sharp weather is actually my quiet time to rebuild and heal. This dark thing, which has had me fearing and withdrawing from winter, has taken me years to learn how to handle. Like a challenging horse, I cannot master her with force, but with calmness, faith and understanding.

Winter is my time to listen.

. 146 .

WELL-FED

It's fruitcake weather!

One morning, all swirling, blowing snow, it will be time to bring down the big blue bowl. I will halve cherries, blanch nuts, chop dates, and set these to soak in a bath of orange juice and tart jelly, just as my great-grandmother's faded recipe tells me.

There will be eggs whisked with brown sugar. Mace, nutmeg and vanilla will be wafting through this old kitchen, while I measure butcher paper, like a child immersed in arts and crafts, just to line the hand-me-down square tins.

Over the years, I have got a bit lazy, to tell the truth. If you want to cut a few corners, you can do so. Skip the brown paper and all the fussy cake tins. I've learned that you can give a spritz of non-stick spray in an ordinary 11" x 14" pan and it actually cooks quicker. If we wait until the cake cools before trying to remove it from the pan, it's all good.

You know there are only two kinds of people, right? Those who love fruitcake — and everyone else! Tell me, who else prefers the dark, rich cake over the light? If you don't like fruitcake, poor dear, you've not had a chance to try a proper one, like nanny's. Moist and boozy, it is made without so much as a pinch of candied peel. We eat ours, with almond paste on top or without, but I like it best kept simple, with slices of aged cheddar.

Oh, summer, how I have loved you — but soon, another enjoyable afternoon will be spent brandying and wrapping fruitcakes in parchment, foil and tartan ribbon. Certain of my friends, who have proved themselves truly worthy, will be the recipients.

This recipe is so good, you won't care that we are what we eat!

When I told my friend that I was including my family recipe for fruitcake in a book of life lessons, she reminded me of the old Gary Larson cartoon. "Unbeknownst to most theologians, there was a fourth wise man, who was turned away for bringing fruitcake."

She happens to like my cake. Nevertheless, we laughed and laughed.

· 147 ·

NANNY'S FRUITCAKE

On the first cold day of fall, find your biggest bowl and mix together:
1 lb. each candied red and green cherries, golden raisins, sliced almonds
½ lb. each black currants, chopped dates
1 cup orange or grape juice over all, then stir a bit
and cover with a cloth. Let sit overnight.

The next day, after occasionally stirring the above
mixture, cream together in a large bowl:
1½ cups brown sugar
½ cup softened butter
6 eggs
3 tbsp cocoa
½ cup blackstrap molasses
¼ cup tart currant or crab apple jelly
½ cup incredibly strong coffee

This mixing is best done by hand with a wooden spoon.

Stir in one cup of flour into the fruit mixture, then add ½
cup of flour to the brown sugar mixture, along with:
1 tsp each of cinnamon, cloves, nutmeg, allspice
½ tsp each of baking soda, salt, mace

Pour over the fruit mixture, stir all together and spoon into greased pans. Bake in a slow oven (300F/150C) 'til it tests done in the centre. When cool, remove from pans, cut into smaller cakes and turn them, upside down, onto heavy foil. Sprinkle generously with brandy. Wrap well and store in the fridge or freezer.

We enjoy nanny's fruitcake year-round, served the
traditional way with slices of extra-sharp cheese.

. 148 .

TROT ON!

Today, I will just say this. If you, like me, have arisen from a sound sleep; if we are holding that first cup of coffee and standing out, listening to the birds singing from burgeoning trees; if we will spend some time today with our horses, just cleaning waterers, checking feet, picking pens; if we will share space with a beloved dog or cat; if we can think of dear friends and family with smiles on our faces ... then this is a good day and we have been blessed.

Should our hearts be heavy with loss or with worry, recalling a voice or the notes of a remembered laugh, we must say this again, until we believe it — this is a good day and we have been blessed.

I am needing to be gentle with myself, mourning the fresh loss of an especially dear friend. One of the world's kind souls, Sharon was a horsewoman, a trained musician, a good cook, a comedian, a lover of all animals; and an empathetic, stalwart, honest guidepost on how to navigate this tricky business called life. Her face flickers throughout the memories of many of my most meaningful days with horses, with laughter and with music. I gasp as I realize that this woman has left behind not a single enemy, not one detractor. Each of us living within her constant circle of light knew only authenticity and love.

For just a moment, clouds drift in front of the morning sun. I shiver and draw in a shaky breath. Yes. This is a good day and we have been blessed.

One of the most painful parts of getting older is saying goodbye. I have decided that healing requires both tears and laughter. Sage and constant friends, like Sharon, will always have our backs, no matter the dimensions between us. I know this now. (Author's Collection)

· 149 ·
SPURRED INTO ACTION

We try so hard to get better. We'll pick something we want to work on, to improve, then we'll get straight to it. Many of us, in our enthusiasm for the task at hand, forget that our horses didn't read the manual. They don't have the same fire in their belly to 'improve'. We need to be aware of that first best effort and reward it. Instead, we so often ride in that place of doubt, where we are never happy, never sure goodness will come around again. We need to trust. We must believe that this one little improvement will become a block on which we can lay a firm foundation.

Our asking is the pressure. Their slightest try is when we must release. Therein lies the learning. Only when we know this can we justly teach.

. 150 .

THERE WILL BE TEARS

Eclipse came to me last night in a dream. I'd fallen asleep wondering and worrying about a new horse. I woke up remembering another I'd not thought about in years.

I was fourteen when my parents purchased the big chestnut on the advice of my teacher. I remember gasping at his pedigree, which read like a racehorse *Who's Who* — Crafty Admiral, Fighting Fox, War Admiral, Man o' War, Fair Play and Mahubah. His mother was linebred to Equipoise. Eclipse was the spitting image of the George Stubbs namesake painting which hung, a cheap and battered print, on my bedroom wall.

Despite his lineage, Eclipse ran with no distinction. He retired after three years' hard slog on the track, a few meagre placings on his race record with The Jockey Club.

I'm tempted to remember only rosettes and sunshine whenever I think of him. Instead, Eclipse taught me that you can still have hair-raising runaways on a third-rate racehorse. Riding him, riding with my teacher, riding constantly taught me much of what I still know and use. Taking the inverted, sweaty, nervous beast — and imagining the assured horse that allowed me the feeling of pirouettes and half-pass, three-tempi changes and extended trot. I still know the feel of that last foot stomping into place for his trademark square halts, the veins standing out on his metallic neck, the unspoken vibration from my elbows, fingers and reins through to his softly-clinking bits.

For four years, we trained and competed. I sat him quietly and proudly, knowing always that I was on the winner. I clearly remember the day and class where he was finally put second. My teacher did not believe in showing horses. To her, dressage was a secret kept between a rider and her horse. To compete for prizes was somehow an exploitation of all the beautiful good that you had done. My mother, meanwhile, was working two jobs to support my riding habit. She and I wanted only to see if we were accomplishing anything at all. We began sneaking away on the weekends, hauling our treasure to every dressage show and hack class we could find.

Eclipse earned his first rosette in his first-ever hack class, a mind-boggling win in a group of over sixty horses. Weeks later, we competed and tied for the elementary win at the provincial dressage championships. We randomly picked this class because my horse was schooling the movements in the test, but we had no real idea of what was going on. I was sixteen and still have the signed tests and long-tailed ribbon awarded by Messrs. von Hopffgarten and de Kunffy, still.

It was not until the local newspaper showed Eclipse and me — with a huge first-prize bouquet — that our teacher caught on to our deceit. She was furious. Not only had we been sneaking around on her but, worse, my horse was published in a trashy manner that had no place in real dressage. She never completely forgave us. But it was not all about the prizes. My horse was my best friend. School was hell and I'd been newly-diagnosed with juvenile rheumatoid arthritis. The pain, the struggle with finding the right medication ... yet on Eclipse, I was graceful. I was not trapped in a stranger's body of molten lead. He gave me wings.

In order to train through the winters, Eclipse boarded out. Those few months he always bore with ill-grace. Worse, the barn help did not warm to my Thoroughbred as he had a habit of wanting his feed on the floor near his water — he was a dunker — leaving him free and clear to poop in his manger. I thought my horse very clever as seldom did his stall need cleaning. His manger, I fear, was something else. Eclipse learned to urinate on command, to lie down when told, to hold up the next foot to be picked, to stamp the leg that needed the wraps off, to nod his head when asked questions, to carry my gloves and whip in his teeth.

To his dying day, Eclipse would run and hide behind the yard light pole whenever I went to catch him. My part in the game would be to call his name loudly then 'give up' and sadly turn back to the gate. Soon, I would hear footsteps coming up behind me, I would feel him carefully pluck my cap from my head and fling it away. Every so often, he would have my ponytail by mistake, but still I would laugh while his neck curled around me for the ritual hug. Our game proved very unpopular with my new boyfriend, who took great pride in wearing a well-brushed and blocked silverbelly hat.

Life went on. The new boyfriend became my husband. The Thoroughbred, though still in his mid-teens, quickly aged. I would tease him about becoming fat and lazy, but eventually I felt that something wasn't right. No longer were his canter strides round and effortless, no longer was he finding joy in all that he knew.

I was not at his last vetting, for some reason, but my mother was. She remembers our friend the vet failing to find a regular pulse and saying, "I don't envy you telling Lee." Eclipse was winding down. We were advised to say goodbye. Later, I went out with the big leather halter and cried into the chestnut mane. I loaded my horse in the trailer and hauled him to be humanely euthanized. Through tears, I unloaded Eclipse and was told to hand over the rope that connected me with my beautiful friend. When it was done, I took the still-warm halter, fired up my truck and drove the long way home.

This horse came to me last night in my dreams. I awoke with joy and soon was beset with tears. Along with Eclipse, my horses have all taught me that great loss can only come when we have been given even greater love.

Eclipse did not start with me as the horse of which I'd dreamed. Instead, with the help of a very gifted teacher, I learned early on to have faith. I learned that nothing lasting is accomplished if we fail to believe. I learned that dreams amount to very little without the seasoning of hard work. I also learned that there may be some terrible rides before one glimpses the longed-for breakthrough. I learned that there must be hardship if we're ever to accomplish anything great. These were all hard lessons for a troubled teen and I'm not at all sure that now, four decades later, I would have the same 'stickwithitness' or the sheer blind faith that he would never let me down.

I do know that when we have that singular feeling, that perfect canter on the still and shining day, that this is heaven on earth. I do know that the animal we shared this with will not likely come our way again. That there is never two of anything, especially when it comes to describing horses.

This overwhelm of perfection has come to me on three separate occasions, only three times in a span of fifty years and counting. Even as a young person, I knew that those perfect miles cantering along the abandoned, grassy roadway would never quite be repeated. Not the rhythm of Eclipse's easy movement, the clinking of his bits, the sun on my face, the sound of the meadowlarks along the verge. Unafraid, the two of us were as one, meeting life in perfect accord.

This will stay my lasting memory of Eclipse — the horse who showed me joy, the horse who taught me what it is to grieve.

. 151 .

KEEPING SCORE

Memories. They're made of strong stuff, and they can haunt us as well as heal us. I was thinking all this, as I stood in the warm sun of the bay window, working my way through a pile of ironing. I'm one of those old souls who still delights in a beautifully pressed shirt, but I digress.

I was thinking of the last time I wore this particular red blouse. We were showing at the fair and I wanted to be seen! Tee, of course, was radiating his usual magnificence. The outing was a good one and will remain rich with recollections of being among friends while riding nice horses. Anticipation. Readiness. Laughter. Challenge. Learning. Victory. Tiredness. Appreciation. All the feels were there, the hallmarks of a truly fine day. I smiled, remembering all this while I ironed. As I reached into my closet to hang this blouse, however, my eye caught sight of something else. It was a valuable item of clothing, given to me by someone who'd once wielded great power over me, without the balance of kindness.

Though the gift was meant to be generous, it came with a comment of having to order an especially large size, as this quality of shop didn't stock anything big enough to fit me. It came as a surprise to find that I am still hurt and ashamed to recall this, no matter how many years have passed. Due to the worth of its label, along with the price tag still hanging from one sleeve, I've hung on to it out of some warped sense of duty. No more. Instead our local charity shop will benefit, while I finally get past the reminder of not being enough. I wonder, how many things do we hold close, whether or not their energy is wholly good for us?

Ah, memories. They can comfort us, heal or hurt us. And, you know, the choice to hold onto them is ours alone.

. 152 .

HALF-HALTS

Today, don't forget to stop and breathe. We've got this.

PULLING BACK

One of the hardest things we can do is to realistically evaluate ourselves. This is why one of the first questions in any job interview is the deadly, "So, tell us about your strengths and weaknesses." We'll fidget and giggle nervously, struggling either with the concept of talking ourselves up, or admitting to inherent character flaws. Some of us have trouble with both ends of the spectrum. Such are the discomforts of being human.

Add horsemanship into the mix and it gets even stickier. How do we go about evaluating our own skills in order to attend clinics or specialized lessons? I ask this because I witness, again and again, good people who either fail to challenge themselves or, as often, they get in over their heads. How do we know if we are afraid to be stretched, made to look imperfect in front of judging eyes — or if we are unaware that before signing up for the specialized clinic, we need to do more riding? How do we know?

Assessing the level of our own horsemanship is difficult if we ride alone, if we don't take ridden tests, if we don't compete, or if we don't have a regular teacher. You can see that each of these scenarios puts us in the uncomfortable position of being judged. I have found that the longer we've been immersed in the horse world, the harder it is to see ourselves honestly.

Having been good in the past is a distorting lens through which to draw any conclusions. While those of us who have long been in the saddle often have an old-money view of the new horsemanship around us, we want to be careful, if we feel this way. Our memories of past glories are not failsafe and cannot always be trusted. The horses who carried us to our greatest heights are not the same horses we are riding today. Our bodies and our courage have changed, and often our methods are growing outmoded. I know this because I have been there and I'm trying to arrive here — an interesting journey, as nothing is staying the same!

A good friend of mine, a professional horsewoman in her own right, has cut to the chase with evaluating unknown riders who wish to attend her clinics and lessons. She simply asks them if they can lope or canter ten consecutive circles, on either lead, without losing the track or breaking gait. It sheds an unwavering light on the training and fitness levels of both the horses and their riders. This simple yet

demanding test has proven to be a pragmatic way of self-evaluating our current skills in the saddle.

In a grand paradox, an underlying fear of failure is one of the reasons we don't sign up for regular lessons or attend clinics or shows. It's something more to think about.

· 154 ·
SHORT STIRRUPS

Today's memory is about the pony against whom all others are judged.

Royally-bred, filled with an unquenchable presence, Roseacres Spartan made me believe in Welsh ponies for life. By the time I'd inherited him from my older sister, Peter had worked through all the flakiness that defines late-blooming individuals, to grow into the noblest equine companion a child could want.

It wasn't easy. Why my father ever imagined this wild-eyed three-year-old chuckwagon pony would be a good fit for his two tiny daughters is beyond all reasoning. Tears and bruises became the norm. A memory of being rushed to the hospital remains in a scar upon my chin. But we were stuck with Peter — and he, with us — and with the passing of time and much mileage, there grew a kind of magic.

Peter took versatility to new heights. He became safe for me to drive down the country roads alone as a young girl. He was my first sidesaddle mount, my first show pony, my first taste of freedom. Peter carried my friend and me happily, confidently, to the riverbank underneath the CPR railway bridge. There, he would stand tied to a willow brush by the bridle reins while freight trains roared overhead — and we dipped and dived in the cold water, uncaring.

Despite losing his vision early on, Peter served his family with pride and honour, living his final years by feel, rather than sight. He died of an aneurysm in the arms of his loving girls at the tender age of nine. Horses were not looked after, once upon a time, as they are today. Nobody thought of chiropractic or dentistry, and we certainly didn't know of the damage parasites could do on a robust body over time. Bless you, Peter, but we know now.

Sensitive, highly-strung, filled with an inner presence, Peter was always a gentleman. Somehow, it never occurred to me that he was also stop-you-in-your-tracks beautiful. (Author's Collection)

· 155 ·

STAYING ON

When Mike throws back the quilts, both he and Glen hit the ground running. I'll wince at the draught they make, opening my eyes long enough to notice that it is a) still dark and b) snowing. I've changed in my old age, choosing not to welcome the day until I can hear affirmative action at the coffee pot. Then, I'll knock back two cups of really strong joe with cream, something I vow to let go as my jeans feel at war with my waistline. Maybe not now, but tomorrow.

Standing in bare feet on the old cast-iron heat vent, sipping, I look out the French doors and down the long stone walk towards the horses. There is a mown grassy break in the trees, with a small ranch gate made of an old rake wheel. It is here that our horses and ponies most always choose to spend their nights, close to the house, safe from the cougars that move silently across the hills sloping down from the yard.

Our house sits in a long shadow cast by two big hills to the east. Long after the surrounding country is basking in heat, we are still waiting for sunrise. The house, dating from the early 1900s, is small and white. It was abandoned entirely in the 1960s and stayed that way, without power or running water, until our young family entered its halls thirty years ago. Set in this old garden with its huge trees, the house is a home with heart. More and more, I cannot bear to leave it.

Mike heads out. I'll not see him again until he remembers that he's not eaten. He'll be home for supper, and I idly wonder what sort of meat I should pull from the freezer, when I turn to do a load of laundry. I forget everything once Glen whines to go outside. He proceeds directly to the horses. The Border Collie and I are kindred spirits in that regard, content to spend inordinate amounts of time just watching them. (I will forget about both the meat and my washing, until hours later, when I see the lights of Mike's truck coming back up the road.)

Atticus has devised a sport of being towed by the leg straps of Pilot's new blanket. I'll have to do something about that. Meanwhile, it explains the high cost of Pi's winter wardrobe. The gelding dresses better than I do, but it's a sure-fire way of keeping up his condition. Pi has struggled with this since coming to southern Alberta. I'm starting to see that he frets in the wind. This wind we have on the eastern slopes rules our days. You can undress for heat and dress for cold, but the wind goes right through you. Our winter, with its lack of snowfall, means that the wind has carved the topsoil from between the grass bunches in the westward pastures. Side roads have had the gravel blown right off them. And still, we ride.

My horses have long found it easier to work in these conditions than when they must 'go to town'. At least once each week through the winter, I'll load three or four up and head in to the public arena. It's a two-hour round trip. One of Mike's frustrations with me, in addition to a resistance to wearing my hearing aid, is the need to have our truck permanently affixed to the stock trailer. As if I must be ever-ready to check out of Dodge. "Well," I say to him, "One never knows ..."

I turn from the doorway and stir my stumps. First, I make a circuit of the creaking house, winding my many old clocks, speaking lovingly to some and chiding others into action. Their varied tickings and chimes give this place the air of a madhouse. I'll post the story that I wrote before bedtime last night. Something will have jogged my memory and it will be all I can do to write the words down as fast as they come to me. There will be emails to answer and messages about ponies for sale (seldom does anyone ask to buy one), sidesaddles to fix, and lessons to teach. I go to my outmoded wall calendar and book these for the coming months. More and more, it comes as a jolt seeing how fast these dates will sneak up.

I try and pay bills, do laundry, clean house or tackle saddle repairs when it's too hot, cold or windy to comfortably ride. My comfort is growing far too important. It has begun to affect my work. Mike has set me up with a beautifully well-lit and organized bench downstairs. And yet the fusty old saddles and I will end up back at the dining room table where the sun streams in through the bay window. I sit here, warming my back, a cup of tea long forgotten, stitch-stitch-stitching to the strains of soprano arias. This, to me, is bliss.

If I'm riding, the first thing is to gather the horses.

If I go out straightaway, they'll still be close to the yard. If I'm tardy, they'll have ranged south or down along the creek, where the hills and brush-filled draws conceal them. I'll be scanning the pasture for traces of horses, but Glen usually finds them first. Once upon a time, our horses were jingled in with the kids' pony, but nowadays, I need the exercise. I'll hike out and bring the boss hoss in with a neck rope while the others follow. The herd comes willingly, for it is in the corrals that they find water and salt. With sale beasts coming and going, it's been years since we've had ranch horses that watered at the creek. Years since we've had horses wise enough to slide down the frozen banks and kneel low enough to drink from holes chopped in the ice. My current horses would rather die of thirst than do this.

I'll close the gate, with hinges that sing the opening bars of *O Canada.* I'll reprimand Glen, who always wants to hurry any stragglers. My pink neck rope goes on the horse I'll first saddle and I'll lead it out to the yard where it gets hobbled or tied to the old tree. This tree has been chewed upon, rubbed against and pulled-back on for so many years that it now stands stunted. At its roots are great hollows where thirty years of horses and ponies have pawed and stamped at flies. This tree has taught my horses as much as I have, and I hold it in high regard.

Once Pilot or Harry, Henry or whoever else is saddled, I'll leave them a while to soak. I'll go for another coffee, or I'll get another horse saddled to work on the fine art of waiting. It is this saddling, riding, tying, waiting, then saddling another, that goes 'round and 'round. If there's ranch riding involved, one or two horses will be saddled, hauled to where the cows are and worked the whole day. Far from cruel, this will be the making of them. Always, my horses enjoy a day of 'real work' far more than an hour of schooling in the sand.

I'll go on this way, stopping for a bite, and maybe a ten-minute nap on the couch, keeping my spurs buckled to my boots, keeping my boots on. This too annoys my husband. I work my way through a succession of second-hand Justin ropers, bought off eBay for ten or fifteen bucks. These I live in, 'til the soles wear through. The leather-soled boots are the only ones I can bear to ride in, as well as the only boots that will pull over my wonky ankle. Long out of style, I still adore them. I can date boxes of old pictures by the era of my boots — purple, black, loden green, red, brown, turquoise. This year, I'm back in black but they're starting to wear thin.

After I'm done riding, lungeing, teaching or being taught, I turn out the horses. The gate still sounds its patriotic tune. My little herd thunders and bucks down the hill until, as one, they stop and begin grazing. Glen leaps with joy at a job well done and we make our way back to the house.

A biscuit for him and the kettle goes on for me. I'll think back to moments of the day that bear saving, ones to be remembered and learned from. Some of these will stay hidden in my own journals, whether they shed light on something precious, private or perhaps shameful. Others, I'll write and post on the Keystone blog, choosing a photo that best tells the story of what my words are trying to convey.

You will read them, we will share our thoughts and then, please God, we will do it all again tomorrow.

. 156 .

MY OLD RIDING HABIT

Some months ago, I offered three beautiful vintage sidesaddle habits for sale. Not easily found, let alone in western Canada, I knew they would find homes quickly. They were like Goldilocks' porridge in a way — one was too small, one was too large, but the third one was just right.

A rare and exquisite Roberts & Carroll, according to its original label, the beautiful hand-tailored, bias-cut jacket hung from the shoulders like no other. I was despondent to think of letting it go but the habit had a mismatched apron. Despite years of trying, I had never been able to find one of the same weight or quality, or that exact shade of navy blue.

Love & RULES

I received a number of heartfelt messages regarding that third habit, the day I sadly listed its picture, along with a hefty asking price. But the messages were all surprising, with one common theme. While each prospective buyer was hoping the navy habit had not yet sold, each was urging me to keep the old coat!

One note stood out from the rest. If I would pass my measurements on to the sender, she in turn would try to make me an apron worthy of the jacket. I pulled the Roberts and Carroll off the market at the same time I sold the other two habits and the mismatched skirt.

Then, we began searching for fabric.

Hundreds of online choices, but nothing new looked right with the mellow lustre of the antique wool. I was hanging the coat back in my closet when it came to me — the memory of a bolt of Duncan tartan saved from a military kilt dating to the Great War. I pulled the forgotten old cloth, pocked with moth holes, from a drawer deep beneath the stairs.

The tartan had a subtlety to it, an untold story of proud service, that somehow made newer cloth seem brash. The white was more ivory; the red, now deep chestnut; the green, almost black ... and there it was, the exact same navy blue.

I said a prayer and sent the tartan by mail to this gifted and knowledgeable seamstress, a sidesaddle rider herself. She worked her magic and sent it back.

The ragged pile of tartan had been transformed into a correctly cut and tailored traditional apron. There was scarcely a handful of scrap left over. As I buttoned the century-old fabric around my hips, then topped it with the 1920s habit coat, they both looked as though, finally, they belonged.

The fact that my maiden name was Duncan, that my grandfathers both saw action in World War I, makes it all the more poignant to me.

I have vowed I will wear this while riding my mentor's beloved Mayhew on Cypress someday. He and I, the old habit and sidesaddle — a band of misfits united by the gift of a second chance.

WESTERN PLEASURE

Old McLean, he had a wife, E-I-E-I-O.

Every morning, Old McLean wakes up, walks past his wife of many years and stoops to pet his cat and chat up his Border Collie. I observed this for some time, then finally asked him if he didn't think his wife was deserving of, at the very least, a fond pat on the rump like some serviceably sound old mare? Keeping the barnyard analogy going for a minute, it's sad to see the old feller so incessantly henpecked, but why does a man need such herding? As in, "Darling, let's work on your aim in the bathroom, you know, narrow it down a bit." Or "You didn't just drop that dead mouse in the kitchen garbage?!" Or "Would you be a dear and fetch all the mugs from your chore truck?"

So, I sit, enjoying coffee in a cup I've retrieved after a windblown trek to the yard in my jammies. I've blown six months' chaff from it, before I can pour and reflect. Being in a relationship raises many of the same questions as does my horsemanship. Do I ride him on a tighter rein? Do I buckle up and put on some more training? Or do I just smile at the memories and turn the old boy out to pasture?

USING OUR CORNERS

Building a confident and reliable horse is akin to working on a new jigsaw puzzle. Excited and filled with anticipation, we dump the heap of unrelated pieces out of the box and into a messy jumble on our table. Now what?

We spread them out a bit and give the pieces room to settle. We look for a corner piece.

Ah, here we are. One piece, on which to build something above, underneath or alongside. We might find the other corner pieces — which are similar to finding the elements of manners, trust, ease and relationship, all of which we need to instill in any horse with whom we seek safe partnership. These are our cornerstones. These pieces shape the entire puzzle. We begin to fill in the spaces in between. How can I get from basic ground manners to a position of trust? Along the way, we will find one piece that is touch, another that is relaxation, then enjoyment — anything other than distrust and fear. One piece, then another piece, then another.

Sometimes, when we think we're in a hurry, or when we're focused on the finishing, we will try to force a piece that looks good, but it isn't a fit. We have a choice here — we can either continue to mash on that piece, or we can replace it with a better fit. Note that just because we chose to try a 'wrong' piece, it doesn't mean that our puzzle is ruined. No, we simply go back a step and look for the right one.

Building a puzzle can be done in several ways. We can build on the puzzle when it is convenient, or when we feel like it, putting it back in the box when it's not high up on our 'to do' list. This is going to take us a long time and we are going to continually be working on fitting the same pieces, over and over again. Doable, maybe, but perhaps not the best and most direct way.

We can build on the puzzle in one sitting, concentrating on nothing else. This too is doable, maybe, but not a well-rounded or gentle approach. Oh, my concentration! Oh, my seat bones! Both the puzzle-building and I would be improved with a break. Or we can build on the puzzle by putting it safely in a place we pass by each day. Like the guitar that waits for us patiently on its stand beside our favourite chair, as opposed to existing in its dusty case under the bed, it is primed and ready for a laying on of hands.

We pick away at our puzzle, with smiles on our faces, with joy, with an uncharted passing of time. Only when we look back can we remember the jumbled pieces. Only then can we see how far we have come. Building puzzles is a lot like building safe and confident horses. One piece at a time, one piece at a time.

· 159 ·

MOUNTING BLOCKS

PART I: This saddle. I pull it down from its high rack today, bring out Eclipse's old bridle, and fish around for a more appropriate bit. You see, all the while I'm working with Pilot, this little thought keeps niggling at me. He wants to be an English horse.

I've sidestepped this issue neatly over the past, oh, forty-five years by telling myself that I'm 'All Western, All The Time'. When last I remember settling into this saddle, my firstborn child is just a baby. He's now fire chief in a nearby town. I didn't know these years would whoosh by so fast — and I certainly didn't know that I would lose my skills. But it happens, just as surely as I've given away my doeskin breeches and outgrown my custom boots.

The saddle, a Kieffer, is the best that my mother's money can buy. I'm fourteen years old when it is ordered and flocked up to fit my exquisite new Thoroughbred. It's an exciting time of plans and dreams. My old riding journal still shows how to properly break in a new saddle, to avoid twisting it or having it not work down to fit the horse. How to keep the stirrup leathers even and train the saddle to stay put. How to look after the leather in a way that the saddle will still be a usable treasure, even when one grows old.

As Pilot stands waiting, I walk out with this saddle over my arm. Oh, the ghosts of horses past! The bouquets of flowers, the trophies, the wide smiles. The tears I've shed in this saddle, while the blood seeps through my knees. My teacher is very hard, very traditional. She believes in hours of lungeing without stirrups or reins, all of this, on her barn of young, well-fed sport horses. There is much picking myself up and appearing brave.

Along with the gift of her knowledge is my fear of her violence and of needing to keep secrets. This is abuse, and as an adult, I am finally able to give it a name.

I set the saddle over Pilot's wither and slide it back, back, back into position. It fits him well enough. He seems to visibly relax when both it and Eclipse's bridle are slipped on. Strangely, the headstall needs no adjustment from the 16:2 superstar who once wore it — horse of my lifetime, now only snapshots in a yellowing album. I warn Pi sternly that he is not to take this gear for granted, that to wear it is both an honour and a responsibility. Take heed! Pi yawns and shakes away a fly.

I fix the stirrups up with the age-old weave, twist the reins, and run the throatlatch through them to secure the gear for lungeing. Pilot stretches at a long walk, then settles into a smooth, flowing trot around me. I'm watching my saddle as much as I'm watching my horse. It looks like a stranger to me and, without warning, I begin to cry. I realize that I am lungeing, not to warm up my horse or because I'm worried about him. I'm afraid to sit in my old saddle again, fearful of reaching out to the past.

I know going in that I won't have control of my legs. Riding a stock saddle has taken care of all that! I know that I will feel uncomfortable. I know that the saddle will now be too small. Most of all, though, I realize that I'm frightened to revisit the girl I was when I was hopeful. When I was first soaking in all the things that make me who I am today. This comes as a surprise.

I call the big horse in off the circle, unclip the lunge rein and take him over to the mounting block. Just as he moves into position, the wind changes and the sky grows dark. I look up at the suddenly ominous clouds through my tears. I can't do it. Not just yet.

PART II: I rode in my old saddle, something I've turned my back on — nay, downright avoided — for over forty years.

The reality was very much less than my imaginings. My body remembered. It said, "Oh. Yes." It was all there. Tiring, too quickly, but all right there, right where I'd left it. If you've done so much of one thing to the exclusion of all else, some muscle memory must remain. How extraordinary we are, how filled with magic!

You know, it wasn't about the saddle. It was never about the saddle. Some of you will get that. Those, I suspect, who have done your share of work on past trauma and the ugly scars left by abuse. The saddle simply triggered all these truths I've so long kept carefully buried. The sun shone, the wind blew — and I was just another woman, out schooling her horse.

. 160 .

TRAIL'S END

We read the books, take the lessons, enter the shows, build up our hopes and dreams, sometimes winning, sometimes crying all the way home. We watch the videos, go to the clinics, saddle up in all weather. All in search of higher horsemanship. This is fine, this is what we human beings do when we want so badly to improve.

But to me, all these notions about learning more and doing the right thing, about holding ourselves to higher standards, are just so much stuff. To me, being a good horseman or woman is in knowing when it is time to lay down our swords. We vet, we treat, we maintain, we do due diligence — all the while knowing that one day, we will have done all that we can.

There will be only one thing left to do, if we are to live in love and kindness.

Horsemanship comes in many guises, but much of it is smoke and mirrors. The real thing is knowing and having the courage to say, "Enough." Being a good horseman or woman is holding ourselves to bravery.

These hard days are ahead of all of us who love and care for old campaigners — and tragically, sometimes, those who are still young or in the prime of life. These horses remind us of the times we were more than we ever imagined we could be. We look in their eyes and are humbled by all the days we've let them down, and still they've held fast to our secrets.

We put our hands on their necks and wish like heck we were more worthy.

Horsemanship, real horsemanship, is stepping up and embracing everything about that last best day. It is the one final act of loving our horses in the way that they deserve.

. 161 .
THE HOME STRETCH

I don't know whether I had an epiphany on this recent road trip with my daughter, or what. By the time we'd returned from the United States and had got so far as her home in rural southern Saskatchewan, I just needed to ride.

We saddled two old favourites, Parry and Cinnabar, then we turned their prows out over the ocean of billowing, golden grass.

The Great Plains stretch in a belt from the middle of the North American continent, all the way up to the Canadian Rockies. An area covering one-point-three million square kilometres (five hundred thousand square miles), this land was appropriated from its Indigenous people and offered, by two governments, as the promised land to new settlers — people who had nothing, packed up their children and their hopes and dreams, then headed west. They tried to farm a land that knew no master.

This land is lonely, even now, even with the comfort of my cell phone sitting solidly in my pocket. I can't fathom what it was like to arrive by boat, then by train, then by horse and wagon, or by foot, to such a place. No grocery store, no lackadaisical 'whatever, there's always next year' when hot winds desiccate the garden. No doctor, no help when birthing pains come in the night. No tidy graveyard in which to bury the children. No counsellor, no Ted Talks or memes, no church on Sunday, no day away to just window shop.

My daughter and I were no doubt thinking all these things as our horses trudged away the miles. We crested a ridge, one of thousands all the same, and there it was. A stone house, smack in the middle of nowhere.

I always feel that old farmsteads are rich with spirit. Certainly, as I looked out the car windows at the landscape flashing past, I saw many such houses as this in the past week. The Great Plains are, as much as our continent's breadbasket, the land of broken dreams. My breath catches in my throat with the sheer weight of this.

Another house, built four-square, walls still standing resolutely on the horizon. Doors hanging from one hinge, blowing open after some family gave it their all and then one day, broken, just left. Owls soaring out of windows that once had held carefully-fitted glass. Barns, once rich with the sounds and smells of livestock, now leaning away from the relentless wind. This keening wind that never, ever stops.

We dismounted and stood, small and inconsequential, before that empty house. Someone had formed all the 'stone' blocks and built it so skillfully piece-by-piece out of cement that resembled sandstone. There was a window where the staircase would have paused and turned to reach bedrooms under the eaves. A shadow along the south wall suggested that once a verandah had sheltered the front door. A beautiful big bay window opened straight to the long west view, a sea of rolling hills that reached all the way to the foothills, hundreds of miles away. To the rear, a kitchen window gazed upon the stone barn, banked solidly into a small hill.

Someone had given it their all in this place, once upon a time. Were their efforts a failure because there were no longer young voices wafting down the hall? Because the apples from those few surviving trees dropped, unnoticed, into the long grass? Because the hand-dug well of saline water had finally caved in upon itself? What had happened to have them, one day, take one last look around and leave?

I leaned against the warm stone and tried to remember this family's untold story. We are here for just a while. We will dream, and try our best, and then we will be gone. The voice of this place told me to be kind. To leave good work. To try every opportunity.

Above all, it said to not waste any more time.

. 162 .

A BALANCED RIDE

Imagine an old-fashioned scale. In the balance hangs discipline, compared to that intangible thing we call 'feel'. If this was your scale, which side would outweigh the other?

Most of us, if we are honest, struggle with balancing the two. Based on our inherent personality traits, along with who has mentored us, we will embrace the one mindset, while struggling with its opposing view.

Those of us who expect obedience seldom have our horses flat-out say no, nor do they ever behave badly. We usually feel safe in the saddle, but we can miss out on a lot of the good stuff. By enforcing rules and concentrating on precision, we sometimes lose our ability to 'give' at just the right moments. Our riding can become laboured while our horses lose their natural flow. We're big on rules!

Those of us who are all about the connection with our mounts can have the opposite problems. In our quest for 'feel', we may not give our horses enough leadership. Sometimes our horses can be unreliable or inconsistent without firm boundaries. We may value peace in our relationship above working through problems or having hard days. We can go years without solving a training glitch. Often, our horses mirror the relationships we've built with the people around us too.

For me, the challenge comes in trying to find the balance between these two extremes.

Basic safety demands that my horses go in a disciplined manner, but the joy in my horsemanship comes from developing the soft feel. I don't necessarily think that one is any better or any worse than the other, for when we live and believe in only one approach, our horses will never rise to be their best. Nor will we. Most days, before I swing a leg over, I stop myself and I breathe. I remember my mantra and gain focus. I set out, strengthened with a newfound balance and intention in my life. Just saying these words settles me. I become clear, fair and resolved.

Love & Rules. Love & Rules. Love & Rules.

CONCLUSION

KEEP ON KEEPIN' ON

Here's to lessons learned and the gift of second chances!

I have been blessed with a rebound not afforded everyone hit with ill health, job loss and the aftermath of depression. Standing tall with my horse, Tee — another comeback kid, if ever there was — I could only blink away tears of humility. Gratitude. Hope. Resolve. This book, my second, is a collection of stories on life's lessons learned with horses. It is the culmination of years of learning, trying, failing and trying again.

So, this notion of 'love & rules' — of self-compassion and self-discipline — applies to ourselves, as much as to our horsemanship. On this day of making our cover photo, I felt a real sense of celebration at the finish of writing this book, along with the release of thirty pounds. Still, my chaps were plenty tight, requiring a helping hand to zip those infernal zippers. I sat my horse, holding the reins stiffly and uncomfortably, as on this same day, I'd also undergone minor surgery on my left hand. This, too, was reason enough to cheer, for I have too long put off seeing to my own wellness. For too many years, like so many of you, I have thought of myself only after everyone else.

The photographer urged me several times to appear fiercer. More like a cowgirl. To be serious, to take the smile from my face. But I could not. The fact that Tee, who has come back to me full circle, improving in his own health enough to lope us effortlessly back and forth across the pasture, was reason enough for my joy riding.

As the day drew to its golden close, as the sun dipped behind the mountains, we posed upon a windblown knoll over the creek valley. We stood resolutely, on behalf of every single one of you who has come back, better than ever, filled with grit and determined to feel joy. We repped all of you who keep on keepin' on, in a world that celebrates youth and accomplishment. We stood for all the people, all the horses, who are still waiting for the strength to seize their opportunities. For it is never ever too late, my friends.

Lessons learned. Second chances. Here's to recognizing them, seizing them, and giving them everything we've got.

"It has taken me a lifetime to realize that I can stop, look back, and not feel shame or embarrassment. Instead, I can see how very far I have come. Strengthened, I will look ahead and ride on." (Mary Durant Photography)

GLOSSARY
GETTING THE DRIFT

APRON —
a type of safety skirt, part of the traditional ladies' habit, worn when riding sidesaddle.

BARN RAT —
a keen student, usually young, who offers manual labour in exchange for free lessons.

BARN SOUR —
a horse who is unwilling to leave the barn to go out for a ride.

BLINKERS —
leather eye coverings on a driving bridle, meant to focus the horse straight ahead.

BRAND —
an identifying permanent mark, humanely applied to horses with extreme cold.

CAMP (ON A HORSE) —
cowboy lingo that means to concentrate training on one particular horse.

CHAPS —
protective leather leggings for the rider, pronounced 'shaps'.

CHINOOK —
westerly wind over the Rocky Mountains, with a dramatic rise in winter temperatures.

COLT —
a young male horse, from birth to four years of age.

COMBINED DRIVING —
a three-day event with carriages, of dressage, a marathon and 'cones'.

CRICKET —
a copper roller in the mouthpiece of a western bit, the original 'fidget spinner'.

DRESSAGE —
the schooling of any horse; also, a competition of skills and compulsory figures.

FILLY —
a young female horse, from birth to four years of age.

GELDING —
a mature male horse that has been neutered; a stallion is left 'entire' for breeding.

HABIT —
the traditional, modest jacket and apron skirt for ladies who ride sidesaddle.

HANDS IN HEIGHT —
a 4" unit of measure. Therefore, 15:2 refers to a horse 62" tall at the withers.

HERDBOUND —
a horse unable to cope or perform when alone or away from other horses.

LEAD —
the leading leg at the canter, generally to the same side as the direction of travel.

LUNGEING —
a method of schooling a horse, whereby it circles the handler on a long rein.

RISING OR POSTING — smoothly easing one's weight up and down, in time with the horse's trot.

ROMAL REINS —
traditional western reins braided from rawhide strips, with a long quirt on the end.

SIDESADDLE —
a saddle with pommels allowing the rider to sit securely, with both legs to one side.

SURCINGLES —
straps fastening a blanket, saddle, or harness securely around the horse's middle.

TRANSITIONS —
changing pace from walk, to trot, to canter, to halt; and in any sequence thereof.

TURNAROUNDS —
a western pivot turn that has the horse spin around on the back legs.

VETTING —
a physical examination for horse health, often performed just prior to purchase.

RECIPES

NOTES

NOTES

NOTES